T0366344

HOW THE TRADING FLOOR REALLY WORKS

HOW THE TRADING FLOOR REALLY WORKS

Terri Duhon

BLOOMBERG PRESS
An Imprint of
WILEY
John Wiley & Sons, Inc.

Library of Congress Cataloging-in-Publication Data

Duhon, Terri Lynn, 1972-
    How the trading floor really works / Terri Lynn Duhon.
      p. cm.
    Includes index.
    ISBN 978-1-119-96295-3 (cloth); ISBN 978-1-119-96601-2 (ebk);
    ISBN 978-1-119-96603-6 (ebk); ISBN 978-1-119-96602-9 (ebk)
      1. Trading rooms (Finance). 2. Stock exchanges. I. Title.
  HG4551.D84   2012
  332.64—dc23

                                                2012029240

A catalogue record for this book is available from the British Library.

Typeset in 11/13 Adobe Garamond by MPS Limited, Chennai, India
Printed and bound in Great Britain by TJ International Ltd, Padstow, Cornwall, UK

To my family and friends: I consider myself unbelievably lucky to have you all and ridiculously proud to be daughter, sister, wife, mommy and friend.

Contents

Foreword

By Gillian Tett

Many years ago, when I was a young financial reporter, I had a chance to walk onto a banking trading floor in London. It was an intense experience, which sparked a frisson of excitement and an insatiable sense of curiosity – and an odd sense of déjà vu. In an earlier part of my career, before becoming a journalist, I had worked as a social anthropologist, conducting fieldwork in places such as Tajikistan and Tibet. At first glance, those remote Himalayan communities might seem to have nothing in common with the young (and they *are* mostly young) men and women who work on the trading desks of the world's banks; on the contrary, in terms of power, lifestyle, aspirations and earnings, the two environments are worlds apart.

And yet what the trading floor of any financial institution shares with the Tibetan and Tajik villages is that they operate as a community and an eco-system; and, as such, they have their own set of rules, traditions and languages which defines the group, and sets them apart from others. Some of these rules and languages are formally stated and "obvious" (just look at in-house bank manuals on compliance for an example of that.) But many other cultural practices and rules are subtle and rarely discussed, either with outsiders or within the group (just take note of the gender differences that Duhon highlights near the start of the book to see this). But both sets of these overt and hidden codes of behaviour are profoundly powerful, and shape how societies are reproduced over time, how power structures develop – and how the participants see themselves and interact with the rest of the world. A bank trading desk, in other words, presents as much material for anthropologists as an exotic village; even, or especially, if the bankers who work there think of themselves as rational "modern" beings who work in a disembodied world of high-tech, cyber-finance.

Given this, Duhon's book is not just illuminating, but valuable and timely for banker and non-banker alike. It sets out to offer a comprehensive picture of how a trading floor works, and how it interacts with the rest of the financial system. But — more importantly — it does this in a way, using real-life stories, that is comprehensible and easy to read; even for people who have never worked on a trading floor, or seen one. This matters. After all, during the past few decades, the operations of these trading floors have often seemed almost as mysterious to outsiders (and some insiders too) as a Tajik village. That is partly because of a widespread aversion among non-bankers towards grappling with technical and quantitative terms; to many non-bankers, complex finance seems so alienating that it is easier to label it as "geeky" and to simply ignore it. However, another reason for this lack of understanding is that the banking industry has long assumed it was in their interests to wrap finance with an air of mystery. This is not necessarily down to any deliberate "plot" or intentional criminality (although, on occasion, criminal acts do occur on a trading floor, as in almost any business sector). Instead, there was a more basic issue: bankers have often assumed that opacity and mystery produces more profit. Banks who have great trading ideas often want to hug them to themselves. Traders with fantastic teams do not want their competitors to steal their staff. And, most importantly of all, many banks have assumed cultivating an air of exclusivity would allow them to charge more for their services. After all, in finance, as in every business, it often pays to be seen as an "expert" who has sole command of some mysterious technology or product; if customers find it difficult to shop around for a service, or compare prices, the profits tend to be much higher.

But while this approach might have seemed to have served the industry well at some points in the past, these days, it is clear that this opacity and sense of mystery has also come at a huge cost. For one thing, the lack of understanding about how a trading floor really works has made it tough for society at large to exert effective oversight, and thus prevent crises before it is too late. Risks have built up within the financial system, and these have gone undetected for years, because journalists, politicians, regulators and central bankers — not to mention ordinary households — had almost no idea what was going on. The recent credit boom and bust is a case in point: if more regulators, politicians, journalists and other outsiders had understood, say, how banks were trading mortgage-linked securities before 2007, the financial crisis would never have spun so deeply out of control. Similarly, if there had been more external oversight of how banks were raising finance in the money markets, vulnerabilities in the system might have been spotted earlier, and possibly even fixed.

Worse still, because traders have been operating in quasi ghettoes, it has often been hard for them to retain that crucial trait: basic common sense. As they feverishly churned out products, or traded instruments, the temptation has been to keep staring at whatever lay beneath their noses (on their computer screens); any sense of wider context to trading has sometimes been lost. As a result, some crazy decisions and practices have emerged. Once again, the pattern of behaviour in the mortgage-backed securities is a case in point; if more traders had been forced to spend time explaining their operations to others, or even visiting some mortgage borrowers, they might have seen how dangerous the bubble was becoming. The lack of public understanding, in other words, did not simply make it tough for regulators to monitor the banks; it also made it harder for banks to engage in wise practices.

And there is a third key point: precisely because trading floors have been swathed in a sense of mystery, it has been difficult for banks to show the rest of the society why trading is a valuable and important endeavour to the wider economy. This is profoundly unfortunate. Since the financial crisis of 2008, there has been a welter of criticism among politicians and the wider public about the antics of bank traders; indeed, the word "speculator" has become the favourite bogeyman of many politicians. And that in turn has prompted calls to ban most forms of trading, and a wider regulatory crackdown. It has also damaged the reputation of the industry, in a manner that has not been seen since the last big financial crash of the 1930's.

In some senses, this development is natural and understandable; some bankers and some traders have indeed done egregious things in recent years, and society has suffered as a result. But what has often been lost amid all this mud-slinging is that economies need financial systems to work; and the trading floors of banks are a crucial pillar of any modern financial system. When trading floors spiral out of control or engage in crazy antics, the consequences are certainly bad; however, if trading floors "freeze", or disappear, this will be very damaging for the economy. That does not necessarily mean that these trading floors need to be as large as they have in the past; the size of these operations and their risk-taking appetites certainly became excessive during the credit bubble, and these need to be reined in and placed on a more ethical and sensible footing. But politicians, journalists, regulators and ordinary voters alike need to recognise that financial trading is a legitimate activity, which is needed to support growth. Sadly, though, it has been hard for banks to make that case — partly because the operations of those trading floors have been so opaque. In that respect, then, what Duhon is seeking to do with this book is crucial. If there was less ignorance about financial trading, and more common sense and transparency, we would have a better chance of building a healthier financial system. And that would not just be good for non-bankers, but bankers — and would-be bankers - too.

Preface

Why I Wrote this Book

Starting off as a 22-year-old analyst at JPMorgan on the interest rate swap trading desk with a math degree from MIT was one of the biggest challenges of my life. I had read a few books and had understood that the trading floor was a high-energy place. I also understood that trading derivatives would suit my analytical background. Yet, despite that and the intense JPMorgan training program, I had no idea what to do when I was told on one of my first days on the job to "trade the short end of the CAD dollar swap book and hedge using BAs and FRA switches."

Later, as I interacted with the middle and back office at JPMorgan, I began to appreciate how little was even understood within the bank itself about the activities and the risk on the trading floor. Even interacting with the bankers from JPMorgan (who advised their clients about using the services of the trading floor) or the loan officers (who made credit risk decisions every day) was eye opening.

After 10 years of trading and structuring derivatives on the trading floor in New York and London, I started B&B Structured Finance with the original goal of training market participants in derivative products and markets. I quickly realized the demand for generic knowledge about the trading floor was our key to being successful trainers. Analysts, middle and back office professionals, bankers and even sales people on the trading floor needed to better understand some aspect of what was going on "on the trading floor" over and above learning about some specific derivative product. If my trainers could tell war stories about their time on the trading floor to put the derivative or risk analysis into context, then everyone in the room had an experience to remember and draw on. Our rule became "stories are sticky and facts are slippy." Thus, in writing this book, I included several true stories that either I experienced directly or I was told by colleagues on the trading floor. These stories not only make the learning more entertaining but also give some context to the personalities that make financial markets go round.

With all the interest in sales and trading from graduates, the huge interest in moving from back and middle office to front office and the intense focus on financial markets and how they work today, there is a real need to teach people lessons they will be able not only to remember but also to utilize. Importantly, there is a real need to give people the perspective of someone who has done it all before.

What this Book Does and Does Not Do

What does it mean to make a market? What value do banks add to the financial markets? What risk do they take as a result? What really happens on the trading floor? What are the key roles and responsibilities on the bank trading floor? When does it all go wrong? These are the questions that this book answers. Because financial markets are continually evolving and there are so many unique financial products that are traded, this book does not attempt to burden the reader with too many technical details, nor does it try to address all the nuances of individual financial products. Instead, many financial products are simplified in order to use them as examples throughout the text. This book aims to establish a framework and some fundamental vocabulary for understanding how markets are made on trading floors and understanding the key roles and responsibilities of the individuals who work there.

Who this Book Is For

For the pending or recent graduate who is looking for a job in financial markets, this book is a must. It is not theoretical; it is practical and easy to read and follow. It clearly explains how the financial markets work and what the purpose of the bank and the bank trading floor is, using clear examples. Anyone looking for a job in financial markets will be able to identify roles and responsibilities which are most appealing and best suited to their skillset. This book starts with a foundation in basic financial products and participants then moves quickly into market making and risk taking. This book does not try to explain every product, nor does it try to teach financial math. It simplifies the financial market and makes it accessible to anyone who is interested. While the financial markets can be very technical, not every role on the trading floor requires a math degree. Most roles require an understanding of financial market dynamics and relationships between products, which this book provides.

For the financial market professional who is not sitting on the trading floor, this book is a crucial handbook. Many financial market professionals are familiar with financial products and financial market participants but still find the trading floor an opaque space. The people who work on trading floors often speak in shorthand and use a lot of vocabulary which is not easily decipherable. Even worse, people on the trading floor don't have the time to help others really understand what's going on. The current financial market professional may not need the first chapter of this book, which provides a financial market foundation, but instead might prefer to start at Chapter 2, "What role do banks play in financial markets?"

For everyone else, this book will put the bank's role in the financial markets into context and explain what really happens on the fabled trading floor. Importantly, this book will help to decipher the conversations and the roles and responsibilities of the key players on the trading floor. The fact is that banks and their trading floors play a crucial role in the financial markets, but they don't need to take as much risk as they have in the past. How to manage this without fundamentally changing or damaging the financial market dynamics is the key issue for everyone to consider.

Finally, Some Key People in the Process of Writing this Book

In alphabetical order they are: Vic Adams, Susan Fleming, Richard Gommo, Bianca Hart, Konstantina Kappou, Betsy Mettler, Marcus Miholich, Anu Munshi, Jannette Papastaikoudi, Megan Rutt and Neil Schofield. They all took time out of their busy schedules to answer some questions about their areas of expertise, give feedback on portions of the early drafts and/or share some of their experiences for inclusion in this book. Needless to say, they were invaluable. Last but not least is my husband, who has listened to me drone on about details I'm sure he didn't want to become an expert on . . .

All Feedback Welcome!

Visit me on www.terriduhon.co with all questions and comments.

Women on the Trading Floor . . . Really?

The trading floor isn't known for being the most balanced place in terms of gender. It has historically been very male-dominated. One female derivatives trader was surprised to hear her boss, on Bring Your Daughter to Work Day, say to his daughter, "Here are the boys. They're here to make money. Here are the girls. They're here to look good." (Yes, that was me . . . the trader, not the daughter.)

Those were the bad old days and much has changed. However, for brevity's sake, I refer to traders and others who work in the financial world as "he" and "him." Conversely, probably because sales teams have more women in them than trading teams do, sales people are always referred to as that on the trading floor, and so they are in this book. So while I tacitly acknowledge the way things are, or are perceived to be, in the financial markets, I do so safe in the knowledge that women, even though they are in the minority, perform as well as men do on the trading floor.

CHAPTER 1

What Are Financial Markets?

This chapter will provide the financial markets foundation, terminology and context to discuss the dynamics of the trading floor. The first step is to realize that every time a financial transaction occurs between two or more parties it has ramifications in the financial markets. Parties on one side of the transaction may include individuals investing in their pensions, saving up for a rainy day or buying insurance. Most of this retail activity gets funneled through larger financial companies such as pension funds, banks, insurance companies and asset managers, which are the main investors in the financial markets. On the other side of many financial transactions are the entities that need money and raise it either by borrowing (debt markets) or by selling part of their company (equity markets). These are generally referred to as the "issuers." Extrapolate from there and the foundation of the financial markets becomes clear. It is where people with money (investors) meet people who need money (issuers). The place where the buyers and the sellers meet or where the issuers and the investors meet is called the "financial market" and the transfer itself often occurs via a bank trading floor. In other words, the buyers and sellers don't physically meet in order to trade; they use the trading floor instead. Throughout this discussion, the broad role of banks as intermediators will become clear. This chapter will also answer questions such as: Who needs money? What is private equity vs. public equity? Why do banks give out loans and how are they different from bonds? Why do derivatives exist?

When I was a senior at MIT, I started doing interview rounds with Wall Street banks for a position in sales and trading. My first interview was conducted by an options trader from a boutique trading company. After a very brief introduction, the trader said, "Make me a market for this pencil." I literally had no idea what he had just said. So the trader says, "OK, let's play a game. I'm going to roll a die. Whatever number comes up, I'll pay you that amount in dollars. If I roll a one, I'll pay you one dollar. If I roll a two, I'll pay you two dollars, etc. How much will you pay me to play that game?" I still couldn't understand what he was trying to get me to say. What did it mean to pay someone to play a game? The trader said, "OK, whatever I roll, you'll at least get a dollar, right? Will you pay me a dollar to play this game?" I immediately said, "Yes." The trader then said, "Will you pay me two dollars to play this game?" I said "yes" again. The trader then said, "Will you pay me three dollars to play this game?" I said "yes" again. I now knew how to get to the right answer but the trader was clearly irritated and was asking rapid-fire questions so I had no time to think. He then said, "Will you pay me four dollars to play this game?" I said "yes" without thinking. The trader said, "Why?" At this point I knew I had made a mistake, but I was so frazzled and nervous that I couldn't think of a good answer. I decided to brazen it out and said, "I feel lucky?" Needless to say, the interview was immediately over and I didn't get the job.

The financial markets encompass everything from shares to derivatives to commodities. They are as broad and diverse in what they offer and who participates as any supermarket is. This seems a daunting space to then try to classify and explain; however, there is one primary driver of the financial markets that is a good framework on which to base an understanding. The financial markets are primarily driven by the supply of **issuers** and the demand of **investors**. Or in other words, the **financial markets** are a place where entities who need money meet with entities that have money. Where do banks and in particular trading floors come into this? They sit in the middle. They facilitate the meeting of the supply and the demand. Within the broader world of financial markets, this particular space is called **capital markets**, where **capital** refers to cash in any currency and the focus of these capital markets is capital raising by the issuers and investing by the investors. Who are the entities who need money? Doesn't everyone need money? Yes, at some point or another, everyone generally comes to the capital markets to raise some money. Figure 1.1 shows the position of banks in the capital markets.

FIGURE 1.1 Banks as intermediators in the capital markets.

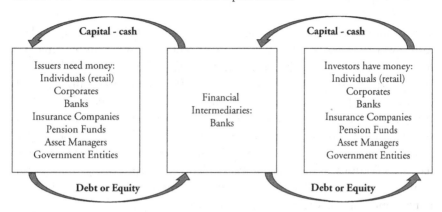

Capital moves from the investors to the issuers via banks acting as financial intermediators. Before going into details of who each of these entities is and what exactly they do in the capital markets, it is important to first distinguish between the equity capital markets and the debt capital markets. All issuers who need money must first decide whether they need **equity capital** or **debt capital**.

Throughout this book, there are references to the price of a financial product in the financial market. A **market** is where buyers and sellers meet. Think supermarket, flower market, flea market . . . Some of these are places which have fixed prices and others are places where a buyer and seller come to an agreement. In the latter case, the price is determined by the number of buyers compared to the number of sellers. This is no different in the financial market. Supply and demand are the drivers of the price of every **financial product**, such as equity and debt. We generally say the price of a financial product is where it recently traded unless some bit of financial news would have likely affected that price since the last trade. The key point to understand about financial products is that their price generally moves all day, every day based on new information. This information can be about the performance of a particular retailer, which will affect their equity or bond price or the state of a particular economy, which will affect financial products in that economy. However, while that information might give general direction of the price (in other words whether the price might go up or down), supply and demand determine the actual price.

Debt Markets

Almost all companies borrow money, or in other words **issue** debt. The easiest way to explain this is by using an example of a young couple buying a home. They don't have the money to buy the entire house, but they have savings which allow them to spend up to 30% of the house price, called "equity," and they are able to borrow the rest via a mortgage, called "debt." They also have an income that allows them to pay off the mortgage debt (plus the interest) over the years. In theory, over time, as the couple pay down the mortgage, their equity in the house increases until they eventually have 100% equity in their house and no debt. Most companies on the other hand almost never pay down their debt entirely. Instead, they continue to borrow more and more as they grow their business.

Companies borrow for a number of reasons. For example, they want to expand their business or they want to buy a competitor. It is exactly the same as an individual going to the bank and asking for a loan. The **lender** wants to know why the **borrower** needs the money and how the borrower is going to pay the money back. If the lender doesn't believe the borrower will be able to pay the money back, the lender won't lend. Governments borrow money the same way and for the same reasons that companies do. For example, they borrow to build infrastructure such as roads or they borrow to expand their defensive capabilities. The lender asks the same questions to governments as to companies as to individuals. Why is the money needed and how will it be paid back?

Years ago, debt and equity were pieces of paper much like paper money is today. Whoever is holding paper money is the owner of it. It was the same with debt and equity. There are stories of people finding boxes of often worthless shares (another term for equity) or bonds (another term for debt) in their attics. They looked like a certificate. Some were very elaborate; others were very simple. Today, there is a legal contract for equities and debt which details the terms and conditions of them, but the ownership is not a function of who is physically holding the contract itself. The ownership is mostly listed in electronic registers.

What is **debt**? Very simply, in the financial markets debt is either a bond or a loan which represents an obligation of one party to make a payment to another party. It is a financial product which gives the borrower (generally called the issuer) an amount of money (called the **principal** amount) and in exchange requires the issuer to pay a **coupon** (also called **interest**) every year and then to repay the entire principal amount at maturity. The **maturity** can be anywhere from 1 day to 100 years, but most company debt has a maturity of between two and seven years. As mentioned above, most issuers re-borrow their debt rather than pay it down. This means that if a corporate borrows $100 million for five years, the corporate is still required to pay the $100 million back to the investors at maturity in five years, but he will often do this by borrowing another $100 million. Box 1.1 summarizes the main aspects of debt.

Box 1.1   Debt summary

- Bonds and loans are the two primary types of debt (Figures 1.2 and 1.3).
- Debt is borrowed money and needs to be paid back at maturity.
- Debt has a coupon (also called an interest payment) which is due until the principal is paid back.
- The maturity of debt can be overnight out to 50 or 100 years but is generally two to seven years.

The coupon on a bond or loan is where the term **fixed income** originates. We talk about the debt markets vs. equity markets but we also use the term "fixed income markets vs. equity markets." Very broadly, the terms "debt" and "fixed income" are the same. The term fixed income is meant to distinguish between a coupon on a bond (Figure 1.2) or loan (Figure 1.3) in contrast to a dividend payment in equity that is an unknown amount and may or may not be paid to shareholders, which we will explore later in this chapter.

What is the difference between a bond and a loan? Historically, **bonds** are bought by investors and **loans** are given and held by banks. Generally, bonds are considered public financial products while loans are considered private financial products. A bond might have several hundred different investors, while a loan will often only be owned by the bank that originally gave the loan in the case of individuals and small companies or by a handful of banks in the case of larger companies. Table 1.1 compares bonds and loans.

In Figure 1.2, the bank facilitates the **issuance** of a bond by finding the investors in the bond. If Supermart needs to borrow $100 million, the bank needs to find enough investors that add up to $100 million. The bank manages both the relationship with the issuers (in this case Supermart) as well as with the investors. The bank facilitates this matchmaking between its issuer clients and its investor clients.

FIGURE 1.2 Example of a bond.

Supermart, a large supermarket chain, borrows $100 million for five years in the bond market with a coupon of 3% per year.

-The principal of the bond is $100 million.
-The coupon on the bond is 3% per year or $3 million per year.
-Supermart gets the principal of $100 million on day one from investors who buy the bond.
-Supermart pays the investors $3 million each year for five years and in five years also pays back the $100 million.

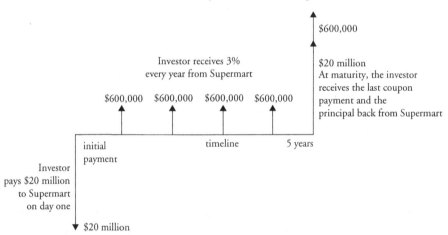

Cashflow timeline for an investor who buys $20 million of the Supermart bond

Another distinction that can generally be made between bonds and loans is that the larger the issuer, the more likely the issuer will use the bond market. This is a function of how familiar investors are with the issuer. While an entity such as a car manufacturer, like Ford or Toyota, can easily borrow in the form of bonds from investors, a small entity such as a coffee shop will likely need to go to its bank where it has a relationship and borrow in the form of a loan. Over time if the coffee shop expands and becomes a recognized brand nationally or internationally, such as Starbucks, it may eventually have access to the bond markets.

There is another distinction we make in the debt markets. It is between the two types of coupons debt can have: **fixed** and **floating**. The first is an interest rate that is fixed for the life of the bond or loan, for example a borrower issues a bond with a fixed rate of 3% per year for five years. The second is an interest rate that is reset with a set frequency based on where current interest rates are. For example, if the coupon is reset annually

FIGURE 1.3 Example of a loan.

Supermart, a large supermarket chain, borrows $100 million for five years from its bank at a rate of 3% per year.

-The principal of the loan is $100 million.
-The coupon or the interest rate on the loan is 3% per year or $3 million per year.
-Supermart gets the principal of $100 million on day one from its bank which gives out the loan.
-Supermart pays its bank $3 million each year for five years and in five years also pays back the $100 million principal.

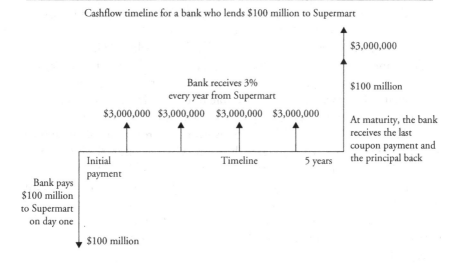

Cashflow timeline for a bank who lends $100 million to Supermart

TABLE 1.1 Comparison of a Bond and a Loan

Bonds	Loans
Bonds are arranged by banks	Loans are arranged by banks
Banks distribute the bonds to their investor clients	Banks may distribute loans to other banks
A bank intermediates between the issuer and the investor	Banks will retain some or all of a loan
There are thousands of investors in some bonds	Loans generally have one to a handful of investors

the interest changes every year. On day one, the borrower knows what his interest is for the first year but has to wait till the end of the first year to know what his interest cost will be for the next year and so on. These are both considered fixed income as defined above because in both cases there is definitely an interest payment to be made as opposed to dividends in the equity markets, which are unknown in both amount and whether they will be paid or not. Why borrowers choose fixed over floating interest payments is not always a case of their choosing as opposed to a case of what the investors are interested in buying at the time. Many borrowers are advised by their bank on what type of debt will be best received by the investors and will thus try to choose what they believe will be the cheapest for them. "Cheapest" means the one with the lowest interest cost. One generalization we can make however is that loans are generally floating rate and bonds are split evenly between fixed rate and floating rate coupons.

The role of the banks is crucial in the debt markets. They are either lending money to borrowers or **facilitating** (also called **intermediating**) the debt issuance to the appropriate investor base. "Appropriate" means that for some smaller borrowers they are only able to borrow from investors in their jurisdiction or region, for example a regional supermarket chain in the United States is likely only to have US investors, whereas a global brand such as a car manufacturer will have global investors. To be clear, the crucial role that banks play in the debt markets applies to the individual who needs a loan, a mortgage or a credit card, through to the largest corporate who needs to do a debt issuance. In fact, one could say that, historically, a bank's main role, other than taking in deposits, was to lend money or facilitate the borrowing of money. Figure 1.4 illustrates how a bank intermediates access to capital.

FIGURE 1.4 Bank intermediating access to capital in the loan market.

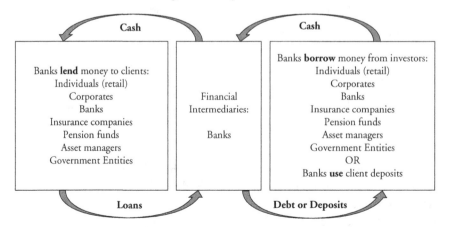

There is an old saying in the banking world in London. Traditionally, bankers were the individuals who gave out loans. The rest of the financial community in London used to say that they operated on the "3–6–3 rule": bankers borrowed money at 3%, lent money at 6% and went home by 3 p.m.

Another big difference between the bond and loan market is what happens after the bond or loan is issued. The bond will change hands (in other words trade) over time, while the loan generally won't. Once the bank has found the initial investors in the new issue bonds (called the **primary market**), the bank continues to play a crucial role in the debt markets because many investors don't keep the bonds for the full life of the bond. They will sell their bond investments for a variety of reasons, which include the price of the bond going up, which means the initial investor made a profit, or the price of the bond going down because the issuer was not performing very well or because the investor no longer liked the sector in which the company operated. All trading activity in that bond after the bank first sold it to its investors is called the **secondary market** (Box 1.2). Because loans are often given to smaller issuers who are less well known in the financial markets, once a bank has lent the money, it is not as easy to sell a loan even to other banks. In other words, there is very little secondary market trading in loans compared to bonds. Table 1.2 compares the primary and secondary markets.

Box 1.2 Reasons for trading in secondary markets

- An investor who purchased his bonds when they were first issued at a price of 100% sees that the price has gone up to 101%. He decides to sell them and make a profit.
- An investor who didn't purchase the debt when it was first issued has decided that he would like to invest in the Supermart bonds.
- An investor who purchased his bonds when they were first issued has a limit to how much the price of his bonds can change. They are now trading at 95% and he bought them at 100%. He is required to sell them now.

When an investor wants to sell a bond, he will ask a bank to buy it from him. He will not necessarily ask the bank that originally sold it to him.

TABLE 1.2 Comparison of Primary and Secondary Markets

Primary Market	Secondary Market
The first transaction of a new issue debt or equity	All trades in a product after the first
The arranging bank sells the new issue debt or equity to an investor for the first time	The investor of a new issue sells the new issue back to the arranging bank or to another bank
The investor buys the shares at the issue price and the debt at 100%	The trade price is likely different from the issue price

He can go to a different bank. A bank's job is to determine the price where the bank can sell it to another investor. The bank will often buy the bond without knowing exactly to whom it will sell the bond but knowing that it has enough investor clients that it will be able to sell the bond to one of its clients.

The price where debt trades is expressed as a percentage of the principal, for example 100% or 101% or 98%. Normally, a bond is originally issued at 100% (a bond price of 100% is called **par**) and over time − based on supply and demand, the performance of the issuer, the performance of the economy and interest rate changes − that price will move up and down. The key relationship in fixed income is between the price of the bond and how interest rates have changed since the bond was issued. If interest rates go up, the bond price will go down and vice versa. The idea is that if interest rates for five years are currently at 4% and a 5-year bond has a 3% coupon, investors will want to pay less for that bond because it is not paying 4%. This is explained in more detail in later chapters.

Trading debt

- An investor buys $50 million of a bond at a price of 100% of the principal amount. Thus the cash price is $50 million.
- The bond price moves up to 101% of the principal amount, which is $50.5 million.
- The investor sells the bond and makes a profit of 1%.
- The cash exchange for a $50 million trade is:
  −$50 million (to buy the bond) + $50.5 million (to sell the bond)
  = $0.5 million profit

Equity Markets

Now, let's focus on the equity part of the equation. As opposed to debt, which is borrowed money, **equity**, also called **shares** in a company, represents ownership in that company. A **shareholder**, also called an equity investor, is an owner of a portion of a company. While individuals and governments borrow money in the same way that companies do, issuing shares is exclusively done by companies and not by individuals or governments. The reason for this is that equity represents ownership, which doesn't make sense in the context of an individual or a government. A shareholder in a company gets a return on his investment via his ownership rights in the company. When a company earns profits, the company can either pay a dividend to its shareholders or reinvest the profits back into the company to fund growth, which will hopefully make the company increase in value. A **dividend** is the distribution of some of the profits of the company to the shareholders. Equity represents the shareholder's right to receive his pro rata portion of the dividend paid.

Supermart dividend payment

Supermart has 10 billion shares outstanding. The market price for them is $10 today. This means that Supermart has a **market capitalization** of $100 billion. Supermart has just gone through its financial year-end and has determined that it has a profit of $10 billion. It has decided to retain $5 billion of that profit for some expansion plans it has and to pay $5 billion to its shareholders as a dividend. This means that each shareholder will receive $0.50 for each share. This is a 5% return compared to the value of the shares.

- 10 billion shares outstanding
- Market price of $10 per share
- $100 billion market capitalization (10 billion shares × $10/share)
- $0.50 dividend per share ($5 billion dividend/10 billion shares)

In the case where the company reinvests the profits back into the company, in theory the value of the shares should go up and thus the shareholder makes a gain. Of course, unless the shareholder actually sells his shares the gain in this instance is simply called a **paper gain**. It is not **locked in** because the price of the shares could go back down for any number of reasons.

Unrealized gains ━━━

An investor buys shares in Supermart for $10 a share. He buys 100 shares. He has invested $1,000 in Supermart. One week later, the investor looks at the price of Supermart shares and sees that the market price has gone up to $12 a share. The investor is excited because his investment is now worth $1,200. He goes out and buys a new TV with his $200 of increased wealth. The next week, he looks at the price of Supermart shares and sees that the price has gone back down to $10. His investment is now only worth $1,000. This investor counted his chickens before they hatched.

━━━

How does this process of having shareholders start? For most entities, it starts in the private equity market then in some but not all cases moves to the public equity markets. Most entities start with a **founder** (also called an entrepreneur), which is the individual or individuals who have the original idea for a new company. They are the 100% owners of the company, called a **start-up**. As the company is starting up, in most cases, the founders will need to use their personal savings or borrow money to pay for the company's offices or general expenses. Any borrowing is generally done through a personal loan because most banks will not lend to a company until it either has a track record of profits or has assets the banks can take from the company and sell if the loan is not paid back. Then, once the founders have exhausted their personal savings or loans, they will sell portions of the company to investors. Initially, this will be to friends and family. Over time as the company grows, portions of the company may be sold to a **private equity company**, which specialize in investing in growing companies. Once investment is made by someone other than the founders, there is more than one shareholder. This private equity market is generally one in which many banks do not participate. While there are some very large private equity investments that a bank might facilitate, on the whole this is a marketplace without central facilitators, which is one of the challenges of this market.

The American reality TV show *Shark Tank* or the UK reality TV show *Dragons' Den* shows a slightly dramatic version of this process. They are good examples and can help to explain what shareholders equity means in the private equity markets, but they are not realistic in terms of the process that most company founders go through in order to find investors. It is a much longer and more arduous process of putting together presentations on the opportunity, the financial projections and assumptions, the growth prospects and the various strategies. Then the founders go through the process of finding private investors to whom they pitch their company. This is sometimes the hardest part. There are a lot of new company ideas and a lot of start-ups looking for money on any given day, so there is a lot of competition.

An entrepreneur who needs a private equity investor

An entrepreneur has developed a lawnmower which automatically mows the lawn by itself every week without the owner needing to do anything. He has called his company Lawnbot and has already sold 1,000 of these at $500 per Lawnbot. This means he has gross revenue of $500,000 so far, but it cost him $500,000 to develop the product and manufacture the first 1,000. He originally raised that money from friends and family and by taking out a second mortgage on his house, but now some of his friends and family need their money back and the entrepreneur would like to be able to pay himself a salary to continue to make the payments on his mortgage. Supermart, a large supermarket, has said it is interested in selling the Lawnbots. The entrepreneur has done some research and figures that he can get his costs on each Lawnbot down to $200 and thus will make $300 per Lawnbot sold. However, he can only reduce his costs in this way if he can build his own factory. The problem is that he doesn't have any more cash, neither do his friends or family, and he can't borrow any more personally. This is a company that doesn't have any earnings' history, hasn't yet made a profit and doesn't have a confirmed way to mass distribute its product; in other words, it is a company to whom a bank would never lend. He needs a private equity investor.

The shareholders, as owners in the company, have a say in how the company is run. Generally this is a function of the percentage of the company they own. Irrespective of the size of the company, the management of the company ultimately reports to the shareholders, who can make changes, such as who runs the company, if they feel changes are warranted to protect their investment. In a small start-up, the founders generally try to retain a majority of the ownership of the company in order to build and grow the company consistently with their original vision. This may or may not be possible and there are several good reasons why it is rare. Many start-ups require more capital to grow than the founders can access through personal savings or loans. So the founders find themselves raising capital more than once. First they go to friends and family. Then they often go back to those friends and family to raise more money. The lucky entrepreneurs are those who are eventually successful enough and big enough to go to a private equity company.

Each time the entrepreneur raises money, the portion of the company he owns gets smaller and smaller. In some cases, the other private equity investors may believe in the business idea but not in the management capability of the entrepreneur. They want to buy a significant enough portion of the equity in order to control the company. This eventually causes tension in most start-ups. It often happens that an entrepreneur or founder of a company is generally not the right person to run the company once it reaches a certain size. One of the most famous of these stories was when Steve Jobs left Apple in 1985. Although officially he resigned, he himself referred to that event as "being fired."

An entrepreneur who isn't the right CEO for his company

An entrepreneur has built an Internet company which sells fresh organic fruit. To build the company he has had to raise money several times. First he went to friends and family, then he went to private equity and then he went to the public markets and, as a result, he only owns 5% of the company now (although it is now a much bigger and more valuable company, of course). He is now the CEO of the company but his shareholders have decided that he's not the right person to build the company into other areas. He was great at starting the company but he's not that great at running large companies. At the recent board meeting, the shareholders decided they needed a new CEO and the entrepreneur officially resigned.

Eventually, if the company is large enough, well known enough and has enough profitability to go to the public equity markets, it can raise equity capital from the public. This is called the **IPO**, the **initial public offering**, of shares in a company. How much the company is able to sell and at what price is a function of the specifics of the company itself as well as down to supply and demand. In the United States, IPOs generally target selling around 20% of the company to the public markets. As opposed to the private equity investment process, which generally doesn't involve a bank to intermediate, an IPO is almost exclusively done through a bank as the intermediator (Figure 1.5). The bank identifies potential investors and helps the company put its **pitch** or presentation together. Then they go on a **road show** (also called a dog and pony show), where the company pitches to potential investors before the **launch** of the IPO.

FIGURE 1.5 Bank intermediating an initial public offering.

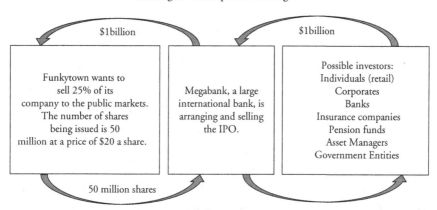

An initial public offering (IPO)

A fashion designer, Funkytown, has decided to go public. It had $800 million of sales globally and $160 million of profit last year. It has 3,000 employees and stores in 20 countries. In the IPO, it sells 50 million shares, which represent 25% of the company at $20 per share. The IPO raises $1 billion. The management and a private equity firm still own the other 75% of the company, which implies a company valuation (also called a market capitalization) of $4 billion.

An IPO moves a company from the private to the public markets because the new shares from the IPO will now be traded on an exchange which allows any investor in the world to buy some. Whereas, before the shares were public, the number of shareholders is generally limited to a handful, there now be hundreds or thousands of different shareholders. Whenever a company sells shares to new investors, be it privately or publicly, the money raised from the sale goes to the company itself. This is not the founder selling his share of the company; this is the company raising capital to invest in resources and assets to grow the business. As a result, the original shareholders in the company all now own a smaller portion of the company because their shares have been **diluted**.

In the Funkytown example, Funkytown sold 25% of its shares to the public markets. This diluted all the original shareholders by 25%. Thus the founder of Funkytown, who owned 35% of the company before

TABLE 1.3 Shareholder Numbers Pre and Post IPO

Pre IPO	Post IPO
Founder 35%	Founder 26.25%
Friends of founder 25%	Friends of founder 18.75%
Private equity firm 40%	Private equity firm 30%
	Public shareholders 25%

the IPO, now owns 35% of the 75% that is still private. In other words, the founder now owns 26.25% of Funkytown (Table 1.3).

Over time, depending on how well the share price of the IPO has performed, the founders or private equity investors may then decide to sell some of their shares to the public markets. This is called a **secondary market offering**. This is how the private shareholders can realize a gain on their investment. The shares which are still private are sold to the public markets. In contrast to an IPO, in which the money raised from the sale of shares to the public is kept by the company to fund growth, in a secondary market offering the money raised from the sale of the shares sold is kept by the selling shareholders.

A new hire in a large European bank was invited to attend a meeting with a senior banker and his client, an aeronautical engineering company. The client was interested in buying another company in the same industry and had authorized the bank to buy a small portion of shares in the other company in the public market on the client's behalf. The senior banker explained that the bank had bought different amounts of shares at different prices as the equity prices had been volatile recently. The senior banker then asked the new hire to calculate the weighted average stock price that the client had achieved. The new hire had no idea what the banker was asking but didn't want to embarrass anyone in front of the client so the new hire pulled out his calculator and furiously hit a bunch of buttons while the senior banker called out the prices and the amounts. The new hire then punched a bunch of ones into his calculator and showed the senior banker and said, "Does this look about right?" The senior banker said, "Let me check," and he quickly did the calculation himself and the meeting went on smoothly. After the client left, the senior banker took the new hire by his shirt and shoved him up against a wall and said, "If you ever embarrass me again in front of a client, you're fired." What's more amazing than anything about this true story is that the new hire still had a job.

TABLE 1.4 Private vs. Public Markets

	Private	Public
Equity Markets	**Private equity** markets are for smaller or younger companies. These shares do not trade on exchanges, although they can be traded	**Public equity** markets are for larger companies whose shares trade on exchanges
Debt Markets	Private debt markets can generally be considered loan markets. They involve smaller companies who can borrow via their banks but aren't large enough for other investors to know who they are	Public debt markets are generally bonds which are issued by larger companies who are well known to large investors

TABLE 1.5 Comparison of Equity and Debt

Debt	Equity
Bonds and loans are the two primary types of debt	Equity is also called **stock** or shares
Debt is borrowed money and needs to be paid back at maturity	Equity is ownership in a company; it does not have to ever be paid back
Debt has a coupon or an interest payment which is due annually until the principal is paid back	Equity may or may not pay a dividend
The maturity of debt can be overnight out to 50 or 100 years but is generally three to seven years	Equity does not have a maturity

In the debt and equity markets, the smaller the entity, the more likely it is to raise capital in the private loan and private equity markets (Table 1.4). As they grow, the more successful companies end up in the public bond and public equity markets. While there are millions of small companies around the world operating in the private markets, there are only thousands of large companies operating in the public markets. However, when people talk about the financial markets they are almost exclusively talking about the public markets. These are the ones people can see and track and that people can easily invest in. And it is on them that the financial media focuses.

Even within those public markets, the focus of most people is on the equity markets. Everyone hears about the S&P500, the Dow Jones, the NASDAQ, the FTSE 100, the DAX, the CAC40, the Nikkei and

TABLE 1.6 Comparison of Upsides and Downsides of Debt and Equity

Debt Investor	Equity Investor
Invests $100 in a 5-year Supermart bond with a 3% coupon	Invests $100 in the equity of Supermart at $10/share
His extreme risk is that Supermart defaults and he doesn't get all his money back	His extreme risk is that Supermart defaults and he doesn't get any money back
His downside is that interest rates go up and he is only earning 3% per year, when he could be earning higher, thus the bond price should go down	His downside is that the equity markets or Supermart don't perform that well and his $100 is now worth $80, for example (or each share is now worth $8)
His upside is that interest rates go down and he is earning 3% per year when he could be earning lower, thus the bond price should go up	His upside is that the equity markets or Supermart perform very well and his $100 is now worth $150, for example (each share is now worth $15), and on top of that Supermart is paying dividends

the Hang Seng. These are all equity market indices in different locations. Why is this the case? One reason is that most investors don't want to invest money to only get a small fixed return, which is what the debt market is about (Table 1.5). Most investors want the opportunity to invest their money and watch this investment grow with the growth of the companies. Table 1.6 compares the pros and cons of debt and equity.

Another reason that most people focus on equity markets is because equity prices are simpler to think about. The price either goes up or down, indicating that the company is doing well or not, and there is some history to show how the price has behaved in the past compared to equity markets generally. Debt prices aren't that meaningful to investors. Debt prices go up and down as well, but they depend largely on interest rates, the coupon of the debt, the maturity of the debt as well as the performance of the issuer so more information is necessary to determine what that means for the investor. (See the Supermart example.)

Supermart shares vs. Supermart bonds and their pricing ━━━━━━━━━

Supermart has 10 billion shares outstanding. The current share price is $10. On average, five million shares trade every day. Every one of the 10 billion shares looks the same and trades at the same price.

Supermart has also borrowed $50 billion via 50 different bonds and loans. Some of the bonds and loans are:

- Supermart 5% coupon $1 billion principal due in Jan 2016: price is 110%
- Supermart 3% coupon $0.5 billion principal due in Feb 2020: price is 99%
- Supermart 6% coupon $2 billion principal due in Dec 2038: price is 117%
- Supermart 8% coupon $0.3 billion principal due in May 2043: price is 112%

They have different coupons, different principal amounts and different maturities; as a result, they have different prices.

This doesn't mean that people are necessarily missing out on vital information about a large portion of the financial markets by only focusing on equity markets. Most investors consider share prices and in particular share indices to be the key indicators of what is happening in the financial markets generally. **Indices** in particular are very helpful because they do not represent just the price of one company. For example, in the case of the FTSE 100 the index represents the price of the 100 largest UK companies. As the FTSE 100 goes up or down, it is an indication of how investors feel about the UK economy and in some cases it is their view on the global economy.

Sample key equity index commentary

Some of the most watched indices globally are the S&P500 in the United States, the FTSE 100 in the United Kingdom, the DAX in Germany, the Hang Seng in Hong Kong and the NIKKEI 225 in Tokyo. Some classic comments on these indices:

- The Hang Seng had the best January in 20 years: it was up 1% for the month.
- The S&P500 is in the red today. (This means that the price is down from yesterday. Negative numbers are generally shown in red and positive numbers are generally shown in green.)

Like the debt markets, after the IPO, the original IPO investors will also sell their shares after a period of time. The reasons are the same as those in the debt market, which include the price of the equity going up so the investor made a profit, the price of the equity going down because the issuer was not performing very well or because the investor no longer liked the sector in which the company operated.

Reasons for secondary trading

- An investor who purchased his shares in the IPO when they were first issued at $20 sees that the price has gone up to $24. He decides to sell them and make a profit.
- An investor who didn't purchase the shares in the IPO has decided that he would like to invest in the shares.
- An investor who purchased his shares in the IPO has a limit to how much the price of his shares can change. They are now trading at $15 and he bought them at $20. He is required to sell them now.

The bank continues to play a crucial role in facilitating this secondary market trading of the shares. Again, investors don't have to go back to the bank that sold them the shares in the IPO; they can go to a number of banks and ask for a price. Secondary equity trading is slightly different from secondary debt trading because investors don't have to ask the bank for a price, they can see the prices on the exchange and decide at which price they want to trade, but most trading is still executed through a bank nonetheless. Chapter 2 explains this in more detail.

Secondary equity trading

- An investor buys 100 shares at the IPO share price of $20.
- The share price moves up to $21.
- The investor sells the shares and makes a profit of $1 per share.
- The profit for 100 shares is:

$$- \$2,000(\text{to buy the shares}) + \$2,100(\text{to sell the shares}) = \$100 \text{profit}$$

There is always a tremendous amount of competition for trading floor jobs in the financial markets from university graduates. In particular, they all want to be sales people or traders. There seems to be even more interest than usual post the 2008–2009 credit crisis when the press has vilified the banks. What they say about the media must be true: Any publicity is good publicity.

Other Asset Classes

Having provided the basis of the financial markets in the form of the two asset classes, equity and fixed income, we can now easily expand into other asset classes, such as currencies, commodities and emerging markets. The **currency market** (also called the **foreign exchange market** or the **FX market**) is simply where different currencies are exchanged. The drivers of the currency market are numerous, although the main ones are global entities with operations in different locations, investors who have cash in one currency but want to invest in a financial product in another currency, governments who are managing their exchange rate and speculators who have a view on one currency vs. another. Like other asset classes, banks play a big role as intermediators in the currency markets.

A currency trade

Often investors around the world invest in financial products which are not in their main currency. An asset manager in Europe who has a fund in euros will need to do a currency transaction in order to buy a bond which is denominated in US dollars. The investor wants to buy $10 million of the bond which has a price of 100%.

European asset manager investing in a US dollar bond

- His investors invest money with him in euros.
- He buys a bond denominated in US dollars.
- The bond price is 100% and the notional is $10 million.
- The current FX rate is €1 = $1.2.
- The European asset manager sells €8.33 million in exchange for $10 million with a bank.
- He uses the $10 million to buy the US dollar bond.

The **commodity market** is the most unique in the financial markets. While most financial markets are about financial products (e.g. shares, bonds or currency), the commodity markets are about physical products (e.g. oil, gold and cotton). Similar to currency markets, the focus is not on issuers vs. investors but on the physical supply chain (e.g. the producers, miners, refiners, distributers and end users). The participants in this market are often those who are part of the physical supply chain. Not all banks intermediate in commodity markets.

A commodity trade

An oil company has one million barrels of oil to sell. It wants to get the highest price possible so goes to the commodity market to sell its oil. The oil company may sell its oil to some oil refiners, who will refine it and then sell the refined product, or the oil company may go to some investors who believe that if they hold the oil for a while they can sell it later at a higher price to other commodity market participants.

Finally, there is a category within financial markets which isn't actually a separate asset class, although it is often considered one. **Emerging markets** are financial markets that are located in countries which are rapidly developing and growing. Examples are countries in Latin and South America, Eastern Europe, Asia (excluding Japan) and some Middle Eastern and African countries. These financial markets are generally less developed and as a result are much smaller than more developed financial markets. They are also more volatile, which means they have a higher tendency to have boom and bust cycles. One historical distinction in these markets is that they were in countries in which the country itself had a real probability of going bankrupt, in contrast to developed market governments, which didn't. This is clearly not always the case today. In fact, there is a commonly used term in the financial markets to talk about the emerging markets that are considered the most stable: **BRICS**. This stands for Brazil, Russia, India, China and South Africa.

The reason emerging markets are not really an asset class is because they are a microcosm of the global financial markets. They consist of equities, fixed income, currencies and commodities, just like any other financial market. The difference is that the equities and the debt are issued by entities within an emerging market country including the emerging market government. The reason they are treated like a separate asset class is because they are more volatile markets and investors will allocate generally only a small portion of their investments into emerging market financial products.

Derivative Markets

Overriding these different asset classes and their markets are the derivative markets. A **derivative** is a financial product which is *derived* from the price of other financial products. The three broad types of derivatives can be categorized as futures/forwards, options and swaps. Every asset class has derivatives of all three types. Because the derivative market is constantly evolving, there are many derivatives which don't necessarily fall easily into these three categories, but on the whole most do.

A future and a forward are similar financial products. The difference is that futures are standardized and traded on exchanges and forwards are more tailored and do not trade on exchanges. This will be explained in more detail in Chapter 2. For now, let's just focus on how the products work. A **future/ forward** is a financial product that allows an investor to buy from a seller a specific amount of an **underlying** financial product at a fixed price at a specified time in the future. For example, in September 2012, the buyer of the December 2012 oil future for 1,000 barrels of oil at a fixed price of $105/ barrel has agreed to buy 1,000 barrels of oil at $105/barrel in December 2012. Rather than waiting to sell its barrels of oil when they are produced, an oil company could decide to use oil futures to sell its barrels of oil in the future and lock in a price today. It would do this if it were concerned about the price of oil going down before the barrels of oil were produced.

If the price of oil/barrel is lower than $105 in December 2012, the oil company has locked in the price of $105/barrel and is happy about its financial transaction. On the other hand, if the price of oil/barrel is higher than $105 in December 2012, the oil company may feel that is has missed an opportunity because it is now obligated to sell its oil at $105/barrel.

In the example of an oil future traded at $105/barrel, if the price of oil/barrel goes higher than $105 in December 2012, the buyer of the future has made money. If the price of oil/barrel goes lower than $105 in December 2012, the buyer has lost money. We normally show this as a graph (Figure 1.6).

An **option** is similar to a future/forward except that the buyer of the option has the right but not the obligation to buy the underlying financial product in the future. For example, an investor has bought a 3-month option on the FTSE 100 (the UK stock market index) struck at 6,000. In September, the investor believes that the UK stock market prices will go higher by December; however, the investor isn't 100% sure of this view so, rather than buy shares in the UK stock market, he buys a 3-month option on the FTSE 100 with a **strike** of 6,000. If the FTSE 100 is higher than 6,000 in three months' time, the investor will exercise his option and will make money. If the FTSE 100 is lower than 6,000 in three months' time, the investor will not exercise his option because it would mean losing money. The right to buy at 6,000 in the future has a cost, though. That is called the **option premium**. If the investor doesn't exercise his option, he will have lost the option premium that he paid in the first place.

FIGURE 1.6 Graph of an oil future.

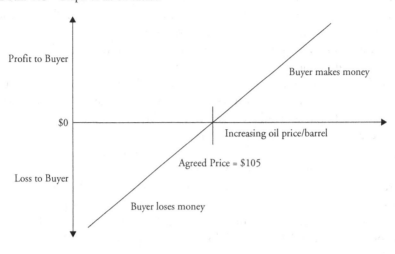

FIGURE 1.7 Graph of an equity option.

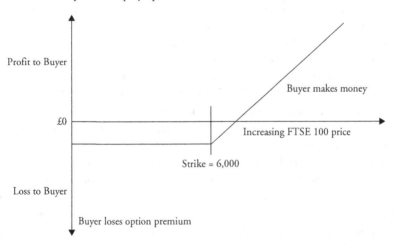

The graph of an option is different from the graph of a future/forward because the option buyer does not lose money if the price is below the strike (Figure 1.7). The option buyer only loses his option premium.

An **interest rate swap** is when two parties exchange a fixed rate for a floating rate on the same notional amount. These were originally driven by loan borrowers who wanted to pay fixed coupons rather than floating coupons, which are more common in loans.

FIGURE 1.8 An example of an interest rate swap.

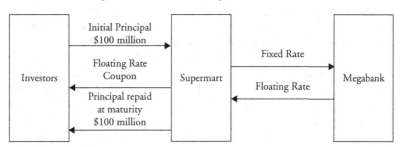

In Figure 1.8, Supermart has borrowed money with a floating rate coupon and has exchanged that coupon for a fixed rate with Megabank. The risk that Supermart wants to manage is the unknown coupon that it had on its debt. If interest rates changed over time, in particular if they went higher, Supermart may not be able to afford the coupon payments. If it can swap the floating rate with a fixed rate, then Supermart knows exactly how much it has to pay each year. The key is that the floating rate coupons cancel out and Supermart is only left with a fixed rate coupon it has to pay to Megabank.

An important point to make about derivative markets is that there is no concept of primary or secondary markets. Derivatives are individual contracts between two parties. A derivative can be created by two parties' agreeing to a contract, and the two parties can agree to **unwind** (i.e. tear up) the contract when one party wants to get out of the trade. However, like every other financial product, market prices move, so there is generally a cost for one party or the other to get out of a derivative early. The size of the derivative market is simply the outstanding notional of derivative contracts between two parties.

To put derivative markets in perspective, the approximate size of some derivative markets are:

- The interest rate derivative market is by far the largest, with approximately $600 trillion notional of contracts outstanding in 2011.
- The currency derivative market has approximately $60 trillion notional amount of contracts outstanding in 2011.
- The equity derivative market has approximately $11 trillion notional amount of contracts outstanding in 2011.

Source: www.bis.org

Because financial markets are global, different cultures are constantly coming into contact with often amusing results. One day, a team of people from the London trading floor of a major European bank went to Madrid to meet some of the clients with whom they often traded. The sales team in the Madrid office told them the day was packed with client meeting so they started early that morning. At around 1 p.m., the Madrid team brought the London team back to the Madrid office and showed them to the boardroom, where there were some sandwiches laid out on the table. The London team said, "Who are we meeting here?" The Madrid team said, "No one. We assumed you wanted to work through lunch." At the time, the working day in Spain was cut in half by a long lunch break, when people often went home to have lunch. The Madrid team were baffled by the fact that their London colleagues worked through lunch but were aware of the practice so had provided a "working lunch" for their London colleagues while they went home to have lunch with their families.

Conclusion

In most cases, entities that need cash go to the equity or debt markets to raise that cash as facilitated by a bank. In almost all instances, a bank will facilitate the raising of cash in the debt markets whether the borrower is large or small. This is because the bank will either lend the money itself in the case of small borrowers (e.g. individual borrowers) or facilitate the access to larger investors in the case of large borrowers (e.g. international companies). In contrast, the equity markets have slightly less facilitation by banks. In the case of private equity, the smaller the issuer of equity, the less likely a bank will be involved even in the facilitation of the meeting of the issuer and the investor. But as the issuer becomes larger, and almost certainly in the case of all public equity, a bank will be involved in the facilitation of the meeting of the issuer and the investor during the IPO.

After the initial sale of a new issue equity or debt product, there is secondary trading that occurs as investors decide whether to sell or buy equities and debt products over time. Banks facilitate this meeting of buyers and sellers in a similar way to the meeting of issuers and investors. And beyond equity and debt there are other asset classes as well as all of the derivative products. Banks are the main facilitators of all of these financial products. Another way to think about a bank's role is that it provides access to global financial markets for all of its clients, both issuers and investors.

In all the upheaval following the 2008–2009 credit crisis, the value that banks add to the financial system has been obscured by the huge losses they and their clients have sustained. The entire world is looking at the banking system and questioning what the point of it is and, in particular, wondering what role trading floors, which is where a lot of these losses originated, should have going forward. Very simply, banks, and in particular trading floors, have a valid purpose and are necessary for the smooth operation of the global financial markets. This book will expand on the role of the trading floor and give many examples to demonstrate that the trading floor remains a vital part of the world's financial systems. Of course, it doesn't mean that banks always get it right.

Discussion Questions

For what reasons does a borrower choose a bond over a loan when he needs to borrow money?

What are the cashflows of a $100-million investment in a bond with a 5% annual coupon, a 5-year maturity and an initial price of 101%?

After the iPad was introduced, why would anyone sell their shares in Apple?

Why don't technology companies generally pay dividends?

How do private equity companies make money?

See www.terriduhon.co for answers and discussion.

CHAPTER 2

What Role Do Banks Play in Financial Markets?

This chapter will explore the role of the banks in more detail. Chapter 1 used the terms "intermediate" and "facilitate," but this is an oversimplification. These terms are fine for primary markets, but they do not provide insight into what it means for banks to be liquidity providers, which occurs in secondary markets, currency markets, commodity markets and derivatives markets. To better understand the role of liquidity provider, we need to explore how banks provide liquidity by looking at the different central trading platforms, such as exchanges and interbank brokers. We also need to understand why providing liquidity is important to the market by looking at a bank's clients and their needs. This chapter will answer questions such as: What is liquidity? What is the difference between a bank trading floor and an exchange? What is the difference between broking a trade and taking risk on a trade? What is financial risk management? Where do most trades occur?

Liar's Poker is one version of a very common game played at dinner parties and on family holidays. This particular version of the game is often played on trading floors and is generally associated with financial markets. Each person starts with a dollar bill, a pound note or some paper currency with a unique serial number. The game is about guessing how many of the same number or letter there are in the group. For example, the first person starts with two 1s. In a group of three or more, with a 10-digit serial number, it is highly probable that there are at least two 1s between all the serial numbers. The next person needs to make at least one of the numbers higher, for example three 1s or two 2s. The person who doesn't think what has previously been called is possible says "liar" to the previous guess. There are then different versions of what happens to the dollars at the end of each round with some versions requiring the liar to pay everyone a dollar if he was wrong or to receive all the dollars if he was right. It is a game of probability; however, another way to view this game is that it's about bluffing as much as it is about reading the other people in the game, hence its name: Liar's Poker.

Banks, in particular their trading floors, play a crucial role in financial markets which is often summarized as "intermediating" or "facilitating" access to the financial markets for their clients. When discussing primary markets in debt and equity, this description is apt. A bank intermediates between its issuer client of debt or equity and its investor clients in the debt or equity. In other words, the bank finds the investors who provide capital to the issuers of debt and equity. And in the case of debt capital, where the form of the debt is a loan, the bank itself acts as the investor. In the secondary markets, and in currency markets, commodity markets and derivative markets, where primary and secondary aren't meaningful terms, the words "intermediating" and "facilitating" are not particularly helpful or descriptive for the role that a bank plays. A better description is **liquidity provider**. For example, if a client wants to sell some stock, and a bank is a liquidity provider in that stock, the bank will put a price on the stock where the client can sell the stock to the bank irrespective of whether the bank can immediately sell the stock on. This is called "providing liquidity." A liquidity provider in a particular financial product is generally a bank that will always put a price on a trade for a client.

To understand the bank's role in financial markets we need to understand how and why banks provide liquidity. How a bank provides liquidity is sometimes via its client base, but often it is via exchanges, interbank brokers and electronic trading systems. We will call these **central market platforms**. When a bank does a trade with a client, for example buys stock from the client, the bank is not guaranteed to have another client who wants to buy the stock from the bank, thus the bank is taking some risk. In providing liquidity to a client, a bank, to some extent, relies on the fact that there are several other liquidity providers in a financial product, many of whom have different clients. Thus, one of these other liquidity providers may want to buy the stock from the bank because it has a client who is interested in investing in that stock. Rather than call up several different liquidity providers, the bank can go to a central market platform.

A bank provides liquidity because it is a service its clients need. Thus, understanding what the different client categories are and what transactions these clients do in the financial markets helps us to better understand the crucial role of the bank as liquidity provider to the financial markets. Financial market texts are full of references to issuers and investors when discussing clients. While these roles are important to understand, we can't forget that many clients also use the financial markets to manage financial risk that they have. Thus, we look at the client as issuer and investor as well as risk manager.

What It Means to Provide Liquidity

The term **liquidity** is often used in reference to how much of a particular financial product can trade each day (this is also called daily volume) or how much can trade at a certain price. It is a relative term which makes it difficult to have a precise meaning for any one financial product. For example, a bond with a total principal amount of £1 billion that only trades £10 million a week on average across all market participants would not be considered very **liquid**; however, if that bond traded £100 million every day on average, it would be considered more liquid. If a company has 10 million shares and only 1,000 trades each week on average, the shares would not be considered very liquid; however, if 50,000 shares traded every day on average, the shares would be considered more liquid. We will explore this in more detail throughout this book. For the purposes of this chapter, the role of the bank as liquidity provider for its clients is to put a price on the trade the client wants to do. The bank provides a price for the size which may or may not be larger than the total amount of that financial product that trades each day across all market participants.

A bank providing liquidity

A client wants to sell 20,000 shares of Supermart today. It asks its bank, Megabank, to execute this trade. In other words, it asks Megabank to buy 20,000 shares today. Megabank knows that the number of shares that trades on average every day in Supermart is 30,000. But that is the result of possibly hundreds of smaller trades. A trade of 20,000 is a very large trade. Megabank will put a price where it is prepared to buy 20,000 shares from its client that day.

When a bank provides liquidity to its clients, it is generally taking the risk that the price of the financial product moves before it is able to close out its position (in the case of stocks and bonds) or hedge its position (in the case of derivatives). To **close out** a **position** in a stock or bond means that if the bank has bought a stock or bond from a client it needs to sell that same stock or bond on to another market participant. When talking about derivatives, we use a different term because derivatives are contracts between two parties. The contract itself does not get transferred to another market participant the way a stock or bond does. We use the word "hedge," which means to mitigate or reduce risk. To **hedge** a derivative means that if the bank has bought an option from a client it needs to sell an option to another market participant. The bank will execute a new contract with another market participant to hedge a derivative.

Coming back to the term "intermediate," a bank's role in the financial markets is not to be the end investor in a financial product when a client wants to trade that product. Its role is to intermediate between buyers and sellers. A bank will sell when a client wants to buy and buy when a client wants to sell by providing a price where the bank can close out or hedge its position while still making a profit either with another liquidity provider or with another client. For example, if the bank buys shares at $9.50/share, it is because the bank believes it can sell them at a price higher than $9.50/share. The bank needs this **margin**, or the difference between where the bank will buy the shares and where the bank believes it can sell the shares to protect it against the risk it takes. The margin also gives the bank the ability to make a profit on the trade. The larger the size of the trade, the more risk the bank takes. Any trade adds supply or demand to the market for a financial product and as a result can move the market price. The smaller the size of the trade, the less the price of the financial product will move as a result of the trade, and vice versa. So, the larger the size of the trade, the more risk the bank takes to close out or hedge the position because the close out or hedge on the part of the bank can move the market price.

Market price and liquidity

In the earlier example where Megabank was asked for a price by a client who wished to sell 20,000 shares of Supermart, Megabank will provide a price where it believes it can sell the shares at a profit. If Megabank puts a price of $9.50 on the shares, Megabank believes it can sell the shares higher than that. But selling 20,000 shares of Supermart in one day when on average across all market participants 30,000 shares generally trade could push the market price below $9.50. Megabank will need to be very careful in closing out this position. Megabank will likely use several different trades over several days to close out this position in a way that does not push the market price against the bank.

Providing liquidity to clients is not something that banks can always do on their own. While in the primary markets banks rely on their own client network to distribute equity or debt, in the secondary, currency, commodity and derivative markets, banks also rely on exchanges, interbank brokers and electronic trading systems (central market platforms). They are distinctly different from the banks in that they are primarily a matchmaking service. A trade gets executed at these central market platforms only if there is a buyer and a seller willing to trade at the same price. A bank, on the other hand, will provide a price to a client whether it is sure it can close out or hedge the position or not. Thus, a bank provides liquidity by taking risk. These trades are often called **principal trades**. A central market platform generally provides access to other liquidity providers. These trades are often called **broker trades** or **agency trades**.

Figure 2.1 is a simplified diagram of a hub and spoke relationship where the dotted lines represent relationships. In the center is a central market platform

FIGURE 2.1 Hub and spoke relationships.

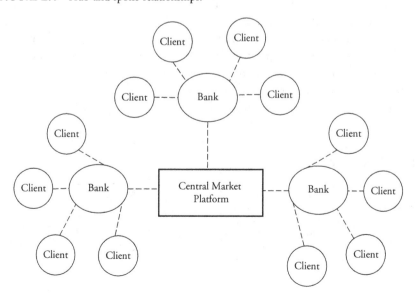

such as an exchange. The banks sit around the exchange and the clients sit around the banks. When a client wants to sell his shares in Supermart he calls up Megabank, with whom he has a relationship, and asks where Megabank is prepared to buy those shares. Megabank then has the following options:

- Megabank can agree to do the trade with the client before it is certain of the price it can close out the trade. This is providing liquidity which involves taking risk. This is called a principal trade.
  - Megabank can then trade with another bank through a central market platform in order to close out its position.
  - Or Megabank can then trade with another of its own clients in order to close out its position.
- Megabank can find a client on the other side before agreeing to do the trade in the first place. While this might be referred to as "providing liquidity," a better term is **broking** the trade because Megabank is not taking risk: it is acting as a **broker**.

Major banks (also called **major dealers**) are liquidity providers for multiple financial products globally. In contrast, there are many smaller banks or specialist financial entities which may only provide liquidity in a few financial products or none at all. These entities may only act as a broker between their client and a major bank acting as a liquidity provider. Figure 2.2 illustrates this idea.

The first client could be the Teachers' Pension Fund of Louisiana (TPFL). It has decided to sell a Supermart bond that it bought a year ago. This client is not very large and so doesn't have a direct relationship with the major banks. It has a relationship with a smaller regional bank called Southern Direct. It calls up Southern Direct and expresses its interest in selling this Supermart bond. Southern Direct does not want to take risk on this bond by doing a principal trade but is prepared to facilitate the transaction by calling

FIGURE 2.2 Trade flow.

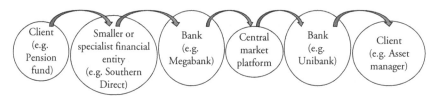

one of the major banks, Megabank. Megabank is a major bank that provides liquidity in US corporate bonds and immediately tells Southern Direct that it will buy the Supermart bond at a particular price. Southern Direct then tells TPFL the price where it can sell the bond. Southern Direct may or may not take a commission on this broker trade, depending on its relationship with TPFL. TPFL agrees to the price and Megabank now owns the Super-mart bond. Megabank now checks to see whether any of its larger clients are interested in buying the Supermart bond. If not, Megabank will go to a central market platform to see whether any of the other major banks are interested. As it turns out, Universal Bank is interested because it has an **asset manager** client who has expressed an interest. Megabank sells the bond to Universal Bank, which sells the bond to its client.

The individuals involved in this decision-making are all likely sitting in an area designated as a **trading floor** in their respective companies. All of these trading floors will look very different from the popular image of the exchange trading floor, which is an image of an **open outcry** exchange. That was where a bunch of wild-haired men ran around wearing colored jackets and screaming "Buy!" and "Sell!" Most exchanges today operate with an electronic trading system, so sadly that fun image is a bit out of date. Today trading floors are a bit more sedate. They generally have rows of desks without partitions of any sort across, in many cases, the entire floor of a building. The employees behind the desks are mostly wearing suits and facing up to six or seven computer screens on their desks while talking on one or more phones and sometimes shouting across to someone on a different row of desks. This can be as seemingly chaotic and loud as that antiquated image of an exchange trading floor but is on the whole, compared to an open outcry exchange, far less physical in nature.

The transaction in Figure 2.2 also illustrates the differences between the different usages of the term "trading floor" in the financial markets.

- One type of trading floor is located within the two end clients. The activity on these trading floors is about research and investment strategy. Financial companies such as insurance companies, pension funds, asset managers and hedge funds have these types of trading floors. These are generally the largest and most active investors in the financial markets.
- The trading floor that is located within the regional bank is about facilitation. These trading floors are designed to facilitate the buying and selling of financial products for their clients. They are not always designed to provide liquidity; they are often merely acting as a broker.

TABLE 2.1 Different Types of Trading Floors

Market participant	Investing	Liquidity providing (e.g. principal trades)	Broking (e.g. broker trades)
Clients (the end user)	Yes	No	No
Smaller or specialist financial entity	No	Sometimes	Sometimes
Central market platform	No	No	Yes
Major bank	No	Yes	Sometimes

- Another type of trading floor is that of a specialist financial entity that might provide liquidity in one type of financial product but not in others. This means that sometimes this entity is a liquidity provider and sometimes this entity is merely acting like a broker.
- The trading floor located on the central market platform is generally designed to do broker trades between major banks acting as liquidity providers. Most clients don't interact directly with a central market platform. That is generally a relationship that only the major banks have.
- Finally, we have the trading floor at the major banks. These trading floors are about providing liquidity, although sometimes they will act as brokers. Table 2.1 summarizes the different types of trading floors.

Principal trades are when a bank provides liquidity and takes risk. If a client wants to sell a bond the bank will provide a price where it is prepared to buy the bond whether it has a client on the other side of the trade or not. The bank will then close out the position by finding a market participant who wants to buy the bond. Because this doesn't happen instantly, the bank is prepared to take the risk that the bond price will move between the time the major bank buys it from the first client and the time the major bank is able to sell it on. The larger the major bank, and thus the more clients and the more trades it is asked to do, the less the risk to the major bank because it is able to find the other side of the trade quickly.

In the trade, described in Figure 2.2, between Megabank and Southern Direct, Megabank put a price on the Supermart bond without knowing for certain that it would be able to sell the bond and make a profit. Two example scenarios are given in Box 2.1 which shows how Megabank could either make a profit or a loss on this trade.

Box 2.1   Risk from providing liquidity

Megabank says it will buy the Supermart bond at a price of 101.5%.

- For a trade notional of $10 million, Megabank will pay Southern Direct $10.15 million in exchange for the bond.
- The market price moves before megabank can close out the position:
  - Scenario 1: The price moves to 102%; Megabank makes a profit of 0.5%, or $50,000.
  - Scenario 2: The price moves to 100%; Megabank makes a loss of 1.5%, or $150,000.

Major banks are harsh places to work. A trading floor within a major bank is an even harsher place to work. Everyone is very busy. Market prices are always moving, and clients always need something as soon as possible. Being nice and diplomatic isn't always the first thing on people's mind. As a result, people often find things out in the most brutal manner. Several stories exemplify this but some of the most extreme are when people get made redundant from the trading floor. Some of the more interesting stories are:

- Being told you were made redundant by the security guard at the door when your card didn't work to let you in the building anymore.
- Being told you were made redundant by the IT support person when your password didn't work on your computer.
- Being handed a box of your things by the security guard at the door to the trading floor because you are no longer allowed on the trading floor.

Central Market Platforms

"Central market platform" is not exactly a standard term used in finance, nor does it roll off the tongue. The term refers to exchanges, interbank brokers and electronic trading systems. These platforms are the background providers of the financial market's matchmaking between buyers and sellers for **standardized** financial products. A standardized financial product is one that is so commonly traded that the financial market participants have over the years agreed to a number of standards. Most public shares, public debt and most derivatives that are traded are considered standardized products.

Exchanges and the products they trade are well known in the financial markets, for example a UK stock that trades on the London Stock Exchange or a US stock that trades on the New York Stock Exchange. The financial products that trade on exchanges are called **exchange traded products**, or **ETPs**. Depending on the exchange, if clients meet certain financial hurdles, such as a minimum cash deposit, they can sometimes deal directly with an exchange for a particular financial product. This means that major bank trading floors do not need to intermediate every transaction for products that are exchange traded. Regardless, most of the time clients deal through an exchange broker, which is often a major bank that deals directly with the exchange (Figure 2.3). This could be executing an **order** to trade a specific notional at a specific price on the exchange on a client's behalf or it could be providing liquidity rather than just taking an order from the client. In either case the trade is always recorded on the exchange. Other well-known exchanges are the NASDAQ, NYMEX, CBOT, EUREX, DAX, FTSE, Hang Seng and Nikkei.

An **exchange broker** can be any financial company from an independent stockbroker to a major bank. Most major banks are designated as a broker by the exchanges with whom they deal. Often major banks will refer to themselves as a broker or a **broker/dealer**. This means that they will execute an order on the client's behalf as broker as well as provide liquidity

FIGURE 2.3 Trading through an exchange.

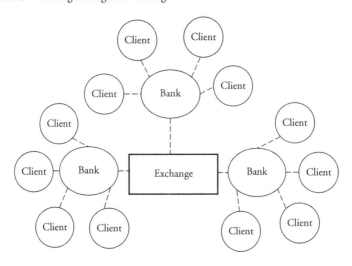

for a client when requested for a particular ETP. But these sound very similar. What is the difference between executing an order on a client's behalf and providing liquidity for a client? The distinction is whether or not the major bank takes risk.

A client calls up its bank and says that he would like to sell 100 shares of Supermart today. The bank says that the price where the client can sell currently showing on the exchange is $9.95. The client says to execute the trade. This is an order. The bank executes the order on the client's behalf with the exchange. The bank has not taken risk, nor has it provided liquidity. It has just provided access. This is broking a trade. Another example of an order is if the client comes back and says that $9.95 is not high enough. The client gives an order to the bank to sell the shares at $10.00. The bank takes this order but cannot guarantee that it will be able to fill the order at this price. The bank will submit this order to the exchange on behalf of the client.

In contrast, in a principal trade, the client calls the bank and says it wants to sell 10,000 shares of Supermart today and wants a price right away. The major bank agrees to buy them at $9.90 without knowing at what price it could sell the position. The reason the client asked the major bank to do this is because the client couldn't immediately sell these shares at the exchange prices. The size of this trade is too large. This is an example of the bank providing liquidity which involves taking risk.

One of the distinctions between ETPs and financial products that aren't traded on exchanges is generally the availability and transparency of historical data about the price and volume of trades on each financial product which trades on an exchange. Because every trade in that product must be reported to the exchange, it is an excellent repository of information. Anyone can look up this data on the exchange websites. For example, look up Apple on Nasdaq. There is historical data as well as current price data.

Sample Apple share prices

The current price data will often show the best **bid** and the best **offer**. The bid is the price where a market participant is willing to buy this stock and the offer (also called the **ask**) is where a market participant is willing to sell this stock. A sample bid and offer for Apple shares might be a bid of $623.91 and an offer of $624.02.

Also, investors who trade ETPs are more likely to give orders to trade specific sizes at specific prices to their bank than in other financial products.

This means that, for ETPs, banks are often acting as brokers more than they are acting as liquidity providers. As a result, one of the technological developments in trading ETPs is the ability of the large major banks who act as brokers to effectively provide a matchmaking service to their clients who give orders to trade on that exchange. This means that the more orders a bank receives over the day, the better that bank is able to match buyers and sellers between its own clients rather than going to the exchange with every order. This has created a phenomenon called **dark pools of liquidity**. While the trades are reported to the exchange, they are effectively happening **off-exchange**. While this is the bank acting as broker, it could also be considered a version of the bank providing liquidity (without taking any risk) to its clients by virtue of having so many clients.

Interbank brokers are less well known outside of the financial markets, primarily because they historically only dealt with major banks – as the name implies (Figure 2.4). For financial products, and derivatives in particular, which are not exchange traded but are standardized, interbank brokers have acted as the primary matchmaking platforms. These products are called **over the counter** products, or **OTC** products. One of the main differences between exchanges and interbank brokers is that often only one

FIGURE 2.4   Trading through an interbank broker.

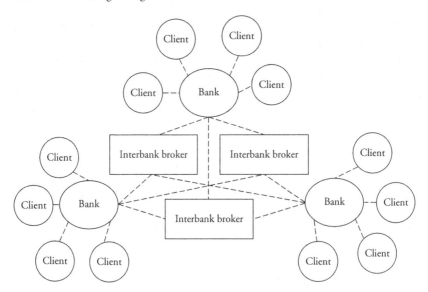

exchange trades any particular product. For example, a stock is generally only listed on the New York Stock Exchange, whereas there are multiple interbank brokers who will broke interest rate swaps. While most exchanges have moved to electronic trading, interbank brokers still practice **voice trading** on the phone with the major bank trading floors despite interbank brokers having invested in electronic trading systems as well. Also, the exchange will have a record of all the trades that occurred that day in a particular product, while there is not necessarily any central database for trades that occur through interbank brokers. Well-known interbank brokers include Icap, Tradition and Tullett.

The distinction between ETPs and OTCs is one that often causes some confusion. One way to think about financial products is that they run the gamut from highly standardized to highly tailored. Most of the products at the highly standardized end of the product spectrum trade on exchanges often via the banks, as explained above. In the middle are products which are mostly but not totally standardized and they trade over the counter, which is a direct reference to the bank trading floors, via the interbank brokers. The highly tailored products, at the other end of the spectrum, trade over the counter only with no interbank brokers. We can *very* generally say that most shares trade on exchange, most bonds and derivatives trade over the counter and all tailored products are over the counter and don't even have interbank brokers. Table 2.2 lists common products in the different categories.

While many people are familiar with derivatives that trade on exchanges, the majority of derivatives are traded over the counter. There are approximately $700 trillion derivative contracts outstanding. Of that, only around 10% trade on exchanges. Thus the majority of derivatives are traded over the counter.

Tailored/structured financial products are often created specifically for one client. This could mean an interest rate swap with a 5.5-year maturity

TABLE 2.2 ETP vs. OTC Products

Common ETP products	All public shares, some bonds, some derivatives (e.g. equity index futures and options)
Common OTC–interbank broker products	Most bonds, most derivatives (e.g. interest rate swaps, forwards and options)
Common OTC-only products	Structured bonds, tailored derivatives. (The word "tailored" is generally used with derivatives and "structured" generally with bonds)

instead of the benchmark 5-year maturity or a bond, generally called a structured bond, which has been designed for one investor or one type of investor, as will be explained in Chapter 4. A bank will create the product and trade it with the client. The bank does this knowing that it will not be able to close out or hedge the position easily because there is no other liquidity provider in that tailored financial product. The bank will use the standardized financial products that trade on exchange or in the interbank broker market to do the best hedge possible. This illustrates another role of a bank, which is to provide liquidity to clients by intermediating between the tailored financial product the client wants to do and the standardized products that the bank can use to hedge. We explore this further in later sections of this book.

An interbank broker's clients are banks. While bank sales people are busy entertaining their clients and maintaining the relationship with a bit of wining and dining, interbank brokers are busy entertaining the traders with a bit of wining and dining and sometimes lap dancing. There was one large US bank which once decided that this created a moral hazard risk. It didn't want its traders to feel obliged to trade with any one particular interbank broker simply because that interbank broker had bought dinner the night before. The traders at that bank were required to pay their own way. This created an awkward social situation for everyone because neither the bank's traders nor the interbank brokers could get comfortable with the role shift. Needless to say, this rule didn't last for very long.

Electronic trading systems augment or even replace existing trading relationships and are thus operated by exchanges, interbank brokers, or banks. It means that everyone can trade via their computers for a certain size for the more standardized ETP and OTC financial products. Electronic trading systems have made the financial market more transparent and open to new types of market participants. For example, a new type of broker has emerged. This new broker operates a system which sits between the major banks and their clients and trades products that are historically not exchange traded. This means that a client can now look at one screen and see bids and offers from different major banks on benchmark interest rate swaps for example. In order for these electronic trading systems to be able to provide this service to clients, they have agreements with the major banks that the major banks will provide bid and offer prices for particular products. In other words, the major banks are still the liquidity providers in the market. An example of this type of trading system is Tradeweb.

Box 2.2 shows the type of information that might be available on an electronic trading system.

Box 2.2   Sample electronic trading system

BIDS OFFERS
SIZE 10,000 8,000 5,000 **4,000 3,500**   5,500   7,500 10,500
PRICE $9.75 $9.80 $9.85 **$9.90 $9.95** $10.00 $10.05 $10.10

Last trade: **3,000 at $9.95**

Above each price is the number of shares that can be traded at that price. This picture highlights the best bid and offer in bold and shows that behind the best bid and offer are other bids and offers for wider prices. There is no further information given here. The number of market participants at each price is not shown. Who the market participants are is not available. The other information that is missing and will never be available is whether this is the full picture of supply and demand or not. Are there other interested market participants who would like to trade at one of these prices but haven't yet put in a formal bid or offer on the electronic trading system? Other electronic trading systems simply show the best bid and offer of $9.90 and $9.95, and nothing else. What information is provided depends on the general convention in a particular financial product and the systems capability of the particular electronic trading system.

Despite the fact that clients can sometimes trade directly with electronic trading systems that are not operated by banks, it is fair to say that, generally, the bids and offers shown on electronic trading systems come from banks acting as liquidity providers in that particular financial product, thus the picture of the financial market where the central market platform is in the center as intermediator, the banks as liquidity providers are around that and the clients as end users are on the outside remains true in most markets.

The question then arises of when does a client choose to trade directly with a central trading platform and when does he choose to trade with a major bank? The two main answers to this are volume and tailored/structured products. The central trading platforms can't always accommodate the size a client might need to trade. This simply means that if the client wants to trade 10,000 shares and the exchange is only showing prices for 1,000 shares, the client will likely go directly to a major bank. If the electronic trading system is showing prices for $100 million for an interest rate swap and the client wants to trade $500 million, the client will likely go to a major bank. On the other hand, if the client wants something which is tailored/structured, he almost always has to go directly to a major bank.

Clients sometimes have an individual whose expertise is executing trades. This individual doesn't necessarily make the original decision to buy or sell but he figures out how to get the best execution, which is another way of saying how to get the best price. He will know the different ways of executing a trade in a particular financial product. Depending on the type of financial product, the size of the trade and the state of the financial markets, different ways of executing will make sense.

Despite the number of electronic trading systems, many financial market participants still like to speak to someone and exchange thoughts on what is happening in the financial market. This is another reason that bank trading floors provide value to the financial markets: they are full of people who are well versed in the dynamics of the financial market. Clients talk to the trading floor and trading floors talk to their interbank brokers. This is how information flows quickest through the financial marketplace.

When banks take risk when they trade with clients, they make money via the price they put on the financial product. If the client asks where the price is, the bank's goal is to put a price where it can make a profit. If it puts a price of $9.90 per share on an equity trade, it hopes to be able to sell the shares at $9.95 and make a profit while remaining competitive with other banks. The brokers, on the other hand, aren't taking risks so they can't make their profits this way. They need to charge a fee per transaction.

Some fees are charged as a function of the notional amount of the trade and some on a per trade basis irrespective of the size of the trade. For example, individual clients of stock brokers often pay a fixed fee per trade, such as $10 per stock trade, irrespective of size as long as the trade is executed electronically. If the client needs to speak to a broker it can be as high as $50 per trade. On the other hand, bank clients of interbank brokers often pay a fee that is a function of the size and maturity of the trade. For example, a $100 million 5-year interest rate swap typically has a fee of $3,000, while a $100 million 10-year interest rate swap has a fee of $6,000.

Trading floors are often frantic, serious places when market prices are moving a lot. Market prices are always moving, but some days are more volatile than others. This means that when financial markets are quiet, or at the end of a day as the financial markets wind down, people on the trading floor let off steam. They do this in a variety of ways. One way is by playing practical jokes on anyone they can. Often, recruitment firms and interbank brokers get the brunt of this activity. Once, an interbank broker was looking to hire a sales person from a major US bank trading floor. The sales person wasn't interested in this job at all and so, in lieu of a professional reply to the interbank broker, he sent through a fax of his bottom.

Who Are the Clients and What Are They Doing?

If the role of a bank is to intermediate, provide liquidity and take risk, what we then need to understand is why these roles are important. To do that we look at the clients of the bank and what their needs are. The starting point for understanding the different clients that a major bank deals with on the trading floor is to classify clients into different types (Figure 2.5). The first major distinction is between **individuals** (also called **retail**), companies and government entities. Among the companies there is then a distinction between **financial companies** and **corporates**. This distinction is made because financial companies are in the business of transacting in the financial markets, whereas this is not the primary business of corporates. Financial companies are

FIGURE 2.5 Simple client categories.

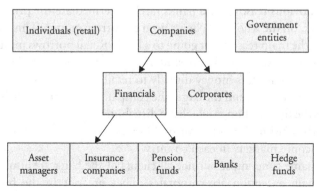

then further broken down into asset managers, insurance companies, pension funds, smaller banks and hedge funds. These financial companies are the main investor base in most financial products.

Major banks are often so keen to keep clients' business that they often turn their clients into monsters. There was a large European client with whom a major US bank had done a lot of business over the years. One particular trader had been working with that client for years as he worked his way up from analyst to associate and eventually to vice president. At the same time, the client's management team had remained the same. One day, this bank vice president was in a car with one of the client's senior managers as they were on a road show in Paris. The client turned to the banker and said in all seriousness, "Look at how far you've come. You're now senior enough to be in a car with me. How lucky you are!"

There are three main reasons for bank's clients to deal with the bank's trading floor:

• to raise capital in the form of debt or equity
• to invest in financial products
• to manage financial risk.

The bank's role as intermediator between its issuer clients and investor clients is crucial in primary equity and debt markets. Not every client of the major bank accesses the capital markets to raise equity capital. That is a space reserved for larger companies. Retail and government entities do not issue shares, for obvious reasons, and banks rarely intermediate the private equity markets. But, on the whole, all clients need to borrow money. This has always been one of the main reasons for going to a bank. Retail borrows money in the form of personal loans, auto loans, student loans, credit cards and mortgages. Banks generally lend this money directly to retail. Companies borrow in the form of bonds or loans, and the larger the company, the more likely it is that it borrows in the form of bonds which are distributed to investors. Government entities borrow primarily in the form of bonds, which are the foundation of the fixed income markets in each country.

At the same time, most but not all clients of the bank are also investors. The one main exception are corporates. They are not in the business of investing in financial products; they are in the business of investing in their core business, for example making airplanes, drilling for oil, designing jeans. Also, while we say that retail invests in financial products; they generally do not do it directly. There are some retail investors who open an investment account with a broker and manage their own money, but most retail investors put their money into bank savings accounts, asset management funds or pension funds. The very wealthy retail investors can also put their money into hedge funds. To further complicate the picture, financial companies don't just invest money from retail: they also invest money from other financial companies, for example insurance companies and pension funds may invest some of their money with asset management funds or with hedge funds. Figures 2.6 and 2.7 illustrate this point.

Outside of the primary market, the banks (via the trading floor) provide liquidity to their investor base for secondary trading in debt and equity as well as for trading in currency, commodity and derivative markets. This is where Figures 2.1–2.4 come into play. The bank clients in those pictures are the investor clients who are trading in financial markets via the banks. Some broad generalizations that we can make are:

- While there are many individual (retail) investors who manage their own money – these include very wealthy individuals as well as **day traders** – most financial market activity is driven by the large financial companies such as banks, insurance companies, pension funds, asset managers and hedge funds. These make up the **institutional investor base**.
- We can conclude that most trading floors are designed to cater to the institutional investor base.
- The products which have more retail investors managing their own money are primarily ETPs and in particular equities and equity derivatives.

Investing does not just mean buying a financial product. It means taking a view that the market price of a particular product will go up or down. The view that the market price will go up means investors will buy particular financial products. The view that the market price will go down means investors will sell particular financial products. This means that investors are both buyers and sellers of financial products. This concept in particular helps people new to the financial markets understand where the concept of a market in the secondary debt and equity, currencies, commodities and derivative markets comes from.

The business of **asset management** companies is to invest their clients' money in financial products. They are generally not acting as brokers for their clients. They are taking the money and investing it as they see fit within

FIGURE 2.6 Bond market issuers and investors in the primary market.

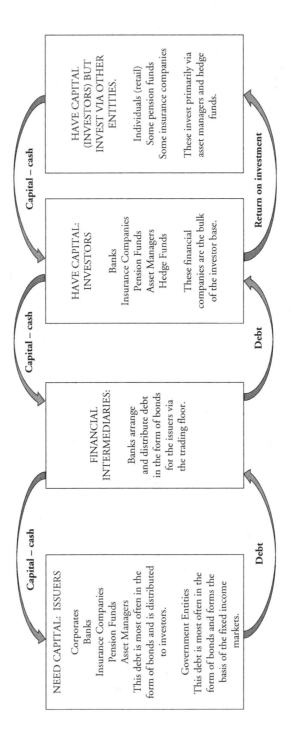

NEED CAPITAL: ISSUERS

Corporates
Banks
Insurance Companies
Pension Funds
Asset Managers

This debt is most often in the form of bonds and is distributed to investors.

Government Entities

This debt is most often in the form of bonds and forms the basis of the fixed income markets.

FINANCIAL INTERMEDIARIES:

Banks arrange and distribute debt in the form of bonds for the issuers via the trading floor.

HAVE CAPITAL: INVESTORS

Banks
Insurance Companies
Pension Funds
Asset Managers
Hedge Funds

These financial companies are the bulk of the investor base.

HAVE CAPITAL (INVESTORS) BUT INVEST VIA OTHER ENTITIES.

Individuals (retail)
Some pension funds
Some insurance companies

These invest primarily via asset managers and hedge funds.

Capital – cash

Capital – cash

Capital – cash

Debt

Debt

Return on investment

FIGURE 2.7 Equity market issuers and investors in the primary market.

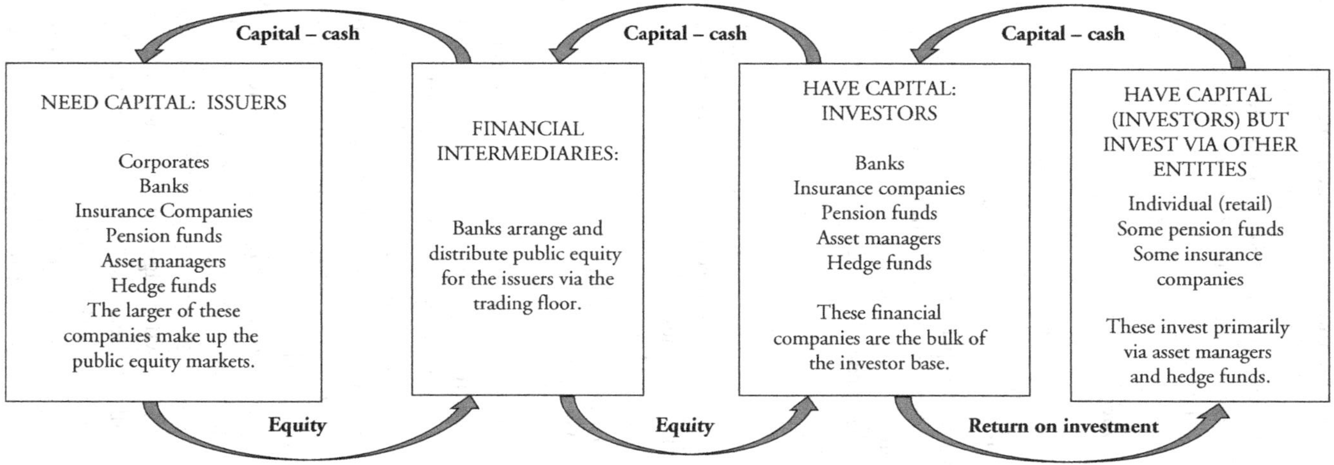

NEED CAPITAL: ISSUERS

Corporates
Banks
Insurance Companies
Pension funds
Asset managers
Hedge funds
The larger of these companies make up the public equity markets.

FINANCIAL INTERMEDIARIES:

Banks arrange and distribute public equity for the issuers via the trading floor.

HAVE CAPITAL: INVESTORS

Banks
Insurance companies
Pension funds
Asset managers
Hedge funds

These financial companies are the bulk of the investor base.

HAVE CAPITAL (INVESTORS) BUT INVEST VIA OTHER ENTITIES

Individual (retail)
Some pension funds
Some insurance companies

These invest primarily via asset managers and hedge funds.

Capital – cash

Capital – cash

Capital – cash

Equity

Equity

Return on investment

a specific investment strategy. The asset management company is paid to invest this money. The amount of money it manages is called **assets under management**, or **AUM**. Some of the largest and most well-known asset managers are State Street Global Advisors, Fidelity Investments, the Vanguard Group, JPMorgan Asset Management, Deutsche Asset Management and Alliance Capital Management.

Asset manager fee income

Current assets under management: $1 billion
Management fee: 0.5% per year
0.5% × $1 billion = $5 million per year
Performance fee: 3% per year
If the asset manager returns 10% in one year, or $100 million, he receives $3 million in performance fees
Total possible fee income for one year: $8 million

Hedge funds are a subset of asset managers. They are the entities that are most often referred to as **speculators**. This term is also meant to distinguish them from the other financial companies which the broader market thinks of as investors. However, there is almost no difference between a speculator and an investor. They are both betting that market prices will move in a particular direction. Mostly, they are betting that market prices move up, but sometimes they are betting that market prices move down. Hedge funds are famous because of the super high returns that some hedge funds have been able to make for their investors. For example, one hedge fund, Paulson and Co, was reported to have returns of over 500% in 2007 for one of its investment funds. However, these big headline returns are often the exception and not the rule. And the rule of thumb is that there is no return without risk and often if a hedge fund is up a lot one year it will probably be down a lot the next.

Hedge funds are often able to charge more fees to their investors than traditional asset managers can. The typical hedge fund fees are **2 and 20**, which means a 2% management fee and a 20% performance fee. However, there are some well-known hedge funds which are able to charge much higher fees as a result of their historic performance. One example is a fund which reputedly charged a 3% management fee and a 50% performance fee. Remember that a 3% management fee means that the returns have to be over 3% every year for the investor to make any money. In an environment where interest rates are very low, (e.g. 2%), it is hard to imagine how a hedge fund can consistently be this good at investing.

Another distinction that has historically been made between traditional asset managers and hedge funds is that asset managers are **buy and hold investors** compared to hedge funds, which are more **active investors**. This means that asset managers used to be known for buying a stock or a bond and holding it for years, while a hedge fund will buy a financial product and sell it the same day if it can make a profit. The truth is actually somewhere in the middle. There is a continuum of investment management style from buying and holding over the long term through to intraday trading. While more traditional asset managers are mostly toward the buy and hold end of the spectrum and hedge funds are mostly toward the intraday trading end of the spectrum, most investment management is somewhere in the middle for both traditional asset managers and hedge funds. A similar statement could be made about the use of derivatives. It used to be said that hedge funds used derivatives while traditional asset managers did not. Again, this is not the case today. Derivatives can be used for investment purposes, in other words taking a view on the price of a derivative, as well as for hedging purposes, and many asset managers use them for both.

For the entire spectrum of investment styles, the role of the bank's trading floor as liquidity provider is a crucial one. These investor clients want to be able to execute trades at a particular price at a particular time on a particular size, and they rely upon banks to provide a price to do that. Investors are very wary of investing in products that are considered **illiquid**. Illiquid financial products are ones that don't trade very often, and/or don't have many liquidity providers. This means that an investor might be able to buy a financial product but will have difficulty selling the product and making a profit on the sale. Hence, the role of banks as liquidity providers to their investor clients is crucial.

In addition to issuing and investing, clients also use the financial markets for financial **risk management** purposes. As a result of their corporate or financing activities, if a company could lose money as a result of a change in interest rates or currency rates, the company has financial risk which needs to be managed. The company will generally look to hedge that risk. "To hedge" means to mitigate or reduce risk. Interest rate risk derives generally from the type of debt products the company uses to borrow money and is hedged using interest rate derivatives. Currency risk derives either from multinational operations or from import/export companies. This risk management activity on the part of companies is a continual re-assessment of the cashflows of the company as they change over time, the capital needs of the company as

FIGURE 2.8 Currency risk management example.

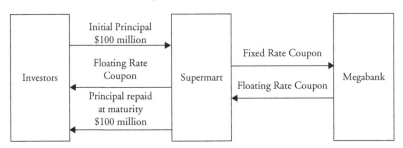

they change over time and the future interest rate and currency rate moves. Thus, companies use banks to discuss and execute hedges.

In Figure 2.8, Supermart has borrowed money with a floating rate coupon and has exchanged that coupon for a fixed rate with Megabank. Supermart has originally borrowed with a floating rate coupon but is concerned that interest rates might go up. This means that the floating rate coupon on its debt could get larger over time. It decides to swap the floating rate with a fixed rate. Now Supermart knows exactly what its future coupon payments on its debt will be.

A classic currency risk management example is an import/export company based in France. Its labor and all its costs are in euros, but its main clients are in the United States and thus it sells its products in US dollars. As long as the exchange rate between euros and US dollars remains fixed, its profits are known and in particular the company knows it is making a profit. But if the US dollar depreciates against the euro, then its profits could disappear. For example, if $1 is equal to €1, and the company spends €0.50 for every $1 of revenue, then the company is profitable. But if $1 suddenly becomes equal to only €0.50, then the company is no longer profitable. The added complexity is that it signs multi-year contracts with its clients. Table 2.3 gives an example of a French import/export company's cashflow profile.

TABLE 2.3 Profile of an Import/Export Company's Cashflow

Year	Income (earn)	Cost (spend)	PROFIT if $1 = €1	PROFIT if $1 = €2	PROFIT if $1 = €0.5
1	$100	€50	€50	€150 = ($100 $\times 2\frac{€}{\$}$) − €50	€0 = ($100 $\times 0.5\frac{€}{\$}$) − €50
2	$110	€60	€50	€160	−€5
3	$120	€70	€50	€170	−€10

As long as the price of €1 to $1 is one or above, the company knows it is making a profit, but the currency rate can move up or down and the impact can be significant depending on how much the rate moves. The company has done some quick analysis to determine what the upside is and what the downside is. It has decided that it doesn't want to take the risk of future currency moves and would rather hedge. A typical hedge will use currency derivatives to give the company a known profitability irrespective of how the currency rate moves.

Many risk management transactions are done using derivatives and many of those are tailored to the specific risk management needs of the client. In this way, we can see how banks as liquidity providers in derivatives and importantly as intermediators between the tailored trades their clients do and the market standard trades they use as hedges is crucial to the risk management of their clients.

The early 1990s had some very well-known court cases (e.g. *Orange County* vs. *Banker's Trust* and *Procter & Gamble* vs. *Merrill Lynch*) of clients who sued major banks because of mis-selling practices or unsuitable transactions done with clients. In one of those cases, the traders at Banker's Trust had reputedly executed high-fives on the trading floor every time they did a trade with their client because they made so much money. As a result, high-fives were no longer allowed on the trading floor of most banks in New York . . . so traders instead did low-fives. These were small finger wiggles behind the back with the hand held low so that there was no ostentatious display of excitement at making money on a trading floor. The unintended consequences are always the most entertaining.

Governments use the financial markets for risk management purposes as well. They are often trading in the currency markets in order to have an impact on their currency. The general idea is that if a currency is too strong then any manufacturing in that currency is expensive compared to other countries, and so jobs and development move to countries where the currency is weaker. The classic example here is China. The Chinese yuan is very cheap and thus it has been very cheap to manufacture goods in China for export around the world, to the detriment of manufacturing and employment growth in countries with more expensive currencies. However, this has benefited China and it is not keen to change this too quickly. Several countries, notably the United States, want China to buy up their currency in the financial market in order to make the currency more expensive. If China buys up its own currency in the financial market, they would be using the forces of supply and demand to change the price of their currency. More buying means the market price of the yuan goes up and becomes more expensive.

While this type of risk management on the part of governments is not necessarily using derivatives or tailored derivatives, it still relies upon the banks to provide liquidity to the governments and intermediate between the government trades and the market generally.

From a bank's perspective, all of these are good general examples of why clients trade financial products and provide a good context for understanding the main financial market participants and the crucial role of the banks. This book will not go into more detail on how each type of client operates and specifically why they trade financial products, because different clients have different drivers for using different financial products. Explaining all of this with some level of detail requires going into more detail on each financial product and each could be the subject for an entire book. Individuals who work in different asset classes and in different financial products will develop **domain expertise** over time in terms of who the primary users of a particular financial product are and how their trades influence market prices. For example, there are individuals at banks who only work with pension funds and as a result are experts in what pension funds do in financial markets. Outside of that team of people, few other people on the trading floor could go into detail on that topic.

KYC is a term often used in finance. It stands for **know your client**, which officially is in reference to money laundering. In other words, know where your client's money comes from in order to ensure that it is legitimate. It is often used in a more general sense, however. A London-based asset manager once offered to do an educational session on financial markets for a client from the Middle East. The session was held in London and the clients had a working sandwich lunch in order to cover as much as possible during the day. When the sandwiches arrived, the clients were starving but quickly realized that they couldn't eat anything other than the potato chips because the sandwiches all had some form of pork. The asset manager had forgotten some basic KYC.

Conclusion

The primary role of a bank's trading floor in the financial markets can be broadly described as providing access to the financial markets for a bank's clients. When a client needs a financial product either as issuer, investor or risk manager, they go straight to their bank, which generally leads to the bank's trading floor. Breaking down the trading floor's role into two broad areas, we identify both intermediating the primary capital markets between issuers and investors as well as providing liquidity and ultimately taking risk in secondary, currency, commodity and derivative markets. Further, for tailored trades, which are generally derivatives trades used for both investment as well as risk management purposes, the trading floors play a key role in providing liquidity and intermediating between the tailored financial product for the client and the standardized financial product that the bank uses to hedge.

Intermediating the primary capital markets is a role that banks generally manage themselves. They match issuer clients with investor clients. However, providing liquidity in secondary, currency, commodity and derivative markets is a role which requires other financial intermediators in the form of exchanges, interbank brokers and electronic trading systems. These other financial intermediators allow banks acting as liquidity providers to close out or hedge positions with each other in the more standardized financial products. While the bank continues to face the client, the bank will close out or hedge with another bank via these central market platforms.

Ultimately, this whole financial system is about matching buyers and sellers in the same financial product in the most efficient form possible. Importantly, if a bank couldn't take risk and thus couldn't provide liquidity for financial products, the financial markets generally would be very inefficient. Thus, the role of the banks is crucial to an efficient financial market system.

Also, financial markets are continually evolving. There seem to be new financial products and new market participants every day. To put this evolution into context, we must look at the needs and interests of the clients and how they have changed. In particular, companies have grown over the years and become large global entities that need more complex financial products. These are companies such as Toyota, Bayer and Dell that have operations in many countries and sales in possibly hundreds of countries. This means that their capital needs are in multiple currencies and they end up with complex interest rate and currency risk that they need to manage. At the same time, the advancement of computing power means that investors have become more sophisticated and interested in investing in more complex financial products. Not only does this mean that financial products are more complicated, but it also means that market participants are more global and market pricing moves faster, which generally leads to more risk. Banks as liquidity providers have evolved and become more complex in order to address these client needs.

At the same time, as a result of the 2008–2009 financial crisis, the financial system has had a lot of criticism over how it operates. Some of the criticisms have been focused on over the counter trading. The claim has been that this results in unidentifiable risk on the part of the bank as liquidity provider as well as opaque marketplaces for the client. While this has been the case in some financial products, it is definitely not the case in most of them. However, the banks and central market platforms have worked since the financial crisis to address some of these concerns, while the regulators and legislators have demanded some sweeping changes to the OTC market. Time will tell what the unintended consequences of these changes will be.

Discussion Questions

Why does a bank add value in an illiquid product?

How are exchanges different from banks?

Can clients access financial markets without speaking to a major bank?

How are hedge funds and asset managers different? How are they the same?

Why do insurance companies have large pools of money to invest in financial products?

See www.terriduhon.co for answers and discussions.

CHAPTER 3

Which Part of the Bank Are We Talking About?

From the trading floor's perspective, all roads lead to Rome. This chapter will describe the different parts of a bank, how they relate to each other and in particular how all banking activity eventually leads to the trading floor. The first step is to be able to distinguish between the different types of bankers that main street sees as all the same. In fact, within banks, people on the trading floor don't refer to themselves as bankers at all. That term is reserved for investment bankers, relationship bankers and generally anyone associated with lending or retail banking. On the trading floor people strictly refer to themselves by their role: traders, sales people, research, structuring, risk management. This chapter will also answer questions such as: Is the Chinese wall really a wall? What is insider trading? What does M&A have to do with financial markets? How does a bank fund itself? What is Libor and why does the financial market care?

One of the many little rivalries within a bank is between the corporate finance people (whom the trading floor calls "bankers") and the markets people. The markets people consider bankers little more than suits who wine and dine their clients. The bankers consider the markets people little more than the missing link.

TABLE 3.1   Major Bank Business Breakdown

Retail Banking	Private Banking	Investment Banking	Asset Management
Taking deposits, providing savings and checking accounts, lending to individuals via loans, credit cards and mortgages	Providing the same services as the retail bank but for wealthy individuals (net worth $2–$5 million) May also offer access to financial markets for direct investment and hedging purposes	Providing financial advice, intermediating the financial markets, providing liquidity and taking risk generally for large companies and governments	Investing money which individuals or companies give them in financial markets in different investment funds with different strategies

Some of the larger major banks operate as several different entities (Table 3.1). They roughly break down into retail banking, private banking, investment banking and asset management. These four entities are often completely independent from each other and many times operate legally as different entities (e.g. Chase the Retail Bank, JPMorgan Chase the Investment Bank, JPMorgan Chase Private Bank and JPMorgan Fleming the Asset Management business).

Retail banking is for individuals and provides savings accounts, credit cards, checking accounts, personal loans, sometimes mortgages and insurance. In the United States, it is performed by banks like Chase, Citibank or any of hundreds of regional banks. In the United Kingdom, it is performed by the likes of Barclays and NatWest. **Private banking** is for high net worth individuals and provides services similar to retail banking and, in some cases, to investment banking. Asset management businesses invest money on behalf of their clients. They invest across products, asset classes and regions. Their clients come from their retail, private banking and investment banking businesses and sometimes simply as a result of their reputation.

Investment banking's clients are primarily companies and government entities. These clients are constantly managing their equity and debt issuance, accessing the capital markets for good issuance opportunities, assessing merger and acquisitions (M&A) opportunities and using the financial markets to manage their financial risk. Some of these clients, primarily the financial companies, are also managing investment accounts either for themselves or for their clients and so are also actively trading financial products.

TABLE 3.2 Investment Bank Business Breakdown

Corporate Finance	Global Financial Markets
Client relationship management	Trading floor activity
Mergers and acquisitions	Primary debt and equity market intermediation
Capital raising advisory for both debt and equity	Secondary trading in debt and equity
	Currency, commodity and derivatives trading
	Providing liquidity and risk taking
	Providing brokerage services for exchange traded products

An investment bank provides services to deal with all these activities. Many of these are advisory services that ultimately end up with some type of financial market activity on the part of the client.

It is easy to see how investment banks are generally divided into two different business units (Table 3.2). One is the **corporate finance** business, which provides advisory services and the other is the **global financial markets** business, generally called the "markets business," which facilitates access to the global financial markets and in particular provides liquidity and takes risk in financial products, in other words, the trading floors.

Most banks also have a **loan business**. Depending on how the bank is structured, the loan business could be segregated and sit as separate business units within the retail business, the private client business and the investment bank or it could operate as one large business unit across all these different businesses. In this book, we will refer to the loan business as one large business unit which could have retail loans through to large company loans.

Note that, like other areas in finance, corporate finance is sometimes, unhelpfully, called "investment banking"; for the purposes of this book, we will only refer to it as "corporate finance." Also, it is simply a fact that no one company looks exactly like another. This is true in every industry and the financial business is no different. This book will use the term "bank" to refer generically to those financial entities which operate a global financial markets business that provide liquidity and take risk in at least one financial product. Thus, commercial banks, investment banks, savings and loans, high street banks, building societies and regional banks (all terms which may be familiar but generally cause confusion) will all simply be referred to as "banks" in this book. Clear distinctions will be made if we are talking about a bank which is different from this definition.

Corporate Finance

Generally speaking, corporate finance is mainly a financial advisory business. This is where the bank looks at all the financial activities of its clients and identifies opportunities to provide financial services to them. As such, we generally call the individuals who sit within the corporate finance unit and manage the clients in this way the **relationship bankers**. There are four different areas that relationship bankers focus on: **mergers and acquisitions (M&A)**, debt or equity capital raising, risk management and financial market transactions. The first two activities are activities that originate within the corporate finance department but ultimately end up on the trading floor. Outside of M&A and capital raising activity, many clients also deal directly with the global financial markets' business for their day-to-day financial risk management as well as their financial market investment activity. While the relationship manager is aware of these activities, he is not generally part of these discussions unless there is a dispute of some sort or the activities are driven by strategic M&A or capital raising activity.

M&A has historically been considered the sexy business to be doing for clients; however, relationship bankers will also provide the more mundane services to their clients, like helping them with their capital management and advising when it might be a good or bad time to raise equity or debt capital. To do this, the relationship banker will liaise with either a **debt capital markets** team or an **equity capital markets** team, which straddles the corporate finance and financial markets businesses. These teams are in touch with the financial markets business and are constantly looking for opportunities for their clients to raise capital (either debt or equity) cheaply. Thus, the client either approaches the bank with a need to raise capital or the bank approaches the client with a good capital raising opportunity (see Figure 3.1). If the bank has a loan business, the relationship banker may also offer to lend money to its clients.

FIGURE 3.1 Debt capital markets and equity capital markets.

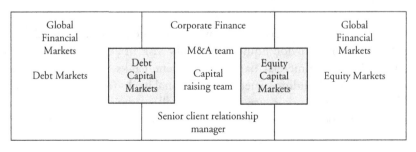

Capital issuance opportunities

While market prices are always moving, there are generally big themes that are happening for months at a time. Themes might be that the stock markets are hot and it's a good time to issue equity. This means that share prices have been rising (or **rallying**) so companies may take the opportunity to issue more shares at a high price. Another theme may be that financial market participants are very nervous so everyone is sitting tight. This means that there is very little financial market activity at the moment. Another theme might be that there has been a re-allocation from equity to fixed income among the big institutional investors. This means companies will have an easier time borrowing money. An easier time means that it might be cheaper (the coupon might be lower) or that the company will be able to borrow a larger principal amount than normal or that there are more investors interested in the debt than normal, which will broaden the investor base for a company's debt. All major banks' relationship bankers will be constantly assessing what the financial market themes are and advising their clients in one direction or another about what the best way to raise capital is.

Mergers and Acquisitions

M&A is all about identifying opportunities for one company to buy another or for two companies to merge and create a larger company. M&A opportunities can be identified by the client and brought to the relationship banker, in which case he will bring on board a team of bankers who also sit within the corporate finance business and who specialize in M&A activity. Or M&A opportunities can be identified by the bank, most likely by the M&A team, which are then presented to the relationship banker, who then decides how to approach the client.

It has historically been a very profitable business for banks. You see, banks don't do anything for free. They either make money by taking risk or they take a fee for their advice. Typical M&A fees are a percentage of the deal size as measured by the market capitalization of the company being purchased. Fee percentages are on a sliding scale and generally get lower the larger the transaction. A good rule of thumb is that the fees are about 1% of the market capitalization of the company being acquired for the larger companies and up to 5% for smaller companies.

M&A opportunities

The Megabank M&A team are constantly looking for the right opportunities for their key clients to expand internationally. In particular, Supermart is a big client of

Megabank. The M&A team at Megabank has recently identified a similar super-market company in the United Kingdom which has had poor results over the last few years. As a result its share price is slightly depressed. It is smaller than Super-mart, which means that Supermart should be able to afford to buy the company. Combine that with the relatively low share price and the similar business and it looks like an ideal target for Supermart. The M&A team at Megabank decides to do some analysis and make a pitch to Supermart.

The Chinese Wall

The relationship that corporate finance has with its clients is generally one where there is an **advisory agreement** and where private financial and strategic information from the client is passed to the bank. This formal legal agreement generally includes a non-contingent fee being paid from the client to the bank for financial advice. Where a formal legal agreement does not exist, the rela-tionship banker is generally trying to secure one. However, it is generally not the case that clients will send private financial and strategic information to a bank without a formal legal advisory agreement of some sort being in place. Individuals who work on the corporate finance side, whether relationship bankers or not, are considered to be inside the **Chinese wall** by virtue of having this private information and are thus restricted in terms of their per-sonal trading ability and their contact with the global financial markets business. A Chinese wall is not an actual wall that separates individuals who have private information from individuals who don't have that information. It is an understanding by individuals that private information cannot be shared with other individuals unless necessary, nor can private information be used to make financial market transactions in which the individual can benefit from having that private information. Corporate finance is generally considered to be inside the Chinese wall and global financial markets business is generally considered to be outside the Chinese wall.

High-profile insider trading

One of the most notorious insider traders was Martha Stewart. In 2001, her Merrill Lynch stockbroker apparently tipped her off to some insider information about ImClone. Martha Stewart was able to sell her shares at a price of around $50 a share shortly before they dropped to $10 a share. Both Martha Stewart and her broker were convicted and served prison sentences as a result.

The reason that private information is so sensitive is that if it is inconsistent with information about the company known in the public markets it could have a big effect on the share price and possibly on the bond prices of the company once it becomes known. Anyone with this type of private information (known as **insider information**) would be considered to be **front running** if they sold or bought shares or debt in that company before the rest of the financial market had the information as well. For example, if someone who knows about a big profit warning that is about to be announced for a company sells shares in that company, that is front running. The regulations restrict anyone who has private information about a company from trading in the shares and debt of that company before it is announced to the financial market and made public. Anyone with insider information has an unfair advantage, which is why it is illegal.

The individuals within corporate finance use the private information they have to advise their clients on various strategic and financial matters including mergers, acquisitions, capital raising (either debt or equity) and risk management, any of which could involve the use of financial products. However, when any of that advice requires the use of the financial market (e.g. in the form of the company raising capital or engaging in derivatives for risk management purposes), there is some contact between the corporate finance business and the global financial markets business but the private information is generally not passed to the trading floor.

Different areas of a bank involved in a capital raising

Supermart has decided that it wants to expand globally by buying a similar company in the United Kingdom. This will require some currency trades because Supermart is most likely to be able to raise capital in US dollars but will need British pounds to buy the UK company. The banker who is advising Supermart will want to bring in a markets person who will be able to advise on how to use derivatives for this purpose. The markets person might now be inside the Chinese wall of Supermart.

Global Financial Markets

The global financial markets business is where the trading floors are and where the relationship with the clients is generally product specific. It is called "global" because banks like to provide global services to their clients,

TABLE 3.3 Sales and Trading Activity on the Trading Floor

Sales Person	Trader
Has the client relationship	Rarely speaks to clients
Talks to the client about financial market activity:	Provides prices on financial products when clients want to trade (this is providing liquidity and taking risk)
• Investing in (buying and selling) financial products • Financial risk management	Manages the risk from doing trades with the bank's clients

many of whom are international. However, most individuals within banks as well as within client organizations work within one region, such as North America, Europe or Asia. So, while most people consider the financial markets global, often individuals within banks as well as within clients are generally focused on one region only.

The individuals who are in global financial markets and who have regular contact with the client are generally called **sales people**. The sales people communicate with the clients about financial products and financial markets and the **traders** who are also in global financial markets determine prices for trading financial products with the bank's clients. This activity all occurs on a trading floor (Table 3.3), where these individuals physically sit.

Note that the issuer relationship for debt and equity is managed primarily by the relationship manager in corporate finance, while the investor and risk management relationship for financial markets products is managed primarily by sales people on the trading floor.

One of the reviewers for this book has worked on trading floors for over 30 years in locations around the world in a variety of roles, primarily in structuring and sales across asset classes. One of his comments (only slightly tongue in cheek) on the manuscript was that in Table 3.3, it should state "fears traders" in the sales person column and "despises sales" in the trader column. When another reviewer for this book, who worked in London and New York as a sales person in fixed income, was asked her opinion about this, she said, "That's probably right. I've blocked out most of the worst of it since I've retired, but the truth is, it's not a nice place."

FIGURE 3.2 Lines of communication on the trading floor.

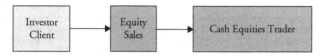

Clients call the trading floor when they need information about what is happening in the financial markets or when they want to transact. A common phone call from an investor like an asset manager might be about doing a large transaction (also called a **large lot**) in the equity markets. While public equities are primarily traded on exchanges, often the amount that the exchange is able to trade at any one point in time at the current price is not large enough for large institutional investors. So, when an investor wants to buy or sell a large lot, which differs depending on the number of shares that trade each day in a stock (in other words how liquid the stock is), the investor will often call his equity sales person on a bank's equity trading floor and ask him for a price instead of giving an order to trade on the exchange via the bank (Figure 3.2).

Depending on the bank and its size, different trading floors will be broken down differently. The larger banks may have several trading floors, for example one for fixed income, one for equity and one for commodities. The smaller banks will have all these different asset classes on the same floor. Figure 3.3 is an example of a possible layout for a fixed income trading floor and Figure 3.4 an example of an equity trading floor. These layouts show a common approach to trading floors, which is to put the traders in the middle and the sales people around the outside all facing towards the middle aisle of traders. Note that Figure 3.3 contains a reference to "credit traders." **Credit trading** generally refers to non-government debt and credit derivatives.

Sometimes the sales person and the trader are the same person for a particular financial product but generally not. There is a role called **sales-trader** in the equity markets which is often confused as a combined role of both sales person and trader, but this is generally not the case. A better way to think about the role of a sales-trader is to think of the role of a sales person being split into a relationship manager and a trade executioner. The equity sales role is more about relationship management while the sales-trader is a role which focuses on getting trades done with the client. This is a term that is specific to the equity markets and is not consistently used in all banks' equity trading floors.

Depending on the size of the office and the structure of the business, a sales person may cover a client for all financial products that the bank trades

FIGURE 3.3 A fixed income trading floor.

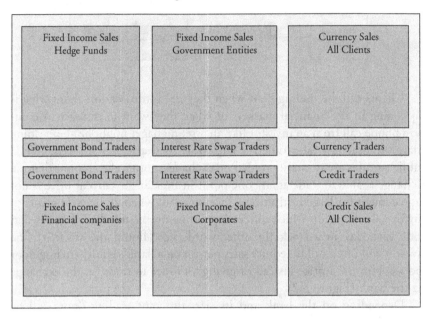

Fixed Income Sales Hedge Funds	Fixed Income Sales Government Entities	Currency Sales All Clients
Government Bond Traders	Interest Rate Swap Traders	Currency Traders
Government Bond Traders	Interest Rate Swap Traders	Credit Traders
Fixed Income Sales Financial companies	Fixed Income Sales Corporates	Credit Sales All Clients

Each sales box represents rows of desks all facing toward the trading desks which are in the center row with the traders sitting back to back, facing the sales desks.

or the sales person may cover a client only for a specific financial product. Generally within the major banks, sales people focus on a type of client (e.g. pension funds or asset managers) and a type of product (e.g. equity indices or US government bonds). For example, in the fixed income markets, there are several different sales teams. One will cover non-financial companies and focus on interest rate and currency derivatives for risk management. Another will cover hedge funds and focus on government bonds. Sometimes it is even narrower than this and there might be a government bond sales person who covers asset managers and an interest rate derivatives sales person who covers the same asset managers.

The traders, on the other hand, are much more consistent across different banks in how their role is defined. Within the fixed income markets, there will be government bond traders, interest rate derivatives traders, non-government bond traders and currency traders. Within equity markets, there will be single stock traders, index traders and derivatives traders. And within these teams, the roles will be even narrower, depending on the size of the business. Most derivatives traders will generally be split

FIGURE 3.4 An equity trading floor.

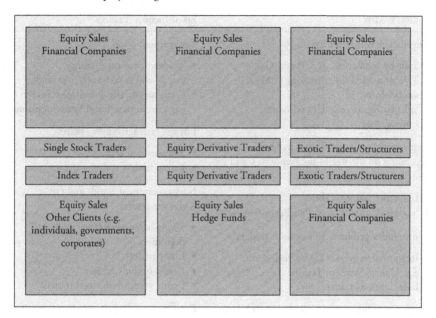

| Equity Sales Financial Companies | Equity Sales Financial Companies | Equity Sales Financial Companies |

Single Stock Traders / Equity Derivative Traders / Exotic Traders/Structurers

Index Traders / Equity Derivative Traders / Exotic Traders/Structurers

| Equity Sales Other Clients (e.g. individuals, governments, corporates) | Equity Sales Hedge Funds | Equity Sales Financial Companies |

Each sales box represents rows of desks all facing toward the trading desks, which are in the center row with the traders sitting back to back, facing the sales desks.

between standardized derivatives (which includes slightly tailored derivatives) and **exotic derivatives** (which includes highly tailored derivatives), and within standardized derivatives the role can be further split between short-term derivatives and long-term derivatives. This highlights that some derivatives which are slightly tailored are still relatively easy to price and trade; however, the more tailored they get, the more exotic they are and the harder they are to price and trade. (See Table 3.4.)

When a client wants to issue debt or equity, another role on the trading floor becomes very important. This is the **syndication** role of debt capital markets and equity capital markets, which sits between the corporate finance bankers advising the issuer and the sales people who will sell the debt or equity to the investors. The role syndication plays is helping to gauge the interest of the investors in a primary bond or equity offering and then to manage the sales force at the point that the bank needs to distribute the debt or equity offering. They do this by keeping track of recent equity or debt offerings at other banks as well as of the general sentiment of the financial market participants. The information they look for is the price, the size, the specific investors if they can get this information and how the offering proceeded.

TABLE 3.4   Trader Categories

Equity Traders	Fixed Income Traders
Single stock equity traders	Government bond traders
• Split by industries e.g. Oil and Gas, Telecoms Media Technology (TMT), financials, etc. • Split by region, e.g. United States, Europe, Asia	• Traders focus on maturity, e.g. 2- and 3-yr trader, 5-yr trader • Government bond derivative traders, e.g. government bond futures, options
Single stock equity derivative traders, depending on the size of the business, could be split by:	Interest rate derivatives traders
• Industries (same as above) • Region (United States, Pan-Europe, Asia)	• Standardized traders • Exotic traders
Equity index products and options traders	Non-government bonds and credit derivative traders
• Index traders who trade by region, e.g. United States or Europe • Index options traders	• Single-name traders in bonds and derivatives • Index traders • Credit options traders • Exotic credit derivatives traders
Structured product traders and exotic traders	Currency and currency derivative traders
• Split by risk classification	• Currency traders • Currency options traders • Exotic currency derivatives traders

Sample debt offering and market color

If Supermart is interested in issuing debt, the debt capital markets team will need to see what is happening in the new issue debt market. The team will get some information on new issues and on how Supermart's old debt is trading by looking at any recent research reports on new issue debt as well as speaking to the trading floor. The feedback from debt capital markets might be: "There is a lot of demand for fixed income products at the moment given the re-allocation of investment funds from equities into fixed income. As a result there has been a lot of new issue looking to take advantage of the demand. However, because of historically low interest rates, there is a view that interest rates could go higher so the investors are really keen on floating rate coupon investments at the moment. Key maturities areas are three and five years. Supermart debt is trading well at the moment."

Keeping track of this information helps the corporate finance team better advise the client on whether the client will be able to achieve the exact capital raise that the client wants to achieve. The debt or equity capital markets team will continually interact with the sales and trading teams in order to have as much **market color** as possible throughout the initial discussions with the client. (Financial market color is a euphemism for financial market gossip.) At the point that the bank and the client are in agreement on what product, what size and what price they are targeting, the bank launches the deal. The first step in that process is often for the client to meet with as many different investors as possible in order for the investors to get comfortable with what the client is trying to achieve. This is also a form of **due diligence** on the part of the investors. It is important that investors meet the companies in which they are invested both at the equity level and the debt level on a regular basis. This road show is set up primarily by the debt or equity capital markets team via the debt or equity sales force. At the end of the road show, the deal goes **live**. At this point, the goal is to immediately sell all of the bond or equity at the target price to the investors as quickly as possible. This process is managed by the debt or equity capital markets team. Figure 3.5 illustrates the timeline involved in a debt offering.

The road show is a key process in the relationship management of investors for both the issuer and the bank. The bank wants to be able to present new investment opportunities to its investor clients on a regular basis and the issuer wants to be able to maintain a good relationship with its investors. For the investors, the road show is a key part of the due diligence process that they go through. They want to ensure that they understand the financial statements of the issuer as well as put the capital raising in context with the issuer's strategy. If Supermart decides it will buy the UK business via a big debt issuance, Megabank will organize a road show for Supermart to meet potential investors and explain its business strategy. This gives the investors, who are both old and new to Supermart, the opportunity to ask Supermart some questions and decide whether they will invest in the new debt issue of Supermart.

While the focus of trading floor activity tends to be around sales and trading, there are many other roles both on and off the trading floor (but still within global financial markets) that are important to the trading floor activities. These include research analysts, quantitative analysts, risk management, structurers, legal, compliance and all the roles and responsibilities within the middle and back office functions.

FIGURE 3.5 Sample debt offering timeline.

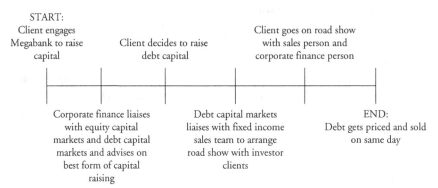

Research is responsible for producing financial market research to send to clients (see Chapter 9). The **quantitative analysts** are responsible for putting together the models that value the financial products and, because many of the models are considered **market standard**, their focus tends to be on the more tailored/structured products (see Chapters 12 and 13). **Structurers** are either part of a sales team, part of the trading team or an independent team (see Chapter 11). This is entirely dependent on the bank and the product on which the structurers focus. As a result, the role of a structurer often blurs with the role of both sales and trading. They are the individuals who help put together the tailored/structured products which banks sell to their clients. The **legal team** is responsible for the documentation that is required to transact financial products with the bank's clients. This includes simple debt or equity trading agreements as well as exotic derivative documentation. **Compliance** is responsible for ensuring that all activity on the trading floor complies with both internal and external regulations. The **middle and back office** teams are responsible for **booking** a financial transaction, which means ensuring it is in the right systems in the bank, that the various documents get filed and payments get made. The **risk management team** is responsible for valuing and reporting on risk throughout the bank (see Chapter 14).

Figure 3.6 shows the different areas of a bank that would be involved in a Supermart new bond issue being sold to a particular investor. The investor would primarily interact with the trading floor sales person. The sales person would liaise with the debt capital markets desk to initially indicate

FIGURE 3.6 Individuals involved and lines of communication in a primary debt issue.

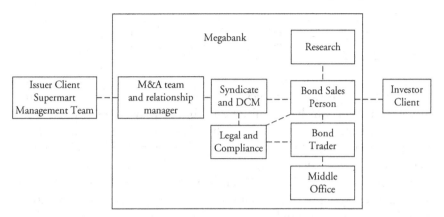

interest from the investor in Supermart bonds and a Supermart meeting during the road show. The sales person would likely accompany the Supermart management team and the Megabank relationship manager on the roadshow to see his investor clients. The investor may want to see any recent research written by the Megabank research team on the supermarket industry in the United States and the United Kingdom, so the sales person would liaise with the research team to facilitate a conference call or meeting. The debt capital markets team will liaise with the legal and compliance team to ensure the documents are approved for the new bond issue. When the investor buys some Supermart bonds when they are issued, the investor tells the sales person, who then tells the debt capital markets team and the trader. The trader liaises with middle office to ensure that the bonds are sold to the investor and the cash is transferred to Megabank and then to Supermart, who is borrowing the money. While these cashflows will generally pass through the trader's book, his involvement in a new issue is limited. The trader's role becomes more crucial in the secondary trading of the debt.

Secondary trading of debt or equity is a much simpler and less time-consuming process (Figure 3.7). The investor calls the sales person and the sales person gets a price from the trader. The investor agrees to the price with the sales person and a trade occurs. The trader then lets the middle office team know that a new trade has happened, which it needs to put into the bank's systems and to ensure that the cashflows occur properly.

FIGURE 3.7 Individuals involved and lines of communication in secondary trading.

Outside of providing financial products or services related to capital raising for a client, which is handled by a debt or equity capital markets team, as mentioned above, the main relationship that the trading floor has with its clients is generally one focused on transacting related to either risk management or investment activities. The sales person will discuss macroeconomics or market price moves and different financial product trades that the client may transact. These could be in the equity, fixed income, currency, commodity or emerging markets using products such as bonds, equity or derivative products such as interest rate swaps or currency options.

Typical client–sales market discussion

An equity investor might call up the sales person to discuss the current financial market environment. The sales person might say, "We've seen a lot of retail outflows in equities recently which is weighing down the markets. We think the economy has really taken a beating and consumers are more risk averse." These conversations are generally very generic and focused on what is happening in the financial markets as opposed to what a client may be doing.

Once a new hire in financial markets lands a particular role, it is very hard to move. Interest rate traders stay interest rate traders and equity sales people stay equity sales people. And most people in middle office, despite often wanting to be **front office** (in other words sales and trading), almost never make it. There was one exception to that rule in the London credit markets. A credit trader was originally in middle office and worked his way up by consistently showing how smart he was and how much about the markets he understood. Once he became a trader, he was known as the nicest guy on the trading floor. He knew what it was to be in the middle office and to be treated shabbily by the front office (traders in particular) and understood the value of helping those around him. He was not only a good trader but also one of the most popular traders with the sales force because they could always ask "stupid questions."

Where Are these Trading Floors?

Most large global banks have active trading floors in New York, London, Tokyo and, increasingly, Hong Kong. However, while each location will have 20 or so major banks operating as the key liquidity providers in that financial market, the top 20 banks will differ slightly in each location. This list of top 20 banks will also differ depending on the product. Not every major bank is a major participant in every financial market. So one bank will be in the top 20 in New York for fixed income but not for equities or will be in the top 20 for fixed income in New York but not London. Also, while some major banks are relatively stable in their top 20 position, there is a lot of movement in the lists from year to year, particularly when there is any sort of financial market upheaval.

With technology, a person could literally work anywhere today, and there are often stories of traders sitting in remote locations, like St Croix, who are very profitable. This is rarely a story about a person who trades for a major bank, because there are generally restrictions to executing transactions anywhere other than the trading floor. One of the reasons for that restriction is that the phones on the trading floor are taped. This is primarily because if there is any question about a trade the tapes can be examined (known as **pulling the tapes**). For the same reason, trading floors don't allow cell phone execution. While there may be business conversations on cell phones, some trading floors even restrict cell phone conversation on the trading floor to force most business conversations to be taped. Trade execution is generally done via recorded landlines on the trading floor, bank email (which is distinct from personal email such as Hotmail or gmail accounts), **bloomberg** mails and any other electronic communication which can be recorded by the bank.

The trading day starts in Tokyo and Hong Kong. Eventually, London's financial markets open. Then about when Tokyo and Hong Kong are closing, New York is just opening. So there is a brief period when financial markets are almost global. When London's financial markets close, New York remains open for a few more hours. Finally, as New York is closing, Tokyo and Hong Kong are starting to open again. The saying goes that you work in New York if you're a morning person and in Tokyo if you aren't. And, the worst place to work from a timing perspective is London. There, you start early and end late because you straddle the trading day.

What this means is that for most financial products the financial market is open almost 24 hours a day for five days straight (Figure 3.8).

FIGURE 3.8 The 24-hour trading day.

Tokyo Monday 7 a.m. Trading Starts	Tokyo Monday 3 p.m. London Monday 7 a.m. Trading Starts	London Monday 12 noon New York Monday 7 a.m. Trading Starts	New York Monday 6 p.m. Trading Stops Tokyo Tuesday 7 a.m. Trading Starts
⇒	⇒	⇒	⇒

This means that most major banks will trade a product at any time of the day on a business day. To do this, the **trading book** for that product is passed around the globe from one trader to another within the same bank. A trading book is the business unit that trades a specific financial product. For example, the Japanese interest rate swap book is primarily traded in Tokyo, but at the end of the day in Tokyo the Japanese interest rate swap trader passes the trading responsibility on to someone in New York. (They bypass London because Tokyo and New York overlap in the morning and evening.)

Passing the yen interest rate swap book around the globe

The yen interest rate swap traders in Tokyo will end their day by contacting the interest rate swap traders in New York to discuss how the trading day went. They normally send an email with any key information and any expected trades overnight during the New York day. They will also show the prices where they are prepared to trade overnight and ask that if the notional amounts are over a certain amount that one of them is called in the middle of the night to approve trades. The email may say something like, "We had a lot of trades today but very little price movement. Call us if there is a major move in the dollar yen market overnight. Any trades over two **yards**, please call for approval." (A yard is a billion.) Here the traders are saying that they did a lot of trades in the yen interest rate swap book that day but that interest rate prices were not very volatile. They do not currently have any risk on their book, but if the currency rates in US dollars vs. Japanese yen move a lot, please wake up one of the traders. Any trade over two yards (or 2 billion yen, which is approximately equivalent to $20 million) needs approval from a trader in Tokyo.

On the whole, the majority of trades in these global trading books are done in the local time zone. This means that most US interest rate swaps are done in New York and most Japanese interest rate swaps are done in Tokyo. The reason for this is that most investors prefer to invest in the things they know the best. So a US company has mostly US investors in its debt and equity and a Japanese company has mostly Japanese investors in its debt and equity. While a US investor might have an Asian investment fund if it is large enough, it will likely be based in Asia. Interestingly, while we believe that we can access all information we need via the Internet these days, proximity is still very valuable.

The banks that make up the major banking community globally are composed of about 40 or so different banks. As mentioned above, the exact list and the order of that list is a function of the year and the asset class and the location. Despite that, the 40 or so different banks don't change that much, with the exception of a few mergers and acquisitions. A few generalizations can be made about these banks. The first is that in North American and European financial markets, the US banks have the largest market share and as a result are generally considered the financial market drivers. Outside of these two regions, the US banks have a more varied market share. In some regions they are very strong (e.g. Latin and South America) and in others they are just growing their market share (e.g. China), while in others it is somewhere in between. The second generalization is about European banks. They have as strong a global presence as the US banks but, generally speaking, a smaller market share. Finally, there are the Asian banks. In general, they have a strong local presence and in some cases a strong regional presence but otherwise have not had a push to grow globally, with the exception of a few banks in Japan.

> There is always a tremendous amount of competition for trading floor jobs in the financial markets from university graduates. In particular, they all want to be sales people or traders. There seems to be even more interest than usual post the 2008–2009 credit crisis when the press has vilified the banks. What they say about the media must be true: Any publicity is good publicity.

The Trading Floor's Relationship with Clients

Financial market activities are considered part of the everyday risk management or investment activities of a sale person's clients and should be seen as separate from any financial market activity which is driven by a strategic initiative, such as a merger or acquisition. The relationship that clients have with the sales person is not explicitly stated or documented as advisory, nor is it considered one. This relationship is one where the role of the sales person is to help the client understand the financial products, how they can be tailored/structured, what the risks inherent to them are and how the market in which they are transacting works.

The term **suitability** needs to be addressed here. A sales person should address the suitability of a financial product for a client in terms of the client's understanding of the financial product itself and what financial markets view the financial product suits, but the sales person cannot address the suitability of a financial product in the context of the specific financial objective of the client, as the sales person will not have this information.

The term **execution only** has been used to describe the relationship between sales people and their clients, but it is not an accurate term. As mentioned above, the sales people must help their clients understand how specific financial products work and what risks are attached to them and how the financial market of which they are a part works, in addition to executing financial products trades. The relationship is also one where market prices are discussed and debated between sales people and their clients.

At the end of the day, banking is theoretically about long-term relationships with clients. Sales people are often the face of the bank for many clients. However, a sales person is paid based on the profitability of the trades he does with his clients, so there is a natural tension between the longer-term nature of the relationship with the client and the short-term gains that can be made in the form of bonuses to the sales person.

The Loan Portfolio and the Funding Department

Two other business units that exist in most banks are the lending business (also called the loan portfolio) and the **funding department** (also called the treasury department). The loan portfolio is the business unit which gives out loans to the clients of the bank, and the funding department is the business unit which manages the borrowing needs of the bank that are often closely related to the size of the bank's loan portfolio.

Megabank could have pitched a UK pound denominated loan to Supermart instead of a bond when Supermart decided to buy a UK supermarket chain. Megabank would have done this if the loan team were interested in lending to Supermart. While historically people have thought of banks as lenders of loans, that is not always their primary purpose today.

As a result of the 2008–2009 credit crisis, banks are more reluctant to lend money today. If Megabank decides to lend UK pounds to Supermart, the transaction becomes much simpler, as Figure 3.9 shows. In this case the trading floor is not involved at all.

The funding team is immediately told that a client has made this request and will want to close the loan in the next few days. The funding team needs to ensure that there is the right amount of UK pounds available to give out this loan to the client. If that amount is not available, then the funding team needs to figure out how it will best secure that amount. One way to do that is to borrow in the Libor market. **Libor** stands for "London interbank offered rate." It is where banks borrow and lend to each other in different currencies for short periods of time, up to one year. And, as the name implies, it is a market which is primarily traded in London.

Like any financial product, the market price, which in this case is quoted as an interest rate where banks borrow and lend to each other, changes over time. The Libor market trades just like any other financial transaction, as described in Chapter 2. There are electronic trading systems and interbank brokers that sit in the middle and facilitate the short-term borrowing and lending of the major banks.

Every business day at 11 a.m. in London, Libor in different currencies is fixed for the day based on the market price at that time, and those **fixings** are made public. The formula is roughly the average of the borrowing rate from a set group of banks. This allows Libor to be used as a reference rate for other products like bonds, loans and interest rate swaps. However, the fixed Libor is not actually where banks borrow and lend to each other during the day. It is merely a snapshot of where banks are borrowing and lending to each other on that day at that time. Table 3.5 gives an example of Libor rates.

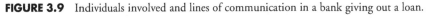

FIGURE 3.9 Individuals involved and lines of communication in a bank giving out a loan.

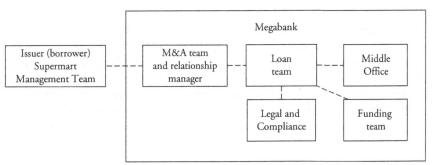

TABLE 3.5   Sample Libor Rates

Maturity	US dollar	UK pound	Japanese yen	Euro
overnight	0.14222%	0.58250%	0.10688%	0.84000%
1w	0.18967%	0.62188%	0.11538%	1.07350%
2w	0.20789%	0.64156%	0.12188%	1.14125%
1m	0.24528%	0.70863%	0.14063%	1.30625%
2m	0.33494%	0.81625%	0.15863%	1.39125%
3m	0.43167%	0.98869%	0.19475%	1.52563%
4m	0.49861%	1.07394%	0.23800%	1.58625%
5m	0.55806%	1.16931%	0.29000%	1.65375%
6m	0.62250%	1.26975%	0.33313%	1.73438%
7m	0.67606%	1.36125%	0.38438%	1.79000%
8m	0.72411%	1.44625%	0.43063%	1.83875%
9m	0.77606%	1.53063%	0.47188%	1.89875%
10m	0.82594%	1.61594%	0.50313%	1.95188%
11m	0.88072%	1.68219%	0.52625%	2.01188%
12m	0.93972%	1.76156%	0.55250%	2.07313%

w = week(s); m = month(s).
Source: British Bankers' Association.

Looking at the Libor rates graphed in Figure 3.10 for different maturities and currencies, we can see the shape of a **yield curve**. This graph shows that banks' borrowing rates on this particular date are highest in euros and lowest in yen. At the same time, all these yield curves are **upward sloping**, which means that they get higher the longer the borrowing term. This is considered a normal shape for a yield curve.

> The credit crisis of 2008–2009 resulted in a lot of questionable business practice on the part of banks. Apparently, banks didn't really want to lend to one other, for fear of the borrowing bank going bankrupt during the crisis, so the Libor market wasn't really operating properly. As a result, the Libor fixing was susceptible to a bit of manipulation, which has resulted in a major investigation on the part of regulators and has caused a huge scandal.

FIGURE 3.10 Libor yield curve.

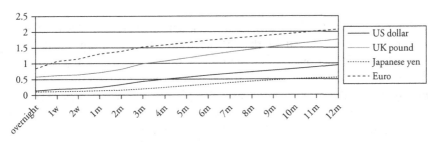

As mentioned in Chapter 1, most loans have a floating coupon. This means that the coupon is not a fixed amount each year; it changes over time based on where current interest rates are. The most common type of floating rate in the financial markets is one that is based on Libor. But most borrowers don't actually pay Libor as a coupon on their loan; they pay Libor plus a fixed percentage. The fixed percentage above Libor is the **credit spread** of the borrower. The riskier the borrower, the more expensive it is to borrow money, thus the higher the credit spread over Libor. Note that this concept also applies to fixed coupons: the riskier the borrower, the higher the fixed coupon. This is true in bonds as well as loans.

Sample loan terms

- Supermart borrows £1 billion from Megabank for five years.
- The coupon is Libor + 2%.
- Thus, 2% is the credit spread of Supermart for five years.

Banks put a lot of money and effort into their graduate training programs. These are the programs into which they hire individuals directly out of university. They are called "analyst training programs" for individuals with an undergraduate degree and "associate training programs" for those with an MBA. They are generally split between the corporate finance new hires and the sales, trading and research new hires. Often these groups get weeks to months of training by the bank before they are allowed into their new roles. This is despite many of these new hires having degrees in finance. It does raise the question of what these grads are learning at university.

Conclusion

From the perspective of the global financial markets business, which is where the trading floors sit, all of the other business units within a bank are designed to channel business to the trading floor. If a bank roughly breaks down into retail banking, private banking, investment banking and asset management, the trading floor sees all of these businesses as sources of potential clients and trades.

Within the investment bank, there are generally two separate businesses: the corporate finance business and the global financial markets business. The corporate finance business is about advising the bank's clients with respect to mergers, acquisitions and capital raising. The people who work in corporate finance see the financial markets as a necessary part of their advisory business, but not the crux of their business, which is ultimately earning advisory fees or deal fees. The global financial markets business sees the corporate finance business as another source of clients and client trades.

Aside from the corporate finance and the global financial markets business, most banks also have a loan business. The loan business is effectively an investor in the debt of the bank's clients. This is where the clients who can't access the bond markets, or who want as many diverse sources of funding as possible, come to borrow money in the form of loans. Finally, there is a funding business in most banks. This is the team of people which manages the cashflows of the whole bank. They try to determine how much cash is needed by the bank, in what currency and for how long and they use the financial markets in order to borrow that cash. Importantly, the borrowing of that cash results in the Libor market and the Libor fixing that is used for many financial market products.

Trying to understand how banks work has become a complex business as banks have grown and merged and become large behemoths. The goal of these large banks could be summarized as "We want to be everything to everyone." This means they want to service clients from individuals to companies to governments in all financial transactions around the world. These large entities are hard to miss. The problem with these banks is that the risk that they take supposedly in order to do business with their clients becomes difficult to understand for any one individual. So the question becomes, "How do the executives and the board of these entities really understand the risk they are taking?"

Discussion Questions

Are there banks which only have retail businesses? Do they have a global financial markets business?

Are there banks which don't give out loans?

What are some examples of some high-profile front running cases?

Post the 2008–2009 credit crisis, the process for setting Libor was criticized. Why was that?

Why is the Chinese wall a key concept to understand for people who work in a bank?

Please see www.terriduhon.co for answers and discussion.

CHAPTER 4

What Does It Mean to Trade?

This chapter will focus on the details of what a trading floor does day to day by looking at three different trades. The first is a US government bond trade for a large US asset manager. The second is a large debt issuance driven by an acquisition where the client issues in US dollars but needs UK pounds. The third is a structured equity product which is created by the trading floor to sell to the bank's retail clients as an investment product. These different trades will introduce different trading floor dynamics, different financial market drivers and different risk taking issues on the trading floor. This chapter will also answer questions such as: What does it mean to "make a market"? Why do clients put banks in competition? What conversations occur between a sales person and a trader? Most importantly, this chapter will highlight the value add of the bank providing liquidity for its clients.

The trading floor is full of entertaining antics by some of the more colorful individuals. These are usually the individuals who are the most volatile and have more extreme reactions to stress. Because a lot of trading conversation is still conducted verbally over the phone or in person rather than electronically, traders have several phones on their desk. The handsets are generally the heavy old-fashioned versions for a reason. They are more robust.

In particular, when a trader experiences a loss or isn't able to hedge or close out a trade the way he wanted or loses a trade in competition with another bank, he will sometimes throw a little temper tantrum. This often involves grabbing the nearest thing handy and throwing it. Phone handsets are the most often used this way.

A **trade** refers to a buyer and a seller agreeing a price and a date at which a specific notional amount of a specific product will be transferred from the seller to the buyer. However, not all buyers and sellers would call themselves traders and even those who call themselves traders are often doing different jobs. As identified in Chapter 2, there are several different types of trading floors and, as a result, several different types of traders. This chapter focuses on the trader who sits on the bank trading floor. This is the individual who provides liquidity to the bank's clients. Officially, we call this type of trader a **market maker**. This means he provides a bid where he is prepared to buy and an offer where he is prepared to sell a particular product for a particular size upon request from a client. The trader is the market maker and thus the client is the **market taker**. This means that the bank gets to buy on its bid and sell on its offer while the client has to sell on the bid and buy on the offer. (See Table 4.1.)

This chapter will walk through three different market making scenarios on a trading floor. They are each representative of different trade drivers:

- The first is a **US treasury** trade for a fictional asset manager (PACAM). (US treasuries are the debt issued by the US Treasury Department. Treasuries are US government debt.) This transaction illustrates the type of relationship a large institutional investor has with the trading floor and the information

TABLE 4.1 Market Maker vs. Market Taker

Market Maker: Bank	Market Taker: Client
Makes a market of $9.90/share at $10.00/share for the client	Sees a market of $9.90/share at $10.00/share from the bank
Buys on the bid at $9.90 or sells on the offer at $10.00	Lifts the offer of $10.00 to buy or hits the bid of $9.90 to sell
Buys at the low price or sells at the high price	Buys at the high price or sells at the low price

flow that occurs as a result of this type of trade, which is in a highly liquid standardized product. We will refer to this as the "PACAM treasury trade."

- The second is an interest rate swap trade which is driven by an M&A transaction and the associated debt issuance by Supermart. This transaction illustrates the different conversations that occur on the trading floor in order to get the debt issuance done as well as the market making decisions that occur for an extremely large derivatives transaction. We will refer to this as the "Supermart interest rate swap trade."
- Finally, we have a structured product originated by the bank to sell to its retail investors. It incorporates a FTSE 100 option and a bank bond issuance to create a structured product. This trade illustrates how a structurer interacts with different parts of the bank in order to create a product which is profitable for the bank and interesting for the retail clients. We will refer to this as the "structured equity product."

Throughout the rest of the book, we will continually refer back to these three trades to illustrate different aspects of the trading floor.

What this chapter illuminates is that the primary business of the bank's trading floor, which is providing liquidity to their clients, is not the sexy exciting business that it is often made out to be. It is slightly more mundane and reactive. It is not necessarily about putting on interesting trades designed solely to make money for the bank. It is about making markets for client trades.

PACAM Treasury Trade

A US treasury sales person at Megabank gets a call from his client PACAM (Perry Allan Carter Asset Management). PACAM asks the sales person, "Where is the market, in size, for the 5-year on-the-run treasuries?" This question has a lot of information built into it, so let's break it down. "Where is the market?" means that the client wants the bank to **make a market**. Making a market means that the trader needs to put a price (a bid) where he will buy something and a price (an offer, or ask) where he will sell. This is the trader's market for a particular product for a particular size. It is also called a **quote**. (See Table 4.2.)

The next part of the question, "in size," means that the client wants to transact a large amount of a particular product. What this amount could be will differ in different markets. US treasuries regularly trade in blocks of $100 million at a time in the institutional investor space. So **size** means anything from $1 billion to multiple billions. In another product, such as

TABLE 4.2 Making a Market in Different Asset Classes

Asset class	Market and what it means
Equity	$9.90 at $10.00 means that the trader will buy shares at a price of $9.90/share and sell shares at a price of $10.00/share
Bond	101.1% at 101.2% means that the trader will buy a bond with a price of 101.1% of the principal and sell at 101.2% of the principal
Currency	76.13 at 76.14 means that the trader will buy $1 at 76.13 yen and sell $1 at 76.14 yen

the corporate bond market, which normally trades in blocks of $10 million to $20 million, size might mean $100 million.

The last bit of information is "5-year on-the-run treasuries." Part of it, "5-year treasuries," is pretty clear. It means a US government bond which has a 5-year maturity. **On-the-run** is a term used in a lot of financial markets and means the current benchmark product. This is significant because in the US treasury market, there are several treasuries which are outstanding with maturities of approximately five years (Table 4.3).

The US Treasury issues 5-year bonds monthly throughout the year every year. Also, because the US Treasury issues 7-year, 10-year and 30-year bonds monthly throughout the year every year, there are many old 7-year, 10-year and 30-year bonds which today have a maturity of approximately five years. The line in bold in Table 4.3 is the on-the-run 5-year that we will use throughout this book.

The question from PACAM is more notable for what it's not telling the sales person. PACAM hasn't told the sales person why it wants to know where the bid and offer from Megabank is. One reason for this may be that PACAM is thinking about a possible trade but isn't yet sure if it will transact. PACAM may be about to trade with another bank and it wants to check that the prices the other bank has shown are fair prices. PACAM may be interested in doing a trade only once the price has reached a certain level and is simply checking on current market prices.

PACAM hasn't told the sales person if it needs **indicative** prices or **firm** (also called **live**) prices (Table 4.4). The difference between indicative and firm is whether the bank is willing to trade on the prices it gives the client. Making a firm market takes more work than making an indicative market; when clients ask for firm prices, the bank generally expects the client to trade. If the client doesn't trade with the bank, there needs to be a reason given.

TABLE 4.3 Treasuries with Approximately 5-year Maturities

			Amount in millions of dollars		
Coupon	Issue Date	Maturity	Issued	Retired	Outstanding
3.125%	02/01/10	01/31/17	$32,521	$0	$32,521
0.875%	**01/31/12**	**01/31/17**	**$35,659**	**$0**	**$35,659**
4.625%	02/15/07	02/15/17	$22,193	$0	$22,193
3.000%	03/01/10	02/28/17	$32,786	$0	$32,786
3.250%	03/31/10	03/31/17	$33,083	$0	$33,083
3.125%	04/30/10	04/30/17	$32,682	$0	$32,682
4.500%	05/15/07	05/15/17	$25,587	$0	$25,587
8.750%	05/15/87	05/15/17	$18,194	$−2,635	$15,559
2.750%	06/01/10	05/31/17	$31,674	$0	$31,674
2.500%	06/30/10	06/30/17	$30,893	$0	$30,893
2.375%	08/02/10	07/31/17	$29,952	$0	$29,952
8.875%	08/17/87	08/15/17	$14,017	$−3,049	$10,968
4.750%	08/15/07	08/15/17	$28,000	$0	$28,000
1.875%	08/31/10	08/31/17	$29,710	$0	$29,710
1.875%	09/30/10	09/30/17	$29,914	$0	$29,914
1.875%	11/01/10	10/31/17	$29,595	$0	$29,595
4.250%	11/15/07	11/15/17	$27,674	$0	$27,674
2.250%	11/30/10	11/30/17	$30,144	$0	$30,144
2.750%	12/31/10	12/31/17	$30,454	$0	$30,454

Good reasons are that the client got a better price from another bank or that the client decided not to trade at these particular prices. However, if the client got a better price from another bank, the bank who gave the original price would expect to be told whether they were **in comp**, which means in competition with one or more other banks. Also, if the client decided not to trade at these particular prices, the bank would expect the client to let the bank know that he has a price target prior to asking for the quote from the bank.

Finally, PACAM hasn't told the sales person which side of the trade it wants to do. Does PACAM want to buy or sell? Traders prefer to know

TABLE 4.4   Indicative vs. Firm Prices

Indicative	Firm
$9.90/share at $10.00/share	$9.95/share at $10.00/share for 5000 shares
Trader makes this market quickly without really thinking about his current trading book position and which direction he prefers to trade. He is just providing information to a client quickly. A notional amount is not specified.	Trader makes this market with a bit more thought. He knows he is likely to trade and wants to make sure he shows a price which is the most sensible for his current trading book risk as well as the direction he prefers to trade. In this example, he has improved his bid compared to the indicative price, which indicates that he prefers to buy rather than sell

which side of the trade the client wants to do in order to have the maximum amount of information possible. The clients, on the other hand, don't want to give too much away and many times prefer to ask for a **two-way market**, which means both a bid and an offer.

How the sales person reacts to this question will be a function of what kind of trades PACAM has done with the sales person in the past. If PACAM regularly asks for Megabank quotes in this same way and PACAM and the sales person have established a routine then the sales person will likely assume this is a similar request to the ones in the past. However, best practice would be for the sales person to confirm that before proceeding, in order to avoid any miscommunication.

If this is the first time PACAM has asked this question then the sales person needs to first ask whether there are any further details PACAM is willing to share with the bank. Importantly, the sales person needs to confirm:

- Is this a firm or indicative quote and, if this is firm, what size is PACAM looking to trade? The trader needs this information in order to give the quote. If PACAM wants a firm quote, PACAM needs to give a size or else the trader will have to put a restriction on the firm quotes it gives (Table 4.5).
- How quickly does the quote need to be given? Is it something PACAM needs as soon as possible or is it something that is being done later in the day/week and this is just to check prices? Usually, all client requests are treated as urgent requests, especially if they are for firm quotes on size.
- Are we in competition with other banks? In general, banks should always assume they are in competition with other banks on quotes, but it is good to check.

TABLE 4.5 Sample Firm Quotes with Size Restrictions

Asset class	Market with size restrictions
Equity	$9.95 at $10.00/share for up to 5,000 shares only
Bond	101.1% at 101.2% for up to $100 million only
Currency	76.13 at 76.14 yen to $1 for $50 million only

The sales person goes to the 5-year treasury trader and asks for the specific quote that PACAM needs. The conversation the sales person will have with the trader might be: "I need an indicative market in size for PACAM on the on-the-run 5-years. Probably $1 or $2 billion because that is what they normally trade when they say size. PACAM has been checking the price of this every few weeks or so. I'm not sure what their price target is and whether they are buyers or sellers. As soon as I get more information I'll let you know."

Alternatively, the sales person could say: "I need a firm market for PACAM for $1 billion on-the-run 5-years. I don't know if they are interested in buying or selling but we're in comp." Traders generally like to know if they are buying or selling and want as much market color as they can get on what the client is trying to do so that the trader can figure out how that might affect the market prices in general. But most traders don't get that luxury.

Depending on the relationship the sales person has with PACAM, after the sales person has passed on the request to the trader (which he will probably put the client on hold to do), the sales person will ask the client what the story is. He will ask questions such as:

- Is this part of a larger transaction?
- Is this a new position or is this taking off an old position?
- Is this the full size or is there more to come?
- Have you executed some of this already?

The intention is to get as much information as possible in order to assist the trader in making the best market possible.

The trader quickly comes back with a market of 16 at 17. While this is meaningful to the sales person and to the client, it is clearly shorthand communication. Traders constantly use shorthand to describe every aspect of a financial product, and they expect everyone with whom they interact to know the lingo too. It may be useful when time is of the essence, but the jargon contributes to the image of the financial world's being impenetrably complex.

Treasuries are an interesting bond market because they trade in 1/32 of 1%. Many other bond markets just trade with prices like 100.45% or

98.26%. The convention of trading treasuries in a non-decimal format is simply convention and nothing more (Box 4.1).

Box 4.1   Treasury quote convention

Treasury price: 100 − 16.
   To translate this price into a decimal, we do the following calculation:

   $= 100\% + 16/32 \times 1\%$
   $= 100\% + 0.5\%$
   $= 100.5\%$

   Thus, the cost of $100 million treasuries with a price of 100−16 is $100.5 million.

   1/32 of 1 percent $= 0.03125\%$
   "16 at 17" refers to the number of 32nds
   16/32nds $= 0.5\%$
   17/32nds $= 0.53125\%$

The **handle** (or the **big figure**) of the trade is known by market participants because they can see the prices on several different electronic trading systems. The reason the handle isn't repeated is because prices don't move that much intraday. The handle is generally constant for several days to weeks to months while the numbers after the decimal move every day. At the moment the handle is 100%.

The phrase "16 at 17," for example, means the trader will buy $1 billion on-the-run 5-years at 100% and 16/32 of 1% and sell $1 billion on-the-run 5-years at 100% and 17/32 of 1%. Box 4.2 outlines a trader quote.

Box 4.2   Megabank trader quote for US treasuries

- US Treasury 5-year on-the-run
- Coupon: 0.875%
- Maturity: 1/31/2117
- Megabank trader quote for $1 billion: 100−16 at 100−17
- Market quote for $300 million: 100−16.5 at 100−16.75

Because treasuries are probably the most liquid fixed income product in the global financial markets, there are live prices quoted on many different electronic trading systems globally so anyone can see quoted prices, but none of those quotes will be for a size of $1 billion so it is important to get a trader on a bank trading floor to make the price for the client.

Following a conversation between PACAM and the sales person, the sales person reports that PACAM is a buyer and wants to buy $1 billion treasuries from Megabank. PACAM lifts the Megabank offer. The exact wording should be from PACAM to the sales person: "I **lift the offer** for $1 billion 5-year on-the-run treasuries at a price of 100 and 17/32nds" or "I buy $1 billion 5-year on-the-run treasuries at 100 and 17/32nds." The sales person will immediately open a line to the trader and repeat those exact words to the trader. (Because PACAM is a client, and thus a market taker, if it wants to buy treasuries it needs to trade at the offer price from Megabank's trader, who is the market maker. The terminology to use is "lift the offer." Conversely, PACAM could have **hit the bid** if it wanted to sell treasuries.)

Open a line means that the sales person presses a button on an open microphone to the trader's desk. The Megabank trader then says to the sales person the following words: "I sell $1 billion 5-year on-the-run treasuries for 100 and 17 thirty seconds to PACAM." The sales person needs to then repeat this verbatim to the client on a recorded line. Box 4.3 summarizes the PACAM trade.

Box 4.3   PACAM trade summary

PACAM says, "I lift the offer for 1 billion 5-year on-the-run treasuries at 101.17/32" or "I buy 1 billion 5-year on-the-run treasuries at 101.17/32."

- Current US treasury 5-year on-the-run
- Coupon: 0.875%
- Maturity: 1/31/2117
- Megabank trader quote for $1 billion: 100−16 at 100−17
- Market quote for $300 million: 100−16.5 at 100−16.75
- PACAM lifts the Megabank offer of 100−17 for $1 billion

Repeating the trade details is very important in the execution process because it helps to ensure there are no mistakes. It is also important to repeat these words clearly to the client on a recorded line. This is because if there is any discrepancy in the settlement of the trade the tapes can be used to confirm what

FIGURE 4.1 Example of how a dispute can be easily caused (and avoided).

Conversation 1

- PACAM calls the sales person and says, "The notional is between $1 to $1.2 billion. Probably closer to $1 billion."
- Sales person gives a quote to PACAM but doesn't repeat the size. The sales person asks for a quote for $1.2 billion.

Conversation 2

- PACAM says, "Can you refresh your price for $1 to $1.2 billion, although I'll probably trade $1 billion?"
- Sales person asks for a refresh from the trader. Sales person doesn't repeat the size to the trader. Convention is to assume the same details for a refresh.

Conversation 3

- PACAM asks for a refresh and repeats that it'll probably trade $1 billion.

- Sales person updates the quote with the trader and again doesn't mention size.

- PACAM says, "I lift your offer and you're done."

- Sales person says to the trader, "You're done." Sales person doesn't repeat notional with either the trader or PACAM but does repeat the price.

- PACAM thinks it's done on $1billion and the trader thinks he's done on $1.2 billion.

---

was actually agreed. The recorded trade is found on the tapes and played back to both parties. This is part of best practice. Unfortunately, best practice is not always carried out and disputes can arise as a result, but most traders and sales people are aware of best practice and try to follow it at all times (Figure 4.1).

The word **done** is a crucial word in the execution of all financial market transactions which are executed verbally. It closes the trade and confirms the execution. Once there was a client who was working on a complicated derivatives trade with the sales person at a large US bank in New York. After days of discussions about this derivatives transaction, the client finally decided to trade. The sales person and the client went through the details of the trade one final time and the sales person got the trader on the line to update prices and let him know that the trade was about to happen. Finally, the client said, "Done." The sales person repeated "done" to the client and then to the trader, who was on an open mic so could hear what the sales person was saying to the client. The trader immediately hung up in order to work on hedging his position, at which point the client started yelling, "Un-done! Un-done!" The client had made a mistake in his calculations and needed something slightly different from what had been agreed. The sales person immediately scrambled to call the trader and started shouting, "Un-done! Un-done!" Needless to say, the trader was not amused but had not yet executed any hedges so agreed to change the deal.

PACAM did not originally tell Megabank whether it wanted to buy or sell and on what size exactly. PACAM could be nervous about telling the bank which direction it wants to go because if it isn't ready to trade yet it doesn't want the bank to front run it. "Front running" in this context means that if the bank knows that PACAM wants to buy a lot of 5-year treasuries and the size is significant enough to move the market prices then the bank may want to start positioning itself to benefit from the trade or to pre-hedge. This means that the bank may start to buy 5-year treasuries ahead of PACAM's buying them. PACAM does not want this to happen as it could move the price against it. This means that if PACAM wants to buy a significant amount and the bank starts to buy a significant amount ahead of PACAM, the price of 5-year treasuries will become more expensive. Note that while there is not a financial regulator in the world who would look kindly on a bank that behaved this way it has been known to happen, which is why clients are often cautious. It should also be clear that front running in any market and for any reason is not considered good market practice and in many instances is illegal.

Front running

Megabank Trader	PACAM
Trader starts buying 5-year treasuries for several hundred million. The average price where Megabank is able to buy is 17. The market quote is now 17.25/−18.25. Megabank knows there is another bank in the market trying to buy a billion to close out his trade with PACAM. The Megabank trader will slowly sell his treasuries into the market while the other bank is trying to buy them and likely make profit of 1/32nd of 1%	PACAM is able to buy its billion from another bank at −18.5. The other bank's trader saw the treasury price moving upward and decided to be conservative in his offer. The other trader now has to buy a billion treasuries to close out his trade with PACAM

In the PACAM treasury trade with Megabank, the Megabank trader has sold something he doesn't actually own. The trader is not sitting around with $1 billion 5-year treasuries on his books waiting for someone to buy them. He will make a price where he is prepared to sell them based on the knowledge that he will be able to buy them from a client or from another bank that same day. This is called going **short**. The treasury trader agreed to deliver something he doesn't yet own in exchange for cash. He can't close out his position until he is able to buy what he agreed to deliver, at which point he will be **flat** or **neutral**. The risk to the trader is that the market price moves up before he is able to close out his position. The opposite of being short is being **long**, which means having a position where the risk is that the price goes down. In most markets this is the same as owning a financial product.

In the financial markets, the concept of going short is often described as "selling something you don't own," which is technically theft. The difference is that what the treasury trader has actually agreed to do is to deliver treasuries to a client which he doesn't yet own. In order to do this, the trader will need to either borrow some treasuries or buy some on the same day he sold them in order to close out his position and deliver what he has agreed to deliver. There is an old saying in the financial markets: "He who sells what isn't his'n, must buy it back or go to prison."

The trading floor has added value by providing liquidity for a large size trade to a client. As mentioned earlier, clients can use any number of electronic trading systems to see prices and trade on-the-run treasuries. These electronic trading systems have live prices from banks that provide liquidity to those systems but the size of this trade means the client needs to call a bank and actually speak to the sales person rather than just use the electronic systems.

Supermart Interest Rate Swap Trade

Supermart is in the process of purchasing a similar business based in the UK called Bigmart. They are both publically quoted entities. One is quoted on the New York Stock Exchange and the other is quoted on the London Stock Exchange. In order for Supermart to buy Bigmart, it needs to buy all the shares of Bigmart in the public market. This means that all the shareholders of Bigmart need to agree to sell their shares to Supermart.

Supermart has been working on the deal for months with the M&A team at Megabank. The deal is supposed to be a secret but the share price of

Bigmart, which is traded on the London Stock Exchange, has increased over the last few months as rumors have circulated that a large US company is looking to buy Bigmart. The fact that discussions are happening is almost impossible to keep secret. Someone will see the Supermart team entering the Megabank headquarters for regular meetings. A junior M&A analyst at Megabank will tell his friend that he is working on a big deal involving a UK supermarket chain. Someone will almost always put two and two together and figure out that there is a possible deal in the works. Officially, Megabank and Supermart will have no comment, which generally only fuels the rumors. It is a known fact that Supermart owns 5% of the shares of Bigmart, which it bought two years earlier, so the financial market participants speculate that Supermart has been looking at buying Bigmart for the last two years. Importantly, while there are always rumors, some of which do turn out to be true, the details of the plan should not be public. Those details include the timing and the financing of the purchase or, in other words, how and when Supermart will pay for the Bigmart shares.

Another common example of front running is when there is a rumor in the financial market about a possible M&A deal. The rumor is that Supermart is looking at buying Bigmart in the United Kingdom and so the stock price of Bigmart has risen because investors are speculating that Supermart will have to pay a premium to buy Bigmart and they want to benefit. The rumor has created a bigger demand for Bigmart shares, which has pushed the price up. These investors are taking a risk that Supermart doesn't buy Bigmart, in which case they will mostly look to sell their shares, which will push their share price down and the investors will lose money (Figure 4.2). Front running in this case is not illegal, nor is it frowned upon necessarily by the regulators. Investors have done a trade based on a rumor and not based on actual insider information. Obviously, there is a gray area between rumor and insider information, which is what ultimately makes these cases complex.

FIGURE 4.2 M&A speculative front running.

M&A Rumor about Supermart buying Bigmart	M&A Rumor proven false
- Bigmart stock was trading at £1.50/share before the rumor	- After some months, the rumor is clearly proven false
- It is now trading at £1.80 due to the rumor	- The price of Bigmart slowly settles back to £1.50/share
- An investor saw the rally in the stock and was able to buy at £1.70	- The investor who bought at £1.70 wasn't able to sell at £1.80 and ended up selling between £1.70 and £1.50/share, losing money as a result

The Megabank M&A team could be working on this deal for months. As part of the process, it has modeled up some costs and benefits of this deal. Obviously, one of the key costs is buying the shares and how Supermart will finance that. The M&A team needs to keep updating the model with current market prices for all the moving parts of this deal to ensure that the economics of the deal still work for Supermart. If any of the market prices move too much, deals are sometimes put on hold indefinitely while they wait for the economics to make sense again.

Part of the plan that Supermart has been working on with Megabank is borrowing money in the public bond market in order to purchase the Bigmart shares. Based on the price that Supermart thinks it will have to pay to make the deal happen, Supermart needs to borrow a total of £5 billion. Because Supermart is a US-based corporate, its main investor base in the bond market is in the United States. This means that it will be able to borrow easier in the United States and in US dollars. The exchange rate Megabank is using in the model between US dollars and British pounds is $1.50 per £1. This means that £5 billion is the same as $7.5 billion. The M&A analyst can easily update the currency rate in his model each day. Box 4.4 summarizes the Supermart trade.

Box 4.4   Supermart trade summary

- 2.5 billion Bigmart shares outstanding.
- Original share price: £1.50.
- Current share price: £1.80 now that there is a rumor about a possible M&A deal.
- Supermart expects to pay £2, which is a premium to the current share price.
- Supermart needs £5 billion to buy Bigmart (£2 × 2.5 billion shares).
- Using an exchange rate $1.5 to £1 means Supermart needs to borrow $7.5 billion.

The discussions within Megabank that will be occurring around this issue will be between the M&A team and the debt capital markets team. The debt capital markets team navigates the capital markets for the corporate finance department. An **analyst**, which is a junior title in a bank, working in the M&A team will call up the debt capital markets team and ask confidentially where Supermart can borrow $7.5 billion. What he means by this is what coupon Supermart will have to pay to borrow $7.5 billion. While Supermart is a frequent borrower in the debt markets, it has never borrowed this much money at one time before so the M&A team wants to know the **premium** Supermart will need to pay.

Supermart has a credit spread of 2% for five years. This means that it would normally borrow at Libor (L) + 2% for five years. But for a possible $7.5 billion issuance, it is likely that there will be a premium of up to 0.05%. This means that Supermart will need to pay L + 2.05% in interest. On $7.5 billion, this is an extra cost of $3.75 million each year (Box 4.5).

Box 4.5   Supermart borrowing premium

- Supermart premium cost for large debt issue
- Issue notional $7.5 billion
- Premium of 0.05%
- Cost per year = $7,500,000,000 × 0.05% = $3.75 million per year

---

The debt capital markets person will have been keeping track of where Supermart has borrowed money in the past and how Supermart's bonds are trading in the financial market today as Supermart is a frequent issuer client. The debt capital markets person will easily be able to tell the corporate finance analyst an approximate coupon for Supermart to borrow this amount. But the debt capital markets person first needs to know the target maturity of the debt. The price of borrowing increases the longer the maturity. The M&A analyst replies that he isn't sure yet. He would like to get prices for 3 years, 5 years and 10 years.

Notice in Box 4.6 that the different credit spreads for different maturities can be graphed the same way that interest rates are graphed. When we graph interest rates for different maturities we call it a yield curve or a **term structure of rates** and we call credit spreads graphed for different maturities a **term structure of credit** or a **credit curve** (Figure 4.3).

Box 4.6   Supermart credit curve

2 years: 1.5%
3 years: 1.8%
5 years: 2%
7 years: 2.5%
10 years: 3%

These credit spreads do not include the premium of 0.05% for the size Supermart wants to do.

FIGURE 4.3 Term structure of credit spreads for Supermart.

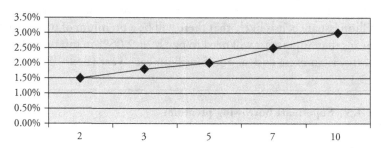

TABLE 4.6 Why Investors Want Floating Rate Bond Investments

	Fixed coupon cashflows 1%	Floating coupon cashflows Libor	What the investor believes will happen
Initial Investment	($100 million)*	($100 million)*	
End year 1	$1 million	Libor = 0.9%	Libor = 0.9%
End year 2	$1 million	Libor = ?	Libor = 1%
End year 3	$1 million	Libor = ?	Libor = 1.1%
End year 4	$1 million	Libor = ?	Libor = 1.2%
End year 5	$100 million + $1 million	$100 million + Libor = ?	$100 million + 1.3%

*Numbers in parenthesis represent investment or payments.

Debt can be fixed rate or floating rate. At the moment, the debt capital markets team explains, investors are concerned about interest rates going up so they prefer floating rate investments.

If the investor has a choice between a bond with a fixed coupon of 1% or a floating coupon of Libor, the investor who believes that interest rates are going up wants the floating coupon of Libor. Today, he doesn't know what Libor will be in the future, but he believes that Libor will ultimately be higher than 1% and he wants to benefit from that (Table 4.6).

Using the Supermart spread curve from Box 4.6 Supermart would borrow at Libor + 1.5% for two years, and so on and so forth. However, Supermart doesn't want to borrow in floating rate because it is concerned about interest rates going up as well and so it wants to borrow in fixed rate. It will need to swap the floating rate to a fixed rate with Megabank when the bond is issued to the investors (Figure 4.4).

FIGURE 4.4 Interest rate swap boxes and arrows.

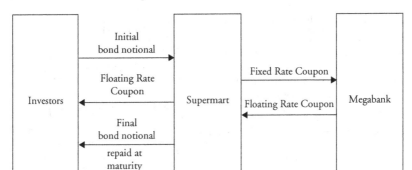

The M&A analyst doesn't necessarily tell the debt capital markets person why he needs this information. There is nothing particularly strange about the request because at any point the M&A team is working on several different potential deals. And, importantly, none of these deals is a certainty until it actually happens.

Because this deal involves currencies, Supermart will need to swap the money it borrows in US dollars into British pounds. So, the second question that the M&A analyst asks the debt capital markets person is, "Where can we swap it into pounds?" This is obviously a more complex question to answer and will be harder for the M&A analyst to keep easily up to date on the pricing for his model because it involves a **cross-currency swap**.

Supermart will borrow in US dollars and pay a US dollar coupon and then repay the money in US dollars at the maturity of the debt. When Supermart borrows $7.5 billion dollars, it immediately wants to exchange that for £5 billion pounds in order to buy the Bigmart shares, which are denominated in pounds. Then, because Supermart owns an asset in the UK that should produce profits in pounds, Supermart wants to pay the coupon in pounds to Megabank in exchange for receiving the cash in US dollars to pay the US dollar coupon that it owes. (See Figure 4.5.) This is called a cross-currency swap and is a complicated product to price. It is complicated because it involves currency, US interest rate derivatives and UK interest rate derivatives. These are traded by three different traders. The debt capital markets person needs the help of a derivatives sales person to help work on this possible trade.

Assume Supermart borrows the entire $7.5 billion for five years. As soon as it receives the $7.5 billion, Supermart will exchange it with Megabank for

FIGURE 4.5 Cross-currency swap.

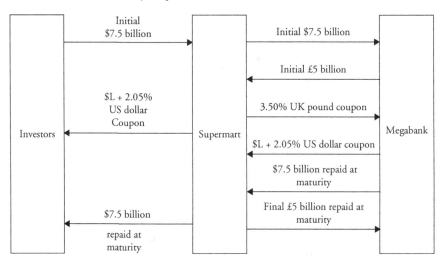

FIGURE 4.6 Supermart netted cashflows.

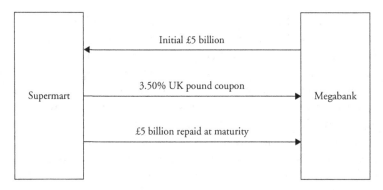

£5 billion. It will also want Megabank to pay the US dollar coupon in exchange for Supermart paying a coupon in UK pounds. This is because Bigmart will make profits in UK pounds so Supermart will use those UK pounds to pay the coupon to Megabank. At the maturity of the borrowing, Supermart will exchange the currencies back. Figure 4.6 shows Supermart's net position. At that point it is likely that Supermart will have built up a bigger investor base in the United Kingdom and, hopefully, it can borrow in UK pounds.

The currency rate and the share price are crucial components of this transaction. If either changes significantly, the cost of the deal could become prohibitive for Supermart. As a result, the M&A team will use a currency rate and a share price that are conservative compared to the current market prices so that any moves in market prices while they are discussing the deal don't kill the deal (Box 4.7).

Box 4.7   Market price move considerations

- 2.5 billion Bigmart shares outstanding.
- Current share price: £1.80, after speculation pushes the price up.
- Supermart expects to pay £2.00.
- Supermart needs £5 billion to buy Bigmart.
- Current FX rate: 1.4 = $7 billion. They use 1.5 to be conservative.

  1.5 = $7.5 billion.

Because Supermart is so large, it has an active risk management team which actively manages its interest rate risk. This team often deals directly with a derivatives sales person on the trading floor at Megabank. The debt capital markets person speaks to this derivatives sales person, who can model the cross-currency swap using indicative market prices for currency rates, US interest rates and UK interest rates. The sales person doesn't normally need to speak to the traders to do this. He is merely using the rates that the traders of Megabank publish regularly on their internal system. They do this so that every time there is a request for an indication the sales person can just use the published rates and not have to call the trader. This situation is slightly different from normal though due to the size of this deal. The traders will need to give the sales person some guidance on the right prices for this large size.

After discussing with the traders, the derivatives sales person says to the debt capital markets person that with a US floating coupon of L + 2.05% for five years (this is the cost of borrowing for five years in US dollars plus the premium for the size) Supermart can swap into a fixed pound coupon of 3.50%. The quote of 3.50% is considered the price of the cross-currency swap because it is the net cost to Supermart of borrowing this money after the swap is done (Figure 4.6). Because this is a tailored trade, it will be more difficult for the M&A analyst to obtain updated quotes on his own. In this situation the M&A analyst will be calling the debt capital markets person and/or the derivatives sales person to obtain updated quotes on this cross-currency swap throughout the deal discussion process.

Initially, the M&A analyst is simply asking for indications. At this point, there is not a firm decision on the part of Supermart to go ahead with the deal. It is merely exploring the idea. Eventually, as the discussions with Megabank advance, the M&A analyst tells the debt capital markets person that if they go ahead with the deal they have decided to do the entire $7.5 billion with a 5-year maturity.

Finally, when Supermart decides to go ahead with the deal, several things will happen within Megabank. The senior person in the M&A team will have a discussion with the head of debt capital markets, the head of bond sales and the heads of the trading teams for US interest rate swaps, UK interest rate swaps and currencies. At this point, these individuals will now be inside the Chinese wall and will be restricted from trading in Supermart and Bigmart. These discussions are important because the size of the deal is so large. When the deal goes live, Megabank will have to sell to its investor clients $7.5 billion of Supermart debt and, at the same time, Megabank will need to do a cross-currency swap to exchange the cashflows that Supermart has on the debt in US dollars into UK pounds all on the same day.

When it is clear that Supermart is seriously considering this deal, the indications that have been given for the cost of borrowing in US dollars and the cost of swapping into British pounds need to become firm. This means that there shouldn't be any surprises when it goes live with the deal. A surprise is when the price that Megabank has to pay to borrow in US dollars suddenly goes from L + 2.05% to L + 2.25%. A little movement is expected but a lot of movement can change the decision of Supermart to do this deal. Because there are so many moving parts to doing a deal like this, the less movement the better on all the inputs to the deal model (Box 4.8).

Box 4.8   All the moving pieces in the Supermart deal

Crucial variables in the Supermart deal

- Bigmart share price: Current share price £1.8; Supermart is prepared to pay £2.
- Current currency rate: 1.4; Supermart modeled based on 1.5.
- Supermart borrowing rate: Currently 2%; Supermart modeled based on 2.05%.

The first step in the deal is for Supermart to propose to the existing shareholders in Bigmart that it will buy the shares for £2.00. They are currently trading at £1.80 so this is a big premium. If the existing shareholders agree to the sale, then Supermart has a short period of time when it needs to go to the financial market and borrow the money to finance the purchase. The existing Bigmart shareholders agree to the sale and the clock starts ticking. Megabank announces that Supermart will be borrowing $7.5 billion in the bond markets in one week with a 5-year maturity and L + 2.05% coupon. The corporate bond sales force at Megabank then immediately goes to its clients to get indications of interest. The feedback will include:

- An asset manager who has been a big investor in Supermart says that it will put in a firm order for $200 million at L + 2%.
- An insurance company indicates that it is interested in $100 million at L + 2.1%.

The sales people report this information to the debt capital markets team. The debt capital markets team compiles this information and keeps it updated during the week leading up to the pricing of the bonds (Table 4.7).

The debt capital markets team is looking for a **clearing price** for the full notional amount of $7.5 billion. When the bond is issued, there are not different coupons for different investors; all investors get the same coupon. The strategy from the investor's perspective is to try to get the

TABLE 4.7 Sample Debt Capital Markets Spreadsheet

Price	Investor	Notional amount
Libor + 2.00%	Ins West	$500 million
Libor + 2.00%	Mondo AM	$200 million
Libor + 2.01%	ADG	$500 million
Libor + 2.02%	IFRG	$200 million
Libor + 2.02%	Ins West	$400 million
Cont.	Cont.	Cont.

notional amount the investor wants at the best price he can get. The "best price" to an investor is the highest coupon possible. Notice that Ins West put in two different bids in Table 4.7. This means that it will take $500 million at L + 2.00% and $400 million more if it can get the investment at L + 2.02%.

On the day of pricing, the information that the debt capital markets team has is the following: it can sell $7 billion at L + 2.03% and $7.8 billion at L + 2.04% and $8 billion at L + 2.05%. This is a good result for both Megabank and Supermart. Megabank really did understand the investor interest in Supermart and the premium for a large issuance. Megabank also managed Supermart's expectations well because Supermart was prepared to pay L + 2.05% but will be able to save 0.01%. (See Box 4.9.)

Box 4.9   Savings of 0.01% on big issuance

0.01% per year is a cost of $7.5 billion × 1/10,000 = $750,000 per year.

The bond is **oversubscribed**. This means that there is more demand at the price point that covers the initial need of the issuer. Supermart needs $7.5 billion so it can't issue a coupon of L + 2.03% as this coupon is only good for $7 billion. Supermart needs to issue a coupon of L + 2.04%, but the demand at that level is $7.8 billion or $300 million more bonds than it needs. One option is that Supermart might decide to upsize to $7.8 billion. Supermart might make this decision based on whether it believes the cost of borrowing is a good price or not. Often, if large corporates are able to get good borrowing prices, they will try to secure as much notional as they can afford when they have the opportunity. If Supermart doesn't want to upsize, the debt capital markets team will need to decide how to allocate to the different investors to get from $7.8 billion of orders to $7.5 billion (Box 4.10).

Box 4.10   Allocation discussion

Possible sizes for different coupons:

> $7 billion at L + 2.03%
> $7.8 billion at L + 2.04%
> $8 billion at L + 2.05%

The difference between how much Supermart wants and what it can borrow is $300 million at L + 2.04%.

The different investors who put in bids for that $800 million at 2.04% that brought the total from $7 billion to $7.8 billion should all be scaled back using the following formula:

$$\$500\text{million}/\$800\text{million} = 62.5\%$$

Each of those investors can have 62.5% of the orders they submitted.

Because Supermart wants to swap its US dollar cashflows into British pounds, setting the coupon for the bond will be done in conjunction with the US dollar interest rate swap trader and the UK interest rate swap trader. What will happen is that the US dollar interest rate swap trader will agree to borrow the US dollars from Supermart and pay the US dollar coupon on the Supermart bonds while the UK interest rate swap trader will agree to lend British pounds to Supermart and receive a pound coupon from Supermart. The currency rate that they use must be a current market rate so they need to check with the currency trader at the point of execution otherwise Megabank is exchanging currencies for Supermart at an **off-market price**. The time when the coupon is set and the bond allocation is done is the exact same time that the interest rate traders each agree to the cashflows they will exchange with Supermart. This is all coordinated carefully by the debt capital markets (DCM) team. (See Figure 4.7.) Box 4.11 summarizes the cross-currency swap rates that were traded.

FIGURE 4.7 Individuals involved and lines of communication.

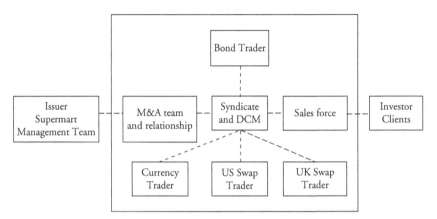

Box 4.11   Summary of the economics of trade

Supermart coupon

- L + 2.04%
- UK swap is fixed at 3.49%

Originally the discussion was a US floating coupon of L + 2.05% where Supermart swapped to a UK fixed coupon of 3.50% but if Supermart only pays L + 2.04% on the US coupon, they can swap for a slightly lower fixed rate in pounds.

This situation is very different from the treasury trade in the first example with PACAM (Table 4.8). The trade with PACAM was introduced by PACAM on the same day that the trade occurred, whereas the Supermart trade was in discussion for weeks or months before it finally happened. The Supermart pricing started off as indication only and then became firmer, at which point the deal became live and the pricing needed to be as exact as possible. The conversations were not necessarily driven by the client, as in the case of PACAM. The conversations were driven by the debt capital markets team, which was communicating with the corporate bond sales force and the derivatives sales person and the two interest rate swap traders regularly from the time the deal was announced. The week of the pricing, each day, they likely met each morning and discussed any financial market news that might

TABLE 4.8 Differences between PACAM and Supermart Transaction Process

Supermart transaction	PACAM treasury trade
Process takes weeks or months to complete	Trade takes 15 minutes
Supermart meets potential bond investors	PACAM as investor doesn't need to meet the US government as issuer
There are several different areas of the bank involved	The only area of the bank directly involved is the trading floor, specifically the sales person and the trader
This is a primary issuance and a cross-currency swap	This is a secondary market trade

affect the deal and the progress by the sales force. On the day of pricing, it is likely that they were in constant communication.

Best practice in this case would be for the derivatives sales person who is modeling the cashflows to have another experienced sales person model the cashflows in order to double check the pricing, given the large size. This is the **four eyes rule**. The derivatives sales person will coordinate the cross-currency swap pricing and execution. The interest rate swap traders will be very clear on the size of the transaction and the direction of the transaction. They will have been giving indicative pricing on interest rates for weeks on this transaction so there should not be any miscommunication about what is going to happen on the execution day.

The derivatives sales person will have agreed a price with each of the interest rate swap traders and the currency trader and said "done" to each of them and repeated the price they agreed at the same time as pricing the bond. The debt capital markets team will confirm the bond coupon and the investor allocations and will send an email to all the sales people sitting on the phone with their clients waiting to pass the coupons and their allocation to their clients. The sales people say the exact coupon and the allocation to their client and they also generally say "done" on the phone.

As soon as the Supermart bond is priced, the bond trader will be asked to make markets for secondary trades. Particularly when there is an oversubscription, there are immediate moves in the secondary market price of the bond. The Supermart bond will have been issued at 100%, but immediately the price might go up if there is interest in buying the bond. This might prompt some investors to take profit on some of their original investment. Within seconds of the bond being issued, the Megabank trader is asked, "Where is your market in the new Supermart bond?" He makes a market of 100.1% at 100.2%.

In terms of the added value of the Megabank fixed income trading floor, Megabank facilitated a borrowing of $7.5 billion between its issuer client Supermart and its investor clients. Then Megabank provided liquidity on a tailored cross-currency swap in order to swap the bond cashflows from US dollars to UK pounds for Supermart. As this was both a large size and tailored derivatives trade, Supermart needed a bank to provide liquidity on the size and to intermediate between the tailored trade and the market standard trades that Megabank will use to hedge.

A Structured Equity Product

Megabank's equity derivatives structurers in London hear about a structured product that another bank is selling to its retail clients in London. Megabank has decided to sell the same product to its retail investors. It is a structured bond, which are very popular with retail investors. The product broadly works in the following way: an investor buys a structured bond for £10,000 today and is guaranteed by Megabank to get at least £10,000 back in five years' time. In addition to this, in five years, if the FTSE 100 is above 5,000 the investor will receive a return over and above his £10,000 investment (Figure 4.8).

The description "in five years, if the FTSE 100 is above 5,000 the investor will receive a return over and above his £10,000 investment" indicates that there is an option in this financial product. The option is a 5-year option on the FTSE 100 struck at 5,000. The investor receives a return only if the FTSE 100 is above 5,000 in five years' time. If it is below 5,000, the investor doesn't receive a return and only receives his principal

FIGURE 4.8 Structured equity cashflows.

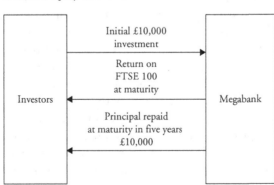

FIGURE 4.9 Option portion of the structured bond.

	FTSE100 price in 5 years' time	Difference to the strike of 5,000	Percentage return	Option return to Investor for £10,000 principal investment
Scenario 1	6,000	1,000	(6,000 − 5,000)/5000 = 50%	£5,000 (=50% × £10,000)
Scenario 2	4,000	−1,000	(4,000 − 5,000)/5,000 = −20%	£0

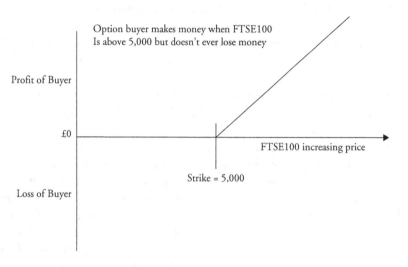

investment back. This means that the investor in this structured bond is implicitly buying an option when he buys this structured bond (Figure 4.9).

This is a classic structured bond, which **guarantees** that the investor gets his principal investment back. It is a very popular structure with retail investors because it allows them to invest their money without the risk of losing their original investment. The risk to the investor, to use the current example, is that in five years' time if the FTSE 100 is not above where it is today then the investor has lost the interest they could have earned on their investment. In a scenario where interest rates are low, this is not significant, but in an environment where interest rates are high or inflation is high, this is very significant. Box 4.12 gives an example of different investment opportunities.

Box 4.12   Different investment opportunities for £10,000

- If interest rates are high, invest £10,000 for 5 years at 8% and earn £800/year.
- If interest rates are low, invest £10,000 for five years at 2% and earn £200/year.

> In either scenario, if the FTSE 100 is below 5,000 in five years' time, the investor will not receive any return/year and will only receive his £10,000 back in five years' time.

This structured bond is a combination of two products (Figure 4.10). The first is a bond and the second is an equity option. This is a bond because the investors invest a principal amount on day one and get their principal amount back at maturity. They also get a return on their principal, which is similar to a coupon.

How does the bond portion work and who is actually providing the guarantee? In other words, who is holding the £10,000 over the five years? The guarantee is often the bank who is selling the bonds in the first place. In this example it is Megabank. Megabank is borrowing the money and Megabank is thus guaranteeing that the money will be paid back to the investor. This guarantee, of course, is only as good as the **credit worthiness** of the bank itself. Credit worthiness means the ability of the bank to pay back the money it borrowed. Lehman Brothers was a large issuer of structured bonds such as this. These products were guaranteed by Lehman Brothers. Most investors didn't consider that there was any risk at all in investing their money with Lehman Brothers. As a result there was a huge surprise for many investors when they realized that the guarantee from Lehman Brothers was worthless as soon as Lehman Brothers had gone bankrupt.

The way a guarantee structure works is that Megabank doesn't get to borrow £200 million, but it does have to pay back £200 million in five years' time. Megabank will be able to borrow £166 million and pay back £200 million in five years' time in exchange for NOT paying any coupons. (Every bond or loan requires the borrower to pay interest which is called a "coupon." Most coupons are paid every year, every six months or every quarter.) Instead of paying coupons every year, Megabank borrows £166 million today and pays back an extra £34 million in five years' time. This is called a **zero coupon** bond (Table 4.9). This means that all the coupons are

FIGURE 4.10 Structured bond creation.

TABLE 4.9 Zero Coupon Bond Compared to a Normal Bond

Normal Cashflows	Principal	Interest	Zero Cashflows	Principal	Interest
Megabank borrows	£166 million		Inception	£166 million	
Year 1		(£6.5 million)*	Year 1		
Year 2		(£6.5 million)*	Year 2		
Year 3		(£6.5 million)*	Year 3		
Year 4		(£6.5 million)*	Year 4		
Year 5	(£166 million)*	(£6.5 million)*	Year 5	(£166 million)*	(£34 million)*

*Numbers in parenthesis represent payments.

paid at maturity (£34 million is equivalent to approximately £6.5 million per year or a coupon of approximately 4% per year on £166 million).

The other part of the structured bond is the equity option. The cost of the equity option and the possible payoffs are shown in the example of the simple equity option.

Simple equity option

Investor buys a £200 million notional equity option on the FTSE 100. The FTSE 100 is at 5,000 today. The investor pays 12.5% of the notional of the trade as the cost of the option. The investor pays the bank £25 million for the option.

At the maturity of the option, if the FTSE is above 5,000, the investor receives a payout from the bank. If the FTSE is below 5,000, the investor receives nothing.

Example:

- FTSE 100 at maturity = 6,000
- FTSE 100 return is (6,000 − 5,000)/5,000 = 20%
- Investor receives a payout of 20%, or £40 million

In this structured bond, the investors are buying a zero coupon bond plus an equity option. The investors don't consider these as two separate products, because they are documented as one investment.

Megabank's equity derivatives structurers have decided to put this transaction together. They need to get prices from two different traders.

The first price is from the Megabank funding desk because this is a Megabank bond. The second price the structurers need is a price on the equity option from the equity options traders.

In putting this transaction together, Megabank will borrow money from its retail clients. So the first question is, "At what interest rate is Megabank prepared to borrow money for five years?" Issuing structured bonds for many banks is a common source of borrowing that the funding desk uses. It is thus a common question for the funding department to receive from internal structurers. The questions the funding department asks are:

- What size do you expect to be able to sell?
- When do you go live with this trade?
- Is this being sold as a buy and hold investment or are we offering any secondary markets?

All of these questions will have an impact on the pricing that the funding department will give to the structurers.

"What size do you expect to be able to sell?" allows the funding department to better manage any other borrowings that it is considering. The fact is that borrowing money costs money in the form of interest. Just because the bond is called "zero-coupon" doesn't mean there is no interest. Megabank doesn't pay a coupon but it does pay interest at maturity. The amount it pays is a cost for borrowing the money in the first place. A funding department wants to make sure it does not have any unforeseen cashflow constraints but, at the same time, it doesn't want to borrow significantly more than it anticipates needing, because it is costly.

"When do you expect to go live with this trade?" Or in other words, "When am I borrowing this money?" This question is also important for the funding department from a planning perspective and ties into the first question.

The structurers reply that they are targeting a size of £200 million and are looking to close the transaction in six to eight weeks. The word "target" here is interesting because it is different from issuing a Supermart bond, where the issuer knows how much it wants to borrow and will pay the coupon required to borrow that amount. Megabank is effectively the issuer in this structured bond, but it isn't doing the trade because it needs to borrow a certain amount. Megabank is doing the trade because it can make a profit, provide an investment product to its retail clients and borrow money at the same time. While Megabank hasn't spoken to its retail clients to know how much they will invest in a structure like this, Megabank has put deals like this together before and has generally been able to sell £200 million each time (Box 4.13). It would expect to be able to do the same in this situation.

Box 4.13   Other Megabank deals

- £220 million 6-year guaranteed structure linked to gold prices.
- €200 million 8-year guaranteed structure linked to US dollar vs. euro rate.
- £180 million 3-year note linked to the S&P500.

"Is this being sold as a buy and hold investment or are we offering any secondary markets?" Structured bonds are important to a bank's funding department because they provide an alternate source of funding. However, if there is a risk that the bank will not have the money for the full maturity of the structure, five years in this case, then the bank needs to take that into account when planning. The contrast is that most bonds are issued solely for the purpose of the borrower to have funding and as a result the borrower only pays them back at maturity. But structured bonds are issued first and foremost to provide a structured investment product to an investor. If the bank offers secondary markets in this structured bond, it means that the bank will offer to buy back the structured bond from its retail clients prior to the maturity of the bond.

Because of the complex compliance process that banks have to go through to sell structured products to retail investors, there is not really a secondary market in retail structured products. If a retail investor wants to sell his investment before the five years is up, he has to go back to the original bank that sold it to him and ask whether the bank will buy it back from him. This is different from a Supermart bond in which an investor can go to any major bank and ask that it buy the bond from him. Most major banks will make a market on a Supermart bond because they know that there are billions of Supermart bonds outstanding and it will likely be easy to find another investor. Also the size a large fixed income investor will be looking to trade, generally $10 million or more, means that the major bank can make some money on the trade, so it will be willing to take the risk. On the other hand, it is not a simple matter of buying back a retail structured product and then calling up a few other retail investors and seeing whether they want to buy it. Being able to sell

TABLE 4.10 Difference between Structured Retail Bonds and Supermart Bond

Supermart Bond	Structured Bond
Supermart regularly issues $1 billion of bonds and has $50 billion of other bonds in the market	This structured bond is a £200 million issue. The borrower is Megabank
Other major dealers will make markets in Supermart bonds	Other major dealers will not make markets in this note
The coupon is a known amount paid each year	The return is linked to the return on the FTSE 100 and only paid at maturity
Supermart bonds are targeted at all investors	This bond is targeted at retail investors

something to retail requires a complex compliance process to ensure that the marketing material is clear and the retail investor has had time to review the material and consider the risks before making the investment decision. This process has to be reviewed each time an approach is made to a retail investor, so it is not simply a case of picking up the phone and calling another retail investor. Because the size we are talking about is much smaller, anywhere from five thousand pounds up, it is generally not worth the time and effort to try to sell the product to another retail investor. (See Table 4.10.)

However, many banks offer secondary markets to their retail investors in their own structured products. If the retail investor wants to sell the structured product back to the bank before the five years are up, the bank will make a price and buy it back from the investor. What is important to stress to the investor at the point that he buys the structured bond is that the price is unlikely to be 100% if he sells before maturity. The investor is only guaranteed 100% at maturity, not any time before. Prior to maturity, the price is a function of the cost of the equity option as well as the cost of borrowing for Megabank.

After the structurers get prices from the Megabank funding desk, they go to the equity options trader and ask for a price where he'll sell a 5-year option on the FTSE 100. The equity options trader asks the same questions as the funding desk. The answers he gets are the same as those given to the funding desk. As this isn't the first time Megabank has issued a structured product, both the equity options trader and the funding desk are familiar with the general process.

FIGURE 4.11 The entire structure.

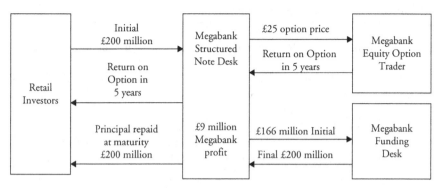

The prices that the equity derivatives structurer gets are a borrowing rate from Megabank and the price of the option from the equity options trader. The equity options trader says the price where he is prepared to sell this option is 12.5%. (Most option prices are quoted as a percentage of the notional of the trade.) If the notional of the equity option is £200 million, the option price is £25 million.

The Megabank funding desk says it'll borrow at 4% for five years for up to £500 million. Because this is a zero coupon bond for Megabank, this means it will borrow £166 million on day one and pay back £200 million in five years' time, as described in Table 4.9.

Together, the cost of the zero coupon bond is £166 million and the cost of the equity option is £25 million, which adds up to £191 million. Megabank will sell this structured bond at a price of £200 million, which includes a profit of £9 million to Megabank. Figure 4.11 shows the entire structure.

The price from the equity options trader is his offer price. It is where he is willing to sell the option to the client. He has not been asked for a two-way market on this product but his two-way market would have been 11.5% at 12.5%. This equity option is not quoted on exchanges, nor is it a very liquid product in the interbank market. The trader will need to determine the price for the option based on his hedge strategy discussed later in the book.

The profit on this transaction over and above the profit to the equity options trader is £9 million for Megabank. This is the difference between the £200 million that the retail investors spend to buy the bond, the £166 million that Megabank borrows and the £25 million cost of the option.

Box 4.14   Megabank profit calculation

- Megabank borrows £166 million and pays back £200 million in five years' time.
- The Megabank options trader sells an option for £25 million and pays the return on the FTSE 100 in five years' time.
- The investor pays £200 million to Megabank on Day 1.
- The difference is £200 − £166 − £25 = £9 million.
- Trader offer to mid of 0.5% is a possible trader profit of £1 million.
- Total trade profit of £10 million, or 5% of the £200 million notional.

Now, the structurers need to put together the marketing material, and get the legal team to put together the legal documents. Then the compliance department reviews everything and after some back and forth and a few tweaks, the deal should be ready to go to the retail sales department. The retail sales team is then sent the entire package of materials via email. It includes an invitation to a conference call where the equity derivatives structurers will walk the retail sales team through the material and how to sell the product to their clients (Figure 4.12). The timeline for closing the transaction i.e. Table 4.11.

FIGURE 4.12   The different parties involved in selling product to retail.

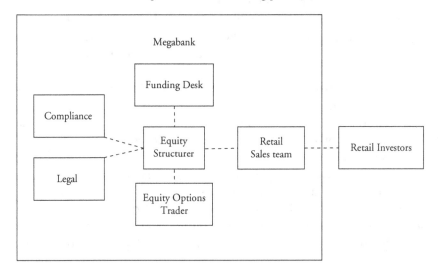

TABLE 4.11 Marketing Overview and Timeline for Closing the Transaction

Timeline	Work to be done
Week 1	Identify the idea, Structurer work with Options Trader, Funding Desk and Retail Sales to agree structure. Get Compliance approval, create marketing docs, educate Retail Sales on structure.
Week 2	Launch product. Contact key retail investors, describe product and send marketing material.
Weeks 3–5	Continue marketing to retail investors. Finalize documentation.
Week 5	Open subscription period.
Week 6	Finalize retail investor interest. Close deal and allocate investment to investors. Distribute final documentation. Receive money from investors to pay Funding Desk and Options Trader.

The marketing commences over a period of generally four weeks. This is when the retail sales team calls its clients and proposes the product as a potential investment. This also gives the sales team time to mail the marketing and legal materials to its clients for them to review at home. At the end of four weeks, there is a two-week subscription period. This is when firm orders are taken from all the interested retail clients. Then at the end of the two-week subscription period, the order book closes and the trade is done. The transaction was a success and the order book was filled before the two weeks were up. Megabank sold £200 million structured bonds to over 10,000 retail clients on sizes between £10,000 and £100,000. On the closing day, the structurer tells both the funding desk and the equity options trader that they are done on the prices that they gave. The conversation is:

To the funding desk: "You have borrowed £166 million in a zero coupon bond for five years starting in two days' time. On the maturity date you will pay back £200 million. Between now and the maturity, we have promised to buy back any structured bonds that our retail investors want to sell. Historically this has been between 5% and 15% of the notional amount in total." For the funding desk, this means the notional they borrow might reduce slightly over the five years.

To the equity options trader: "You have sold £200 million FTSE 100 options with an expiry date in 5 years. In 5 years, if the FTSE 100 is above 5,000, you will pay the return to the retail investors. You have received £25 million for that option. There is a secondary market in this structured bond so you may have to buy 5% to 15% of these options back before maturity."

Because of the long process, the prices that the equity options trader and the funding department give need to be firm prices that they hold for several weeks until they know they are done and on what size. From the equity option trader's perspective, he has to be happy to sell that option for 12.5% for six weeks before he is done on the trade. There is a chance the trade doesn't happen and there is a chance that the notional amount is smaller than he was originally told. The biggest risk is that the price of this option goes higher than what the trader quoted and he isn't hedged because he hasn't yet been told he is done. (See Box 4.15.)

Box 4.15   Equity options trader risk calculation

Megabank trader market on equity option:
    11.5% at 12.5%.

- Megabank trader sells £200 million options at 12.5% and the price is now 13%.
- Megabank trader will lose 0.5% on this trade or £500,000.

The added value of Megabank in this transaction is the ability to put together an appealing investment for its retail investor clients. Megabank intermediates between the more complex derivatives market and constructs an investment which has relatively simple cashflows that the retail investor can understand. Megabank will also provide liquidity in the secondary markets for this product.

Conclusion

To trade means agreeing a price at which someone buys or sells a financial product. But unlike the picture we often see in the media, where traders are running around screaming on the stock exchanges, most traders on the trading floor of a bank are carrying on a more sedate and sometimes much anticipated transaction. This chapter gives three examples of common transactions which happen on the trading floor. They are interesting because while one happens within 30 minutes, one takes months and another takes weeks to plan and structure. What is crucial in all of these transactions is the amount of communication that is required between different parts of the bank and the market makers. Also crucial is clarity on the point of execution and the exact words that are used. These three trades give a sample of the types of conversations which occur on the trading floor all day and thus the type of information flow that a trader is processing as part of his job as market maker.

These three trades also show the value of the bank intermediating the financial markets for its clients. The PACAM trade was a large enough size that PACAM might have struggled to execute the full size on any of the electronic trading systems without moving the price significantly. PACAM needed the Megabank trader to provide liquidity and take some risk. The Supermart transaction was a very large size and tailored and needed the trading floor to intermediate, provide liquidity and take risk at different points in the process. The primary issuance of the Supermart bond was about intermediating between issuer and investor clients. The corporate finance department, the debt capital market department and the sales force were instrumental in making this possible. Swapping the currency and the cashflows for Supermart's risk management purposes required Megabank derivatives traders to provide liquidity on a tailored transaction. Providing secondary market liquidity for the Supermart bonds required the Megabank bond trader to make markets as soon as the primary issue was priced. The structured equity product was one which originated on the trading floor but was created to provide retail investors with a principal guaranteed investment. These types of trades simply wouldn't be possible without the bank trading floor intermediating, providing liquidity and taking risk.

These three trades give a sense of the day-to-day client trading activity that occurs on a trading floor. They also give a sense of the risk that banks take to provide liquidity to their clients. The key to taking risk is about putting the right price on the risk in the first place. This is why bank traders are market makers and clients are market takers. Market makers decide where they are comfortable buying or selling a financial product such that they make a profit in exchange for the risk that they take.

Discussion Questions

Why do clients often ask to see both the bid and the offer from the market makers?

Are clients always the market takers?

Why is it so important that trade execution is on a recorded medium (either phone or a form of electronic communication)?

Why is clear communication in trade execution so important?

Please see www.terriduhon.co for answers and discussion.

CHAPTER 5

What Is the Market and Why Does It Move?

This chapter will begin with a focus on the term "the market" and the numerous ways it is used and what it means in different contexts. Generally, the term means either financial market participants or market price. Ultimately though, when talking about the market, what financial market participants are really trying to figure out is how the market prices will move. The next question then is: Why do markets (and thus market prices) move? There are macroeconomic and microeconomic reasons that govern price changes, and these should be studied and understood. But all the models and analysis in the world won't change the fact that at the end of the day the forces of supply and demand determine what the right price is. This chapter will also answer questions such as: Is the financial market a sentient being? Is fundamental analysis valuable at all? Can the financial market be controlled?

One story that gets told in the financial markets is about monkeys and darts. The idea is that investing in financial markets is a 50/50 bet and those asset managers who make money are simply lucky. In other words, investing is no more complex than throwing darts when the dartboard is covered with different financial products. If there are 16 monkeys in the room, at the end of the first quarter, 8 of them will have made money and 8 of them will have lost money. At the end of the second quarter, of the 8 who made money in the first quarter, 4 will have made money and 4 will have lost money. By the end of the year, only 1 monkey will have made money each quarter. At the end of the day, no one knows with certainty what will happen in the future, but the thoughtful, informed investor is probably the one who will do better over time.

The financial market is such a difficult concept to describe. Ask people who work in the financial markets to define the financial market and they will often struggle to be concise and even give wildly different answers. This does not mean that people in financial markets don't understand it. It means that the term is used in different ways in different contexts. It also means that few people in financial markets are ever required to explain what financial markets are to anyone. "It is what it is" (as someone first unhelpfully explained to me). At the same time, market dynamics are a fundamental part of understanding what the market is, and everyone has different theories on those. To some extent, that is what makes a market.

At the end of the day, regardless of the nuances of the meaning of the term "market," we are all focused on what market prices will do in the future. Will they go up or will they go down? Will they be very volatile or will they be more stable? There are days of commentary, reams of research and hundreds of models dedicated to answering these questions. This chapter introduces a framework for how to approach market prices. First, there are some fundamental relationships between financial products of which we should all be aware as well as some fundamental analysis that should give us a good idea of the direction of price movements and the relative value of financial products. This is the basis of the theoretical price. Second, supply and demand ultimately determine the price at which something trades. We call this the "actual price" or the "fair market price," which may be very different from the theoretical price. This difference is what drives investors to believe something is cheap or expensive and ultimately what compels people to trade. From the perspective of the trading floor, this drives the client business that the trading floor does. However, traders on the trading floor are busy doing all the same analysis their clients are doing because the trader needs to make a market for the clients who have a view and want to trade.

What Is the Market?

The most common use of the term "market" is a place where buyers and sellers meet. As mentioned in Chapter 1, a supermarket, a flower market or a flea market are good examples of these. They are easy to visualize because they are physical places where people go in order to buy or sell physical items such as flowers or old furniture. Financial markets are harder to visualize because they don't refer to a physical place, nor do they refer to a physical product. Financial market participants don't need to physically go to a trading floor to walk away with a treasury bond or an interest rate swap or an equity option. Also, there is not one place that financial market participants meet to buy and sell any one financial product.

A good image of how the financial market works is when someone is in the market to buy a new car. The first thing they will do is figure out how much their old car is worth. They will look at a bunch of information on the Internet about where the specific brand and model of car they own has recently traded or is being offered for sale. They will contact a few local car dealers and see whether the dealers will be able to give them a reasonable deal on their old car. Ideally, the buyer wants the highest price he's seen on the Internet, and the dealer clearly wants to pay the lowest price possible. The dealer will also be looking on the Internet and thinking about the customers he's seen recently. He needs to figure out if he buys the old car whether he will be able to sell it at a profit. The financial markets work in a very similar way. There is a lot of data available on historic market prices for a particular financial product as well as current bids and offers on a particular financial product for a particular size. The client should be able to see all this data and make a decision about what the right price for his particular financial transaction is. He will then go to a trading floor where the trader needs to make a decision about where he can close out or hedge the trade with the client and still make some money.

This is the financial market. It is a space which encompasses all the different buyers and sellers of a particular financial product and the prices where they are willing to trade. It takes into account all the available information that could affect the price of the transaction. Sadly, all the snide remarks about used-car dealers come to mind as well and, unfortunately, in some cases those also apply to the financial markets. (See Box 5.1.)

Box 5.1 The financial market

Generically: where buyers and sellers meet.

In finance: the known bids and the offers of the market participants interested in trading a financial product plus all the peripheral information around those prices.

Peripheral information might include:

- At what price previous trades were transacted
- Who the buyers and sellers are
- What financial market participants think about the future direction of the price

Financial markets are similar to used-car markets...

Nowadays, the idea of a financial market isn't that hard to grasp when everyone is constantly looking on the Internet for the best place to buy different goods and services and negotiating the price as a result. But what does market mean when a client says to a trader "Make me a market"? As described in Chapter 4, this is what a market maker does. He makes markets in specific financial products. He will buy at a certain price and sell at a certain price. He will use broader financial market information about recent trade prices and current bids and offers from other banks to determine his bid and offer, but this is his little financial market: it is specific to him and often specific as to its size and client. In the PACAM example from Chapter 4, the Megabank trader made a market of 100−16 at 100−17 when the market that he saw on the screens was 100−16.5 at 100−17.75.

Another similar question is "Where is the market?" This is often asked by clients to sales people, by sales people to traders and then by traders to their interbank brokers. This is sometimes interpreted as a request for the trader to make a market but it can also be a more general question about financial market color.

For example, in the PACAM treasury trade in Chapter 4, PACAM asked, "Where is the market in size for 5-year on-the-runs?" PACAM didn't specifically say, "Make me a market," but the sales person interpreted the question that way. Another example would be if PACAM had generally asked, "Where is the market for 5-year on-the-runs today?" This may have been interpreted as a more generic question. The sales person wouldn't have necessarily gone to the trader to answer this question. Sales people and traders discuss what is happening in the treasury market several times an hour throughout the day. Sales people are as versed in market color as the traders because it is their job to be able to communicate that type of information to their clients. The sales person might answer with the following: "The screens are showing 16.5/16¾ for average size, around $300 million a side. There's not a lot of flow today and the market doesn't feel like it's going to move one way or the other."

Another common use of the term "the market" is in a phrase such as "What do you think about the market?" or "What's your view on the market?" These are commonly used within financial markets between clients and sales people, between sales people and traders and between traders and interbank brokers. These questions are generally used to start a conversation and are very open ended. All of these financial market individuals are ultimately focused on the question of what market prices on the particular financial instrument they trade are going to do over some time horizon (Table 5.1). The time horizon the client is looking at is a function of who the client is and what their investment or risk management strategy is. The time horizon the sales person is looking at is generally a function of the client they are talking to, and the trader is generally focused on a more short-term time horizon, such as a day.

The question about the markets is an open-ended one because any number of issues could be the main focus of the day. There could be some much-anticipated financial news about to come out that day, such as new regulation or unemployment rates. Depending on the asset class and the

TABLE 5.1 Different Time Horizons

Individual	Time horizon	Reason
Investor client	Trade strategy dependent	If the investor is a day trader who makes money on **intraday** price movements, he will focus on price changes today. If the investor is a buy and hold investor, he will focus on the longer term such as months or even years
Sales person	Client dependent	The sales person needs to be well versed in views about one-day price moves as well as long-term price moves, depending on which client he is speaking to at the time.
Trader	Hedge or closeout dependent	The trader needs to be focused on how he can hedge or close out any position he gets from a client. Ideally that is on the same day, so he is mostly focused on intraday price movement

particular financial instrument being discussed, this question will elicit different answers even on the same day.

For example, on one particular day, there is some macroeconomic indicator being released such as non-farm payrolls. This is a number that is used to help calculate the unemployment figure in the United States. It is released every month and gives the number of jobs that have been added or lost in the last month. This number will have an impact on almost every asset class in the US financial markets. Depending on the state of the global economy, it could also have an impact on financial markets around the world. However, each regional financial market will generally be focused on its own macroeconomic data first and foremost.

The conversation in the US equity markets could be something like:

Client: What do you think about the market?
Sales person: Our guys are expecting the number to be much higher than expected. So we think the markets could rally off the back of this. The market is desperate for some good news.

The client used the standard conversation opener. The sales person automatically referred to the non-farm payroll number that is being announced that day. The sales person didn't specify what number he was talking about because everyone in the US financial markets is talking about the same number on the day it comes out.

Macroeconomic statistics, such as the non-farm payroll, are monitored by any number of agencies and economists. Many of those economists will have developed a theory or formula for predicting the non-farm payroll number well in advance of its release. Those economists who are more often right get a following of financial market participants. They rely on this research to position themselves ahead of the number being released. Given the numerous predictions ahead of the number being released, there are also reports which provide a summary of the different predictions and give the average prediction, which is called the **consensus**. This becomes the generally expected number for the financial market participants. When the sales person says that they are expecting the number to be much higher than expected, he is referring to his internal economist's view in contrast to the market consensus.

The sales person uses the term "market" in two different ways in this conversation. The first refers to market prices. "The market could rally." This means that equity prices could go up if the number that is released is higher than expected. More employment means the economy is doing well and companies and their share prices should benefit from that.

This conversation also highlights another usage of the term. When the sales person says, "The market is desperate for some good news," he means that the financial market participants have been hearing a lot of bad news about the economy recently and want to hear some good news. This is more human nature than anything. When the economy is not doing well in any region, jobs are lost, companies don't make as much money and share prices generally go down. The professional investor finds it hard to make a positive return when anything he buys in the equity markets is likely to go down in price or not move. This is a classic bear market situation. Investors will latch on to any good news and see it as an opportunity to buy.

When bulls walk, they walk with their heads up in the air; when bears walk, they walk with their heads hanging down. A **bull market** is one where the market prices are on an upward trend; a **bear market** is one where the market prices are on a downward trend (Figure 5.1). Bull or bear markets can last as long as a few months out to several years. Bull markets are when economies are strong and bear markets are when economies are weak and the market prices for financial products reflect this.

Financial market participants are the various individuals who trade in a particular financial product. Specifically, these are the individuals within the financial companies whose job it is to invest in the financial markets. They are busy looking at the market in which they invest every day and deciding when is a good time to buy or sell. What they generally think about

FIGURE 5.1 Bull and bear markets.

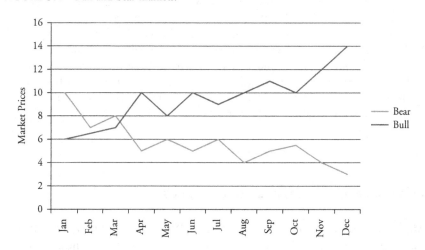

the market will either push market prices higher as the majority of them decide to buy or they will push market prices lower as the majority decides to sell. Their decision to buy or sell generally gets transacted through a trading floor via the sales person to the trader, who has to hedge or close out the resulting position. Thus, while the main market price movers are the investors, the traders will also have an impact on the market prices, depending on their hedge or closeout strategy.

PACAM treasury trade moving the market

PACAM has told its main bank sales people at three different banks that it has a program of buying US treasuries at the moment. PACAM has not disclosed total size but, generally, every time it asks for a market it trades $500 million to $1 billion.

These three banks have all had their offers lifted several times by PACAM. As a result, these three banks are always in the interbank market lifting offers of other banks.

The price of treasuries is going up as a result.

In the United Kingdom, many people refer to **Black Wednesday**, the 16th of September 1992. The United Kingdom had agreed to keep the UK pound at a certain price against other European currencies. Unfortunately, the financial markets didn't believe that the pound was worth that price so market participants began selling the pound because they thought that it was overvalued. The British government was forced to try to counteract the impact of the market by buying the pound to try to keep its value up. Eventually, the British government gave up against the force of the financial market and allowed the value of the pound to fall. It is reputed that one investor in particular, George Soros, made over $1 billion by trading against the British government.

Price Fundamentals: Macroeconomics

Market prices move for two main reasons. We'll call the first **price fundamentals** and the second supply and demand (Table 5.2). These two are highly related, but to understand them we will look at each separately. The

TABLE 5.2 Market Price Movers

Price Fundamentals	Supply and Demand
1. Macroeconomics: Is the economy doing well or not? 2. Company specific news: Is a particular company doing well (i.e. making money or losing money, growing quickly or slowly, winning market share or losing market share, financially stable or unstable)? These fundamentals lead to market price direction. In other words, they indicate that the price should go up or down	Where a financial product actually trades may be influenced by fundamentals, but is ultimately a function of the number of buyers vs. sellers The **fair price** has little to do with theoretical price and everything to do with where the financial product last traded and what the current bids and offers indicate about the market price now Supply and demand determine the market price

first is the fundamentals. We'll break fundamentals down into two main areas: macroeconomics and company specific news.

Macroeconomics is how the broader economy is performing. It is not about the performance of any one company or issuer: it is about the US economy or the European economy or the German economy. The example of non-farm payrolls is a classic macroeconomic statistic which has the ability to move financial markets in the United States and sometimes around the world. Every day, there are statistics released and government announcements made which give financial market participants a better idea of how an economy is performing today and how it will likely perform in the future. Table 5.3 is a sample **financial market calendar** for one day. This is a list of different publications of statistics or speeches which are being released that day around the world. The consensus number and the previous number are also included for market participants to assess what might happen to market prices if the number being announced is different from consensus.

The markets constantly focus on macroeconomics because an economy is never stable. It is always growing or shrinking. When it is growing, it is generally considered a bull market in that particular region and share prices go up; when it is shrinking, it is generally considered a bear market and share prices go down.

Most economies are cyclical over periods of years. This is called the "business cycle" or the "boom and bust cycle." The ability to predict when the cycle will change is what the whole financial market is focused on. In other words, when is the right time to buy or sell a financial product?

TABLE 5.3 Sample Financial Market Calendar for One Day

Country	Event	GMT	EST	CONSENSUS	PREVIOUS
Europe	Euro-Zone Sentix Investor Confidence	09:30	04:30	−16.50	−21.10
Europe	German Factory Orders (YoY)	11:00	06:00	−0.40%	−4.30%
United States	Fed's Bullard Speaks on Inflation Targeting in Chicago	13:55	08:55	—	
Canada	Ivey Purchasing Managers Index	15:00	10:00	57.00	63.50
United States	Fed's Fisher Speaks on Economy in Washington	17:15	12:15	—	
New Zealand	Average Hourly Earnings (QoQ)	21:45	16:45	0.50%	1.30%
United Kingdom	New Car Registrations (YoY)	—	—	—	−3.70%
Australia	Reserve Bank of Australia Rate Decision	03:30	22:30	4.00%	4.25%

YoY means "year over year." It is the percentage change of this year's numbers from last year's numbers. QoQ means the same thing but for quarters rather than years.

Every one ideally wants to buy at the end of a bust cycle and sell at the end of a boom cycle (Table 5.4).

Being able to predict the perfect timing every time is as much art as it is science. There are some financial market participants who are well known for this ability. In September 2008, when Lehman Brothers defaulted and caused global market prices to go into a downward spiral, in particular the market prices of bank stocks, Warren Buffett decided that it was the right time to invest $5 billion in Goldman Sachs shares. Market participants thought he was crazy. The world was about to end right? Well, not yet and in the words of Warren Buffett, "Be fearful when others are greedy and greedy when others are fearful."

The key things to keep in mind with regard to economic statistics are:

• When the economy is growing, most prices go up.
• Things such as share prices go up because companies are more profitable.

TABLE 5.4 Buy Low and Sell High

Boom Cycle	Bust Cycle
Bull Market	Bear Market
Share prices going up	Share prices going down
But, what goes up, must come down...	Most economies are generally on a long-term growth trend but still have bust cycles every few years
Ideally, an investor would have sold his equity investments in the summer of 2007 when the S&P index was at a high of 1,500	Ideally, an investor would have bought equities in March 2009 when the S&P index was at a low of 700
But this was the height of the boom. Selling at that point seemed ridiculous. No one believed it would ever stop...	But this was the bottom of the bust cycle. Buying at that point seemed ridiculous. Everyone was worried about the end of the world...

- Real estate prices go up because more people are employed and able to buy new homes.
- Commodity prices such as oil and gas go up because people can spend more.

At the same time, bond prices generally go down because the financial markets will expect the governments in those locations to try to prevent bubbles. The housing bubble in 2003–2007 is a good example of this. The economies in North America and Europe were growing. People felt wealthier and bought more houses. House prices were suddenly sky high. They no longer made sense to most people. This is a bubble. To combat bubbles due to economies growing too fast, governments will try to influence interest rates and push them higher. The converse is also true. If the economy is not performing well, share prices go down and bond prices go up because the governments are expected to try to stimulate the economy with low interest rates.

The way that a government influences interest rates is to borrow more money by issuing more debt or to buy up its outstanding debt. The government is using the forces of supply and demand. When there is more supply of government debt, the interest rates are higher. This is because when the government needs to borrow more money there is more supply (bonds) against the same amount of demand (investors interested in buying the debt). Thus, the government needs to pay more interest in order to borrow more. This raises interest rates.

Governments do this deliberately as part of their monetary policy. The idea is that if a mortgage on a house is a function of where the government

TABLE 5.5   How Interest Rates Influence the Economy

Possible Homeowner High Interest Rates	Possible Homeowner Low Interest Rates
Current Mortgage Rates of 8%	Current Mortgage Rates of 4%
This means that for a $100,000 mortgage, the monthly payments will be around $600/month	This means that for a $100,000 mortgage, the monthly payments will be around $300/month
This is an annual interest cost of $8,000	This is an annual interest cost of $4,000
The possible homeowner may consider this too high and decide to wait	The possible homeowner may consider this doable and decide to buy a house
This depresses house prices and makes individuals feel less wealthy and thus spend less	This improves house prices and makes individuals feel more wealthy and thus spend more

borrows money, then people are less likely to buy new houses if interest rates are higher and thus the economy slows down. On the other hand, if the economy is too slow, the government can lower interest rates by buying up its outstanding debt and having less debt outstanding. This lowers interest rates and is meant to spur the economy toward growth. (See Table 5.5.)

In a difficult economy, when the government is trying to push interest rates lower, the impact on bond prices is that they go up. This is the key relationship to keep in mind. If interest rates go down, bond prices go up, and vice versa. For example, in the treasury market when the on-the-run 5-year that PACAM traded in Chapter 4 was first issued, it was issued with a price of 100% and a coupon of 0.875%, but over time there has been more demand for that bond, which has pushed the price up above 100% to 100−16 or 100.5% (Figure 5.2). The coupon hasn't changed, but the price has. This changes the effective return to an investor because he has to pay more cash to buy the bond. The effective return is now 0.77%, as opposed to 0.875%.

This investor pays more than 100% for his investment, but he still receives the 0.875% coupon. This means that his return over time is 0.77% which is less than 0.875%, which is the fixed annual coupon amount. When bond prices go up, the return (or **yield**) goes down, and vice versa.

The next time the US government borrows money for five years, it won't have to pay a coupon of 0.875% to borrow money: it will pay a lower coupon closer to 0.77% if the market price of the current on-the-run 5-year hasn't moved.

FIGURE 5.2   Picture of investor paying more than 100%.

Cashflows for an investor who buys a 5-year on-the-run treasury at a premium

Investor receives 0.875%
every year from the US government

$875,000 $875,000 $875,000 $875,000

$875,000

$100 million
At maturity, the investor
receives the last coupon payment
and the notional back from
the US government

Investor pays $100.5
million to the seller of
the treasury on day one

$100.5 million

Within the same currency, most debt products have a similar relationship to government debt that mortgages have. The easiest to understand are fixed rate bonds. The coupon on a fixed rate bond issued in US dollars will always refer to the current yield on US treasuries. The idea is that the US government borrows at the lowest interest rate possible and everyone else borrows at a higher rate than that. We can say the same for the UK government and debt in pounds or for the German government and debt in euros.

Figure 5.3 is a simplified picture of a normal yield curve. This shows that the longer the maturity that an entity borrows, the higher the yield (or the coupon) gets. This also shows that a government borrows at a lower interest rate than a bank and other companies generally borrow at a higher interest rate than a bank. As a result of the 2008–2009 credit crisis, we've seen all variations of this picture, for example a picture that is entirely reverse of this with the government borrowing at a higher rate than any other entity in the local currency. However, Figure 5.3 is the theoretical relationship in normal financial markets.

On the other hand, when a government is distressed, for example Greece during the euro crisis of 2010 and 2011, it can no longer control the interest rates at which it borrows. There was so much concern about Greece's ability to pay its borrowings back that investors were unwilling to lend to Greece at a low interest rate. (See Table 5.6.)

While financial market participants can see the statistics as they come out, what they can't predict is how the governments will react to these statistics and whether they will attempt to move interest rates as a result. Table 5.7 lists the key macroeconomic relationships of when an economy is in trouble and when it overheats.

FIGURE 5.3 Government vs. corporate borrowing.

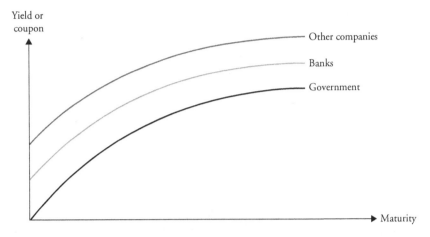

TABLE 5.6 Greek Government Cost of Debt*

Greece pre-crisis	Greece in crisis
Current interest rates of 4%	Current interest rates of 10% because investors consider Greece a high-risk investment
Current borrowings of €100 billion	Current borrowings of €100 billion are maturing. Greece needs to borrow another €100 billion over the next few years
This is an annual interest cost of €4 billion	10% means an annual interest cost of €10 billion if Greece re-finances today.
Greece can afford this amount as long as its economy remains stable	Greek economy is faltering and Greece can't afford the current interest cost of €4 billion a year, much less €10 billion in the future if it re-finances today

*Numbers have been simplified for this example.

In the fixed income markets, calculating bond prices and yields is a time-consuming, detailed process called "bond math." Everyone needs to be able to go from a bond price to a yield and vice versa quickly. The terminology is misleading because the theory is not just for bonds: it applies to most derivative products which have cashflows in the future. The financial calculator is the tool that people on the trading floor are seen running around with regularly. Advice: "If you work in fixed income, learn how to use a financial calculator. You never know when you're going to need it."

TABLE 5.7 Key Macroeconomic Relationships

Scenario	Share prices	Government Reaction	Supply and Demand	Bond prices	Economy
Economy in trouble	Share prices go down	Issue less debt	Less supply	Bond prices go up, yields go down	Improves because money cheaper to borrow
Economy overheating	Share prices go up	Issue more debt	More supply	Bond prices go down, yields go up	Stabalizes because money more expensive to borrow

Price Fundamentals: Company Specific News

Aside from macroeconomics, the other key fundamental that influences market prices is **company specific news**. This is information about individual companies and how they are performing. While we generally say that companies thrive in a strong economy and suffer in a weak economy, this is a very general statement. In fact, some companies are **countercyclical**; in other words, they do well in a weak economic environment. An individual company can do well or poorly depending on how it is managed and the industry it is in, irrespective of the general economy. The equity markets in particular focus on company specific news, which is often the main driver of share prices moving up or down.

Company specific news often relates to the publication of a company's financial statements, which provide a record of the company's growth, profitability, financial stability in the past and, perhaps, a clue to future performance. Every company operates on an annual basis. This means that every year each company produces a set of accounts that details its income and expenses for the previous year. Many public companies operate on a calendar year-end basis, which means that they produce their financial statements for the period from January 1st through to December 31st for each year. It then takes two to three months for a company to produce its financial statements and double-check them. The double-checking is done by an accounting firm, which audits or reviews them. The company is then in a position to announce its earnings and financial statements for the year. February and March are generally big months for annual **earnings announcements**.

TABLE 5.8 Sample Earnings Calendar

Earnings Announcements for Wednesday, February 15th		
Company	EPS Estimate	Time
Aastra Technologies Ltd	0.69	After Market Close
Aastrom Biosciences Inc.	−0.23	Time Not Supplied
Abercrombie & Fitch Co	1.12	Before Market Open
Acco Brands Corp	0.27	07:00 ET
Acer Incorporated	N/A	Time Not Supplied
Advance America Cash Advance Centers Inc.	0.28	Time Not Supplied
AF Gruppen ASA	N/A	Time Not Supplied
Agnico Eagle Mines Ltd	0.48	After Market Close
Akva Group ASA	N/A	Before Market Open

Table 5.8 shows a sample from the earnings announcement on one day. There are a few hundred being announced on this date. This is a few of them, in alphabetical order.

Earnings announcements aren't just made on an annual basis. Shareholders want to know what's going on throughout the year. As a result, most companies produce earnings announcements on a quarterly basis for each quarter. Then on an annual basis, they produce earnings announcements for the full year. The earnings announcement includes a snapshot of some key information for shareholders, commentary from the management of the company as well as the full financial statements. The key headlines come from the snapshot.

Box 5.2 gives a snapshot or sense of how this company is performing. Some of the key information that the market focuses on include: the **EPS (earnings per share)**, growth and profitability both overall and within various lines of business, and the financial strength of the company. For many companies, the market focuses first and foremost on EPS, which tells shareholders the earnings of the company on a per share basis. Shareholders compare this number to the EPS for previous years and to what the market expected the company to earn in the current period in order to assess how the company is doing in general and how it is doing relative to its competitors.

Box 5.2   Sample earnings announcement snapshot

- EPS, up double-digits for ninth consecutive year; $13, up 13%.
- Net income: $16 billion, up 7%.
- Revenue of $100 billion, up 7%.
- Free cashflow of $17 billion, up $300 million.
- Growth market revenue up 16%.
- Cloud revenue more than tripled 2010 revenue.

Each quarter when the quarterly announcements come out, the equity market is furiously trying to predict what the annual number will be. However, it is not as simple as multiplying the quarterly number by four. Many businesses have different earnings over different quarters. For example, the Christmas shopping period is a huge boost to retailers and shows much higher earnings in that quarter than in the other three. Box 5.3's quarterly earnings report when compared to the annual report in Box 5.2 shows that one quarter isn't a perfect way to estimate annual earnings.

Box 5.3   Quarterly earnings

- EPS: $5, up 11%
- Net income: $6 billion, up 4%
- Revenue of $30 billion, up 2% as reported, 1% adjusting for currency

---

These earnings are used to calculate the **PE ratio** (the price/earnings ratio). The PE ratio is the market price of each share divided by the earnings per share. In the above example, with a share price of $190 and annual EPS of 13, the PE ratio is 14.5 (Box 5.4).

Box 5.4   PE ratio calculation

If the share price is $190 and annual earnings per share are $13, this is a PE ratio of 14.5. $190/$13 = 14.5

The PE ratio is considered one of the main ways to value a share. Different industries are valued with different ranges of PE ratios, which provide a benchmark of whether a PE ratio is high or low. Typically, a company or industry with a high expected growth rate in future EPS will trade at a higher PE ratio than a company or industry with a low expected EPS growth rate. Another way of thinking about this is how much will an investor pay for every dollar of future earnings. In the example in Box 5.4, investors are willing to pay $14.50 for every $1 of next year's earnings because they know that they will benefit from not just next year's dollar of earnings but all future EPS of the company and that EPS is likely going to grow over time. If the company was later expected to grow its earnings at a lower rate, then the PE ratio would go down because the stream of expected future earnings would be lower. Generally utilities have low PE ratios and tech companies have high ratios; this difference is largely based on expectations for future growth.

If a company produces very poor results in one year but the outlook for the company doesn't really change, the share price should go lower to reflect those results while the generally agreed PE ratio for that company remains relatively constant. However, if the poor results indicate future poor performance or lower growth, then that company's PE ratio also will likely fall. Further, in some instances, a company may have had a bad year and lose money rather than earn money. For these companies, the PE ratio is meaningless for that period and thus it is harder to determine fair price for them. Table 5.9 summarizes these key company specific relationships.

While earnings have a big impact on share prices, they have a slightly smaller impact on the bond prices for the same issuer. The reason is that bond prices change based on interest rates and credit spreads. Interest rates move, as described above, as a result of macroeconomics. Credit spreads are specific to an issuer and are meant to reflect the issuer's ability to pay back

TABLE 5.9 Key Company Specific Relationships

Scenario	Share prices
Economy in trouble	Share prices go down
Economy overheating	Share prices go up
Company earning more money than last year	Share prices go up
Company earning less money than last year	Share prices go down

TABLE 5.10 Rating Scales

Moody's	S&P	Fitch	How we refer to the rating	Broad market categories
Aaa	AAA	AAA	Triple A	Investment grade
Aa	AA	AA	Double A	Investment grade
A	A	A	Single A	Investment grade
Baa	BBB	BBB	B double A or triple B	Investment grade
Ba	BB	BB	B A or double B	Sub-investment grade
B	B	B	Single B	Sub-investment grade
Caa to Default	CCC to Default	CCC to Default	There are several levels between triple C and default	Generally considered distressed

the money borrowed. The larger the credit spread, the more risk that a borrower can't pay back the money borrowed. Earnings give some indication of the borrower's ability to pay back the money but another type of financial analysis is important for fixed income investors.

A **rating** is a way of indicating the credit worthiness of an issuer. Credit worthiness means the likelihood of being able to pay back the money an entity has borrowed. Table 5.10 shows rating scales. A triple A rating means an entity is considered to have very little risk. Sometimes the jargon used is **risk free**, but that is not 100% accurate. For the very low risk the investor takes, he gets a lower return when he invests in that issuer's debt. In other words, the coupon a triple A borrower has to pay for the money he has borrowed is lower than for any other borrower in the same currency with the exception of the government in that country. Government entities have historically been considered risk free when they borrow in their own currency because they can print as much money as they need to pay down their debt. This is the only place when the term risk free can be used, and today we know that is even a bit of a stretch.

The three major **rating agencies** are Moody's, S&P and Fitch. Rating agencies do an analysis of a company's financial statements and then form a view on the company's ability to pay back the debt issued. They then make those ratings public. Most entities can't issue debt without a rating from one of the major rating agencies. This is primarily because most fixed income investors have rating requirements and restrictions on their investment portfolios.

Investment grade entities are those whose rating is between triple A and triple B. These entities have the most investors in their debt because many investors have an investment grade requirement on their investment portfolio. This means that borrowers have to be investment grade for most investors to buy their debt. Sub-investment grade entities (also called **high yield**) are entities whose rating is below triple B. These are primarily double B and single B entities. These entities have fewer investors in their debt because they are considered riskier. However, as the term indicates, the coupon on their debt is higher to compensate the investor for the higher risk. These entities borrow as much and sometimes more in the form of loans from their banks than in the bond market from investors. This is primarily because there are fewer investors who are allowed to invest in non-investment grade debt.

While earnings announcements are closely watched by rating agencies and a company's earnings are taken into account in the rating process, the rating agencies do not change ratings every quarter or even every year. They review ratings at a minimum once a year and definitely when there is any company specific news that might change the rating; however, ratings are supposed to be stable, long-term assessments. Thus, while investors in a company's debt look at earnings announcements, they are often as focused on the rating announcements for a company. These announcements also tend to have a bigger effect on the prices of a company's debt.

Supply and Demand

The above sections show that there are theoretical prices or relationships for every financial product based on some assumptions about what we have observed in the past. But theoretical analysis is merely that. It doesn't actually tell an investor what the current market price is. The reason is that theoretical analysis is generally based on historical relationships and historical data. It doesn't tell us anything about the future. What has happened in the past might influence how an investor feels about the future, but it won't necessarily tell the investor what will happen in the future. When discussing market views, what people are really talking about is what investors expect to happen to market prices in the future based on their assumptions about some future events, for example economic indicators or company specific news.

One way to look at **supply and demand** is the following. Based on some fundamental analysis, issuers decide whether they need more capital, and that decision affects the amount of supply. Based on some fundamental analysis, investors decide whether to invest, and that decision affects demand. Irrespective of what the fundamentals tell us the **theoretical price** or theoretical relationship should be, it could be vastly different in the actual market. The value of this difference is that investors have differing views on whether financial products are cheap or expensive which drive their trading decisions. The fact that all fundamental analysis is subjective means that some investors end up buying because they think somthing is cheap and someone else ends up selling because they think the same thing is expensive.

Some interesting examples of wildly different market vs theoretical pricing are the government borrowing rates versus company borrowing rates during the 2010—2011 government debt crisis and PE ratios during the dot.com bubble.

During the **dot.com bubble** in the late 1990s, the average PE ratio for technology companies was in the 40s. However, comparing the long-term historical average PE ratio of 15 to a PE ratio in the 40s was considered silly by market participants because technology was "going to change the world" and new rules applied to those companies. Eventually, in 2000, the dot.com bubble burst and the NASDAQ, the US stock index for technology companies, dropped by almost 80%. For example, Amazon.com saw its share price go from over $100 per share to under $10 per share.

What financial markets people say is that the fair price is the market price. This is where the financial product last traded or where most market makers are prepared to make a market in that financial product. No theoretical model can determine the market price. While theoretical models help investors decide whether the market price is cheap or expensive based on their views, they don't determine the market price. As a result, a trader on the trading floor is keen to see as many client trades as he can to get a sense of the supply and demand for a financial product which helps him to make markets for his clients and hopefully make money at the same time.

When theory and the market price are reversed

Example 1: A new company is about to do an IPO. There is so much excitement about this company that the share price, even before the IPO, goes higher and higher every time it is discussed.

The average PE ratio of the industry in the country where the company is based is 10. But this company has never had any earnings. That means that the PE ratio is infinite. This does not make sense theoretically, but investors in this IPO have a view that this company will make a lot of profits in the future so are happy to ignore the PE ratio as a theoretical price guide for now.

Example 2: On the same day, the US government and a large company in the US borrow money for five years. The US government borrows at 2% for five years and the large company borrows at 1.8%.

This does not make sense theoretically. All US borrowers should borrow money at a higher rate than the US government. Historically, the US government was riskless but today there is some concern about the US government making all its payments on its debt. At the same time, the US company is a large international company that doesn't rely entirely on the US economy for its profits.

Conclusion

When listening to financial market participants throughout the trading day, it appears that they are obsessed with the market. What do you think about the market? Where is this market going? How does the market feel? What's interesting about this is that while indigenous people of the Arctic tundra have multiple words for snow, financial market participants seem happy to use one word with multiple meanings and, amazingly, still understand each other. The trick is in how the question or sentence is phrased rather than the word itself.

The obsession with the market is driven by a need to figure out whether market prices for a particular financial product are going up or down. While there is a lot of fundamental information out there about how the economy is performing or how a company is performing, it is all historical data. Financial market participants are then trying to judge how what has happened in the past is going to affect market prices in the future. The obsession about the markets generally is because market participants know that supply and demand are the ultimate drivers of price of every financial product. This does not mean that fundamental analysis is not valuable. It should tell an investor whether something is cheap or expensive, but it does not tell investors what the market price is going to be.

The complexity of working on the trading floor is about understanding the different theoretical models that different investors use as well as having a grasp of market supply and demand. The sales person needs to help his clients interpret different financial news and different market price movements. The trader needs to interpret all this information and be able to put a price on a trade for a client.

Following the financial crises that started in the first decade of this century, the media began portraying the financial markets as a sentient being. The idea is that the markets have become a complex decision-making beast that decides whether governments go bust and whether a company can issue shares. The reality is that the financial markets are a complex series of relationships and information. They are almost impossible to predict but it doesn't stop financial market participants from trying to do just that.

Discussion Questions

Why do we generally say that when equity prices go up bond prices go down?

Why is macroeconomics important to all asset classes?

What type of events might only affect one asset class?

Please see www.terriduhon.co for answers and discussion.

CHAPTER 6

How Do Traders Make a Market?

This chapter will explore how traders make markets. Putting a price where a trader is prepared to buy or sell something is not a simple decision. It is a complicated process of filtering through the barrage of financial data that is constantly coming to the trader, assessing the liquidity and volatility of the market prices and understanding the risk and return targets that the trading book has. The trader's job is to keep focused on what is happening not only in his specific market but also in other financial markets that may affect his market. This is why traders rarely speak to clients. They don't have time. They need to focus on their markets. This chapter will take the three trades from Chapter 4 and look at how the trader makes the market for them. This chapter will also answer questions such as: What is the fair price for a financial product? Why does the bank make a margin on trades? Why do market makers need to have a view on financial markets and the ability to take risk?

There is a well-known story in the financial markets about a currency trader who had been asked for a market in US dollars vs. Swiss francs (SFr) in the 1980s. This was before technology allowed instant information flow globally. The trader made a market of 1.70 at 1.80. This meant that he would buy $1 for SFr1.70 and sell $1 for SFr1.80. The client lifted the offer for $1 million.

This meant that the trader sold $1 million in exchange for SFr1.8 million. This was a big notional in those days. About half an hour later, the client called again and asked for a market. The trader said 1.75 at 1.85. The trader moved his market because he was interested in buying the US dollars back to close out his position. The client lifted the offer again for $1 million. Now the trader was short $2 million and long Swiss franc at an **off-market** level. This happened a few times until the trader made a market of 2.00 at 2.20. The client then said, "Now you know where the market is." Any trader who has ever heard this story will generally tell a story of their own along these lines. The point is that not all markets are liquid and transparent all the time. Often market makers are put in a position when they have to make a market but have only a vague idea of where the market really is.

In each of the three examples from Chapter 4, the trader made a market and provided liquidity to a client. While we explored the process that led to the need for a price, we didn't explore the process that led to the price itself. So the following questions need to be answered: How did the trader decide what the right price was? What risk was he taking when he traded with the client? Why was he comfortable with the risk he was taking at that price? What does he do next?

Traders get information to make a price from the following: interbank market, exchanges, electronic trading systems, clients, financial market research and general public knowledge. Different financial products will trade in different ways, for example some only trade on exchanges and others only in the interbank market; increasingly, others are a combination of the two in the form of electronic trading systems which can be anything from interbank brokers to an exchange. "Information from clients" means the knowledge that the trader gets from understanding what the bank's clients are doing in the financial market. Financial market research is the vast amount of research that is published every day about financial markets. General public knowledge is the information that comes from **financial media** such as Reuters, Bloomberg and CNBC. All together this comprises the information flow that the trader must synthesize in order to come up with a price.

Over and above this, a trader needs to consider the following:

- the liquidity and volatility in the financial market for hedging, which ultimately drives the price/value of the trade

- the trader's interest in taking on this position which is a function of whether the new trade puts on risk or takes away risk in his trading book and in what size
- the competitive environment
- the size and complexity of the trade
- the bank's relationship with the client
- the credit worthiness of the client
- the other trades previously done with the client.

When the financial market is very volatile and clients are very active, a trader's job can seem very hectic and stressful given all the considerations that need to be made at the same time (Box 6.1).

Box 6.1   Market making considerations

- Current market information:
  - previous trades and trade prices that day
  - the liquidity and volatility in the market
  - recent market price moves for similar financial products
  - recent market price moves for other key market indicators
  - financial news expected to be released that day
  - any expected major flows in the market that day.
- Trader's position:
  - the trader's interest in taking on this position which is a function of whether the new trade puts on risk or takes away risk in his book and in what size
  - the competitive environment.
- Client situation:
  - the size and complexity of the trade
  - the bank's relationship with the client
  - the credit worthiness of the client
  - the other trades previously done with the client.
- Trader's relationship with the sales person.

Underlying all of the above considerations is the understanding of what a trader on a bank's trading floor is doing. His job is to be a market maker. He provides liquidity to the financial markets and as a result he takes risk. Even if he doesn't know exactly how he will hedge or close out a position as a result of a trade with a client, he will make a market. He facilitates his client's access to the financial markets. He is not supposed to be taking large amounts of risk on his books and sitting on it. His job is to take on risk and move it on into the financial market in the most efficient way he can such that he makes a profit from the client trade. His job is to take on risk and hedge or close out the position. His price at the end of the day is fundamentally a function of where he can hedge or close out his risk and still make some money for the bank.

PACAM Treasury Trade

In the PACAM treasury trade example from Chapter 4 (Box 4.3), PACAM initially asked, "Where is the market, in size, for the 5-year on-the-run treasuries?" So let's look at a snapshot of what information the 5-year treasury trader might have at that point in order to make a market.

Traders sit all day in front of their computer screens. Some traders have as many as six computer screens in front of them crammed with live data. Individual traders will organize their screens in different ways, but often traders who trade the same financial product will have similar types of information. The live information they need to see throughout the day is a combination of price information on the financial product they trade, price information on similar financial products, price information on major indicators and updated financial headlines.

The 5-year treasury trader will have several interbank broker screens showing either live prices or indicative prices for all the on-the-run treasuries as well as several off-the-run treasuries. One screen might look like Table 6.1.

TABLE 6.1 Sample Prices of Current On-The-Run Treasuries

Benchmark	Coupon	Maturity	Price/Yield	Price/Yield Change	Time
2-Year	0.250%	01/31/2014	100-01/0.22	0-005/−0.004	15:43
3-Year	0.250%	01/15/2015	99-27.5/0.30	0-00/0.000	15:35
5-Year	0.875%	01/31/2017	100-16.5/0.77	0-00/0.000	15:40
7-Year	1.250%	01/31/2019	99-28/1.27	0-1/0.005	15:20
10-Year	2.000%	11/15/2021	101-15/1.84	0-3/0.012	15:45
30-Year	3.125%	11/15/2041	102-11.5/3.00	0-7/0.011	15:33

FIGURE 6.1   US Treasury yield curve.

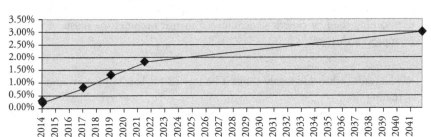

Table 6.1 shows a sample screen with the current on-the-run treasuries. The Price/Yield shows where the bonds last traded and the Price/Yield Change shows how much they've changed on the day. The Time shows the time of the last trade. The trader might have this yield curve graphed against other government yield curves. Note that the yield curve isn't based on the coupons of the treasuries but on the yield that the investor gets as a result of paying a price that is not 100%. Figure 6.1 shows a yield curve.

There are several different electronic trading systems which will generally have approximately the same bids and offers. For the PACAM treasury trade, the best market on the electronic trading systems is 16.5 at 16.75. The differences might be on the size indicated at each price. While a lot of US treasury trading is electronic, the traders will often speak to the brokers who manage the electronic screens, and thus voice trading still occurs. When the trader talks to the different brokers, he figures out that the size that he can trade on each side of the market is $300 million. But PACAM asked for a market in size which is larger than $300 million. What the trader needs to figure out is what happens when he lifts the offers of 16.75 for a total of $300 million. Does that move the price up or is there a lot of selling interest in the market today? Initially, he is making a two-way market so he needs to also assess what happens if he hits the bid for $300 million.

Notice that when the trader trades with the client he is the market maker, but if he wants to hedge in the interbank market immediately he needs to hit the bid or lift the offer, in which case he is the market taker. Alternatively, he could put in a bid or offer in the interbank market and wait to see whether another bank hits the bid or lifts the offer. Neither strategy is ideal, of course. In the first, he is making a market for $1 billion, not $300 million. In the second, if he sits and waits, the market price could move before his price gets hit or lifted.

Some individuals on trading floors have quirky personalities which are entertaining the first time it's encountered then it becomes the norm. A few examples of this are:

- The trader who could only think if he carried his baseball bat around the trading floor.
- The sales person who had to have a fan under his desk otherwise he would overheat.
- The trader who couldn't work with his shoes on.
- The sales person who took phone calls under his desk for privacy.

Because the trading floor is a little more quirky than other places, a lot of this behavior is tolerated . . . some is encouraged.

There will also be a screen showing the price of major equity indices around the world and the change on the day (Table 6.2). These equity indices represent broad financial market sentiment globally and as a result are very liquid and transparent financial markets. They are very quick to respond to financial market sentiment changes so they are considered market indicators.

Because interest rate swaps are a function of the treasury market, treasury traders will often have a US interest rate swap screen up to be aware of major movements in interest rate swap prices. While we say that interest rate swaps are a function of the treasury market, sometimes big moves happen first in the interest rate swap market which then affect the treasury market. While this might sound like the tail wagging the dog, the fact is that while derivatives are defined as a function of another financial product they are independent markets in their own right. This means that the market participants in the treasury market are different from those in the interest rate derivatives market. Remember that supply and demand drive price more than the "theoretical right price" does.

Treasury traders will also look at price volatility indicators. These include options on treasuries which are traded on exchanges as well as options on equity indices. These give indications of the financial market sentiment about future price volatility. Price volatility is important for the trader to have an idea of how much the treasury price might move on any

TABLE 6.2 Picture of Eq Indices

Index	Previous Level	Current Level	Change (Current − Previous)	% Change (Current − Previous)/ Previous
DJIA	12,632.95	12,716.50	83.55	0.66%
S&P 500	1,312.41	1,324.09	11.68	0.89%
NASDAQ	2,813.84	2,848.27	34.43	1.22%
EURO STOXX50	2,470.79	2,477.17	6.38	0.26%
FTSE 100	5,790.72	5,789.10	−1.62	−0.03%
DAX	6,616.64	6,638.24	21.6	0.33%
NIKKEI 225	8,809.79	8,876.82	67.03	0.76%
HANG SENG	20,333.32	20,739.40	406.08	2.00%

day. The more volatile the treasury prices, the more risk the trader takes when he makes markets for his clients.

Since the 2008−2009 credit crisis, there are likely to be credit index screens showing some key credit indices. These indices have become popular as indicators of broad credit sentiment. There is a North American index, a European index and a European Sovereign index which are constantly monitored to determine whether markets think there is more or less credit risk in the system. This is an indication of the state of the economy in a weaker economic environment.

And finally, there is likely to be a screen showing currency and commodity prices and their intraday moves. They are also broad indicators of market sentiment.

Outside of financial market prices, there is news and research. There will be a few screens with rolling financial news. This is just headlines in the financial markets and keeps the traders informed about key events as they occur. If something catches a trader's eye, he can click on the headline to expand and see the full story. At the same time, there are often television screens around the trading floor with different financial news channels from around the world playing 24 hours a day. Finally, he will be inundated with internal research reports from the bank's economists and interest rate strategists as well as external research reports and calendars of key financial market data, such as those listed in Chapter 5 (Table 5.3).

While a trader monitors all of this information every minute of every trading day, he is often on the phone chatting about financial market sentiment or discussing financial market color. Financial market color is a euphemism for financial market gossip. This includes rumors about what big financial market participants might be thinking or doing in the financial market, what someone thinks about particular financial market data and rumors about new regulation or legislation which will affect the financial market. Traders will chat to various individuals throughout the day: their interbank brokers, traders at other banks, other traders on their own trading floor, sales people or major clients among others.

So when PACAM asks for a market the key information the treasury trader has is:

- There is no major financial market data being released today. On a day when major financial market data is being released, the financial market has the potential to make large price moves. This is because the financial market anticipates what the data is going to be well ahead of the data being released. Take an example of non-farm payrolls in the US. Depending on what treasury market participants believe ahead of a number, they will either have a net long position or a net short position before the number is released. What this means is that the treasury market will either have rallied or fallen ahead of the number being released in anticipation of the number. Then depending on how certain the predictions were ahead of the number, there might be further market price moves after the number is released. If the number is what was expected, then most of the financial market has already traded on that data, and there is no further market price movement. If there is some but not a lot of discrepancy about where the number will be and the number comes out with the majority predictions, there will be further movement after the number. But if the number comes out with the minority predictions, there will be a big move in the opposite direction while treasury market participants reverse their positions. On a day when a number is being released, a trader will often want to pre-position ahead of the number based on his view of what the number will be and how the financial market will react.
- The financial market rallied overnight on strong economic news out of Europe but has given up most of those gains since the New York open. Because the US treasury market is slightly less liquid before New York opens, it is often the case that US treasuries move **in sympathy** with other financial markets but then revert when New York opens. A rally in the

bond market means that the bond price has increased while the returns (or yields) have decreased.
- There are no major bond deals being priced today, and no major flows of which the trader is aware happening in the financial market. This simply means business as usual and no one is anticipating any large trades that are going to have an impact on the financial market prices.
- The stock markets have roughly been stable around the world since the Tokyo open and there are no major earnings announcements or IPOs happening today.
- The 5-year on-the-runs are currently quoted on screen as 100−16.5/16¾. The screen quote is good for $300 million a side. In talking to the interbank brokers who run the screens, it is clear that there are equal amounts on the bid side as there are on the offer side outside of the screens and there is no gossip indicating that any of the banks have large positions to unload in the financial market.
- None of the other treasury traders at Megabank is anticipating any major moves, nor have they seen any significant trade flow to report. The other treasury traders are the T-bill trader, the 2-year and 3-year trader, the 10-year trader and the long bond trader. There is likely also a head of the treasury trading desk who is involved in major decision-making and positioning across the treasury trading desk.

How major financial market data moves financial markets
Non-farm payroll

- May non-farm payroll was 54,000. This was down from the April number of 244,000. The consensus for May was 165,000, and the lowest economist prediction was 65,000.
- The market was expecting the economy to show improvement. Many investors would have bought equity (pushing share prices up) and sold bonds (pushing bond prices down) ahead of the number being released.
- The minute the non-farm payroll was announced, share prices went down and bond prices went up as investors re-assessed their view on the economy.

All of this information points to a benign financial market environment today. There is no anticipation of any price volatility or any event which will disrupt financial market trading or move market prices significantly. In this type of trading environment, traders are more likely to consider other factors as more significant in the market making process. Some of those other factors are:

- size and complexity of the trade
- bank's relationship with the client
- credit worthiness of the client
- other trades previously done with the client.

These factors are all client driven. On this particular request, neither the size nor the complexity is a particular problem. While "in size" does indicate that PACAM wants to transact a large notional amount, because of the high **daily volume** in the treasury market (Box 6.3) and the fact that the financial market environment today is relatively benign, a size of $1 billion would not necessarily be considered a difficult amount. If the client wanted to transact $10 billion or if the client wanted to transact $1 billion at 6 p.m. in New York, this would be a different issue.

The bank's relationship with the client is also crucial to the pricing that the bank will make for the client. If PACAM had a historically difficult relationship with Megabank, the trader would not feel inclined to try to win the business. Winning this business means making a very **tight** market and potentially taking a lot of risk as a result. A tight market is one where the difference between the bid and the offer (also called the **bid–offer spread**) is smaller than most other traders would make. The risk is that the trader isn't able to close out the position and retain any profit on the trade or, worse, the trader loses money when he closes out the position.

Difficult relationships with clients come about in any number of ways. There could be a trade dispute in the past which hasn't really settled. PACAM could put Megabank in competition on every trade, which means that Megabank is always forced to take more risk than the trader is comfortable taking in order to win transactions. PACAM could have accused Megabank of front running in the past and there is still some concern about this issue on both sides. Alternatively, PACAM and Megabank could have a long-standing good relationship and there is genuine goodwill on both sides to ensure that this relationship continues to the benefit of both parties. In this example, it is closer to the latter rather than the former, so the trader is keen to give a good market to PACAM and win the business even if it means taking on a bit more risk than he would like.

The credit worthiness of the client is a question of how financially stable the client is. The key questions to ask are different for different trades, though. In this case it is a question of whether the client has the cash on hand or in the future to do the trade it is proposing. If PACAM buys $1 billion of treasuries, does it have the cash to pay for them? In this case, PACAM is a client with a solid credit history and is large enough to be able to have the cash for 100 times the size of this particular trade, so there is no immediate concern on that front.

What other trades has Megabank done with PACAM? This question is important primarily when trading derivatives with a client. For treasury trades, it is not a consideration other than as an indication of the depth of the relationship with PACAM.

The next set of questions is about the bank and the financial market:

- the trader's interest in taking on this position, which is a function of whether the new trade puts on risk or takes away risk in his book and in what size
- the liquidity and volatility in the financial market for hedging, which ultimately drives the price/value of the trade
- the competitive environment.

Taking these one at a time, we start with the bank's interest in taking on this position. In this example, the trader doesn't actually know what position he's going to be taking on. He is being asked to make a market, which means he could either be buying $1 billion of 5-year treasuries or selling $1 billion of 5-year treasuries.

The important word here is **axe**. "Does the trader have an axe?" which refers to "an axe to grind." This means does the trader really want to buy or does he really want to sell, in which case he is axed to trade in a certain way. This highlights a key element of making markets. Traders *must have a view* on whether market prices are going up or down in order to make good markets and make money from client trades. This trader does not have a strong view either way today. This means that his view is that market prices are **range bound** for the next few days. This trader is thus focused on making money as well as hedging each client transaction and not building up a large position in either direction.

In this example, while the trader doesn't have a strong view he is axed to sell treasuries because he is long $400 million from a trade done overnight with a Tokyo client. The trader shows a market which is slightly skewed toward selling rather than buying. The screens show 100−16.5/16¾, so he shows a market of 16 at 17 (Box 6.2).

Box 6.2   Financial market vs. Megabank trader quote

- On-the-run US treasury 5-years
- Megabank trader quote/market for $1 billion: 100−16 at 100−17
- Market quote for $300 million: 100−16.5 at 100−16.75

Finally, the liquidity and volatility in the financial market and the competitive environment will have an impact on the quotes that the trader will show on any trade. The trader always needs to know how liquid the financial market is for his product. In other words, how much can he trade at any one price? In this example, he knows that he can trade $300 million on each side of 100−16.5/16¾. But he needs to do $1 billion. If he sells $1 billion to PACAM at 17, and buys $300 million at 16¾, will he buy the next $100 million at 17 and the next $100 million at 17¼? If this is the case, he will lose money on this trade quickly. Box 6.3 shows the daily volume in different government bond markets.

Box 6.3   Relative liquidity in the US treasury market

Government bond market daily volume

- US treasuries: approximately $400 billion trade each day.
- UK **gilts**: approximately £20 billion trade each day.
- German government bonds: approximately €20 billion trade each day.

To put these sizes in Box 6.3 in context, they are not all being traded through Megabank's trading floor. They are going through at least 50 different bank trading floors within the United States and another 50 bank trading floors outside of the United States. These are trades across all of the outstanding US treasuries in the market today, not just in the on-the-run 5-years. These are being done by individuals through to large institutional investors. This number represents thousands of different trades throughout the trading day at different prices as the market price moves throughout the day.

The Megabank treasury trader has put a price of 17, where he's prepared to sell $1 billion. He has made this decision based on a combination of things. He wants to sell rather than buy. This is because he is already long some 5-years (e.g. $400 million) and thus he will be net short $600 million if he sells. He knows that in benign financial market environments he will be able to trade a minimum of $500 million between 16¾ and 17. He has decided that he wants to win this business with this client and give this client a good price even if it means taking some risk on hedging the last $100 million. (See Box 6.4.)

Box 6.4   Treasury market liquidity analysis

- Trader owns (is long) $400 million.
- 100−16+ market bid for $300 million and 100−16¾ market offer for $300 million on the screen.
- Trader sells $1 billion at 100−17 to PACAM.
- Trader is now short $600 million.
- Trader can buy at least $500 million between 16¾ and 17.

Figure 6.2 is another way to look at the close out strategy of the trader. The line represents the price of the 5-year treasuries, which gets higher to the right and lower to the left.

FIGURE 6.2   Treasury price line.

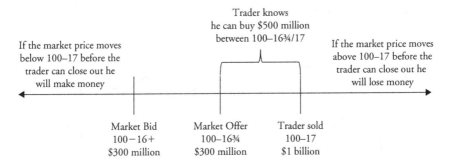

Traders often play games with the financial market to try to move market prices one way or another. One example is that traders provide interbank brokers with firm prices on bids and offers on benchmark products. When there is a lot of volatility in the financial markets, traders don't like to provide firm prices; they prefer to provide indications only. However, providing firm bids or firm offers and then pulling one side only might worry a financial market that is already skittish. This is not a tactic that can be used often or at all in some financial markets but has certainly been done.

Supermart Interest Rate Swap Trade

To simplify the hedging discussion for the Supermart interest rate swap trade from Chapter 4, we will change the example slightly. Instead of Supermart doing a cross-currency swap from floating US dollars to fixed UK pounds, Supermart will simply do a US interest rate swap from floating to fixed (Figure 6.3).

A standard US dollar interest rate swap is an exchange of a fixed rate for a floating rate. The floating rate is often Libor, which resets quarterly. For the purposes of this book we will use a 12-month Libor to make the examples easier to discuss and illustrate. The price of an interest rate swap is the fixed rate coupon that is necessary to pay in order to equal receiving the Libor rate today and the Libor rates that the market expects in the future. While cross-currency swaps include an exchange of principal, in order to exchange the initial currency, same-currency interest rate swaps are an exchange of coupons only. They do not involve exchanging any principal. In

FIGURE 6.3 Supermart interest rate swap trade overview.

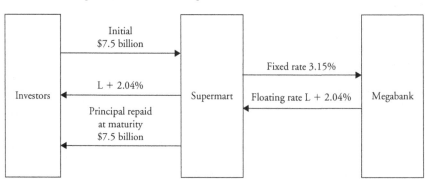

TABLE 6.3 Supermart Debt Cashflows vs. Interest Rate Swap Cashflows

	Supermart debt cashflows (borrows)	Supermart receives interest rate swap	Supermart pays interest rate swap
Start Date:	$7.5 billion	0	0
End year 1	(Libor + 2.04%)*	Libor + 2.04%	(3.15%)*
End year 2	(Libor + 2.04%)*	Libor + 2.04%	(3.15%)*
End year 3	(Libor + 2.04%)*	Libor + 2.04%	(3.15%)*
End year 4	(Libor + 2.04%)*	Libor + 2.04%	(3.15%)*
End year 5	($7.5 billion + Libor + 2.04%)*	Libor + 2.04%	(3.15%)*

*Numbers in parenthesis represent payments.

the Supermart example, Supermart has borrowed money in the form of debt. It now only wants to exchange the floating coupons for fixed coupons. The cashflows for an interest rate swap compared to the cashflows for Supermart debt are shown in Table 6.3.

This figure shows that Supermart's floating coupon on the debt and the floating coupon of the interest rate swap cancel out. The only cashflow Supermart is left with is the borrowing of $7.5 billion and the fixed rate on the interest rate swap.

In this example, the market making request coming to the US interest rate swap trader is not coming directly from the client but from a series of conversations within the bank starting with the client and the M&A team, and moving to the debt capital markets team and then to the derivatives sales person. The market making request is:

• not for a two way market
• nor is it in competition with other banks
• nor is it for today
• nor are the interest rate swap traders told who the client is.

The specific request is likely to be communicated along the following lines:

We're working on an M&A transaction. It's not 100% firm, but one of the financing options is to issue debt in floating dollars and swap it into fixed. The size of the transaction is $7.5 billion dollars. We're looking at 3-year, 5-year and 10-year maturities and are likely to go with 5-years at this point.

Can you give me a good indication of where we can do this trade today? I'll need updates every morning for the next several weeks and I'll keep you in the loop on the likelihood of the trade happening and the timing.

This means that Megabank will pay the floating coupon on the debt to Supermart in exchange for receiving a fixed rate. This is a common trade, but not a standardized trade. The reason is that the standard interest rate swap is a fixed coupon in exchange for Libor flat. The Supermart bond has a coupon of Libor + 2.04%. The cashflows in this interest rate swap will be non-standard. Megabank will thus need to be compensated for paying extra on the floating leg by receiving more on the fixed rate. (See Box 6.5.)

Box 6.5   Standard vs. non-standard interest rate swap cashflows

---

1.11% vs. Libor − is the Megabank trader's offer for large size 5-year interest rate swap market standard trade.

Supermart wants to exchange the coupon of Libor + 2.04%, which is higher than Libor:

1.11% $\neq$ L + 2.04% (if 1.11% on the market standard trade is equal to Libor, it is not equal to Libor plus 2.04%).

So add 1.04% to both sides to make them equal:

3.15% = L + 2.04% (non-standard interest rate swap where Megabank will pay L + 2.04% and receive 3.15%).

This is a simplification. The actual fixed rate is likely to be slightly different from 3.15%.

What the interest rate swap trader really cares about, though, is not what the cashflows are but at what rate he is effectively agreeing to trade an interest rate swap. Box 6.6 shows that the rate he's agreed is 1.11%. This is his offer. He is the market maker so if he is going to receive fixed from a client he gets to receive the higher rate.

Box 6.6   Interest rate swap quote

Current interbank interest rate swap market as seen on the electronic trading systems: bid 1.05% and offer 1.07% $400 million a side.

The **mid-market** price is 1.06% (this is the middle point between the bid and the offer).

Megabank trader says he will receive fixed on this trade at the equivalent of 1.11%.

If 1.11% is his offer, and the mid-market is 1.06%, this means his market for $7.5 billion is 1.01% at 1.11%.

This is a wide market because of the size.

The price of an interest rate swap is the fixed coupon.

Ideally, the US interest rate swap trader could go into the interbank market and pay fixed at 1.07% (which is the current offer in the market) and thus lock in a profit of 0.04% a year. But that is unlikely to happen, particularly because of the size of the trade at $7.5 billion. Similar to the treasury market, $1 billion isn't that difficult to hedge in the US interest rate swap market, but $7.5 billion is a bit more of a challenge. The US interest rate swap trader will need several days to hedge this position. Megabank is a major bank in the US interest rate swap market and as a result expects to trade hundreds of millions of US dollars of interest rate swaps with clients every day so that is another source of hedges in addition to the interbank market.

A US interest rate swap trader will be looking at many of the same screens that the US treasury trader looks at in addition to all the screens that he needs that are specific to US interest rate swaps. Identifying the right market price today is relatively easy. There are several interbank broker screens and several electronic trading systems which have bids and offers. The challenge is to put the right price for this size. The trader needs to determine how liquid the market is. In other words, what notional amount can he trade at 1.07% if he lifts the offer in the interbank broker market? What notional amount can he trade at 1.08%? Also, he needs to determine his hedging strategy. Will he try to hedge this immediately? In which case, he will likely move the market price very quickly. This notional amount is too big to go through the financial market at once.

The analysis of the volume in Box 6.7 is the same as the analysis for the treasuries in Box 6.3. This is not the volume that Megabank will see in any one day, nor is it the volume of trades that occur in the 5-year maturity. Interest rate swaps trade with maturities of 1 day out to 30 or 40 years. However, as Megabank is one of the large traders in US interest rate swaps, Megabank will see a lot of this trade flow.

Box 6.7   Interest rate swap market liquidity

Daily trade volume:

- approximately $400 billion in US interest rate swaps
- approximately $400 billion in euro interest rate swaps
- approximately $75 billion in UK interest rate swaps
- approximately $40 billion in yen interest rate swaps.

While the total notional is high, the average trade size is also high. This notional represents approximately 1,000 trades per day in each currency.

Every day that the interest rate swap trader is asked to provide indications to Supermart, he is being asked to provide prices where he would actually be able to trade that day. The client in this case is very active in the financial markets and will be monitoring interest rate swap rates through a variety of sources (e.g. Bloomberg, Reuters and any electronic trading systems he has access to). US interest rate swaps and treasuries are two of the most liquid financial markets in the world. The interest rate swap trader knows this and knows that, although he is providing an indication every day, it needs to be as close to the firm offer as they will give on the day of the execution. If not, the day of the execution the client will be able to see a difference and will not be amused (Box 6.8).

Box 6.8   Example of indication anomalies as seen by the client

Market mid: 1.06% (the point between the bid and the offer). Supermart can see this on the electronic trading systems it uses.
Megabank offer: 1.11% (the offer price from Megabank).

This is a mid to offer of 0.05% (the difference between the mid-price and the offer price).

Supermart is thus expecting to see a constant mid to offer of 0.05% as that is what it is being told is the margin Megabank needs to do this large size.

If on the trade date the market mid = 1.08% and Megabank's offer is 1.15%, this is a mid to offer of 0.07%.

Supermart wants to know why!

The interest rate swap traders will go through the same process as described above for making a market for PACAM in the treasury trade above, with one exception. The size in this transaction would be considered very large. The PACAM trade was for a market in size, meaning large, but not extra-large. A treasury trader will recognize that "in size" means something around $1 billion, or a yard. The trade with Supermart is a total notional of $7.5 billion, which is much larger and needs much more consideration.

Equity Structured Product Trade

The equity structured product trade from Chapter 4 (Figure 6.4) involves two different market makers. The term "market maker" is a slightly interesting term to use here because the equity options trader is a market maker, but the funding department is rarely considered a market maker when it borrows money. Externally, when it needs to borrow money, it generally

FIGURE 6.4 Equity structured product trade overview.

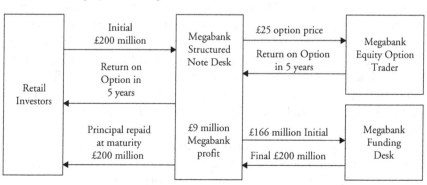

FIGURE 6.5 Megabank risk due to holding a price open for a few weeks.

borrows at the price where the financial market allows, like every other debt issuer, as opposed to the price it sets itself. However, for this trade, it is telling the trader where it is prepared to borrow money.

Two other points make this an interesting transaction. The first is that the market makers must make a market on an uncertain size for weeks at a time rather than for a known size at one point in time. The size of these transactions are considered average compared to the normal sizes that the market makers are used to dealing with, which makes the unusual pricing request easier to manage. The funding department of Megabank deals with funding in the tens of billions, and the equity options trader often deals with hundreds of millions. Thus, a size of £166 million of funding and an option size of £200 million is manageable. However, the unusual pricing request will still create more risk for the bank and cause the bid—offer spread for the options trader to be wider than it would for a normal request.

The risk that the equity options market maker faces is that he puts a price where he will sell an option at 12.5%. He needs to be able to hedge that option for less than 12.5% in order to lock in a profit. If over the period of several weeks the price of the option goes above 12.5%, he will lose money on the trade (Figure 6.5). He thinks the right price for this option is 12%, thus he shows a price of 12.5%. He is comfortable with that price because he doesn't believe that the price for these options will move that much over the next six weeks. He has also gone through the similar list of considerations as were outlined in Box 6.1 and is comfortable with this price for up to £200 million. Even if he only ends up trading £50 million, he is originally being conservative and assuming that he will trade the maximum notional amount.

This is a similar situation for the funding desk. It will provide a price where it is prepared to borrow up to £166 million. It will show a lower rate than the market rate because it doesn't know what notional amount it will end up borrowing. Imagine a scenario where the funding desk has the opportunity to borrow at a very good rate from the bond market during the four-week offering process. It needs to borrow £200 million, but it doesn't want to borrow more than it needs, because borrowing costs money. It also doesn't want to borrow less than it needs because this is a good rate and it may not get this opportunity again. However, it may be borrowing up to £166 million in the structured bond—but it won't know for six weeks. So, there is opportunity cost associated with this trade for the funding department and, as a result, it asks for a lower borrowing rate to compensate for this risk.

Both traders know that the structurer will build in the right profitability for Megabank as a whole. Because the client is retail and less experienced in financial products, the client will not be able to break down the product into its different pieces and check to see whether the pricing is fair. Banks understand this but also understand that they have a position of trust with the retail client and must not take advantage of that. The rule of thumb in Europe is that a structured product cannot make more than 1% per year of profit, which means that a 5-year product can make a maximum 5% profit for the bank, which includes the profitability of the options trade.

The second interesting point is about the secondary market making of the product after it has been sold to the retail investors. Offering to buy the product back from the investors throughout the life of the product is simply asking the market makers to provide a price for the **other side of the trade** later in the life of the trade. For the equity options trader this is easy to do and something he does often.

For the funding desk it isn't that straightforward. They are originally being asked to borrow money for five years. Then, two years later are possibly being asked to give the money back. Again, this is a planning issue. The funding desk borrows at a different rate for two years than they do for five years. So, they must make a decision about how much they are prepared to pay for this type of borrowing. Ideally, they will consider the buy-back stats given to them by the structuring team and look at the different rates where they borrow for different maturities and come up with a price that makes sense.

Imagine a scenario where the structuring desk says that on average it buys back the entire notional amount from retail investors within three years. Megabank will need to price this as if it is a 3-year borrowing or a 2-year borrowing but not a 5-year borrowing. If the structuring desk says that on average it is only asked to buy back 10%, then this is more like a standard 5-year bond and Megabank will likely consider that it is borrowing

90% of £166 million rather than rely on the full 100% of the money over the five years.

These considerations are slightly different from the considerations for the PACAM treasury trade or the Supermart interest rate swap trade, but at the end of the day traders are making markets and taking risk, so the end result is that they need to know where they can hedge the risk that they've taken which drives the market that they make.

A Typical Trader Day

Most traders start the day relatively early and get to their desks around 6:30—7 a.m. because they need to prepare for the trading day. Note that the exception to this timeframe is in San Francisco and Chicago. Trading floors in those locations generally operate on New York time, which means that their day starts one to three hours earlier in their time zone.

The preparation for the day consists of:

Review the trading book positions and P&L from the day before. **P&L** stands for profit and loss in the trading book from the change in market price between **end of day** (EOD) the day before yesterday and the end of day yesterday. What happens every day is that all the new trades that the trader executed that day are entered into the bank's systems either by the trader, the sales person or a middle office person depending on the complexity of the trades and the systems and the regulations of the bank. Then, sometime that afternoon or sometime overnight, the systems process the new trades and produce a new position report for the trader which also includes the P&L of the book for that trading day. Each morning, the trader needs to review those positions and the P&L and confirm that they are what he expected to see. If not, with the help of the middle office, he needs to go through the new trades entered from yesterday and double-check that everything is correct.

Check for any trades done overnight. All trading books are generally passed around the globe within one bank in case any client in a different location wants to trade that product overnight. The trader needs to check those trades, the prices agreed and how his position changed as a result.

Review any market events which happened overnight. This is checking the financial news for any big stories which might affect the markets.

- Check for any big events expected that day: any new debt or equity issuance expected, any big client trades expected, any economic data coming out that day.
- Go to the **morning meeting**. The morning meeting could be just the traders or it could include traders and sales people for the same financial product. It depends on the financial product and the convention within the bank. The morning meeting is where any big events for that day are discussed, where the trading desk's positions are discussed and where any axes for the desk are identified. It also might include a recap on the previous trading day and a **postmortem** on client trades missed.
- Send out the **morning market commentary**, which goes to all the relevant sales people, interested parties in the bank and sometimes outside of the bank to clients, although this is something that sales people are generally responsible for. This commentary informs the sales people about events expected that day in the market and any axes the trader has.

After the morning meeting, the trading desk is generally considered open for business. What this means is that the traders sit at their desks and look at their screens all day. They often don't go outside even to get coffee; the most junior person on the desk is responsible for that. If the day is busy, they don't even leave their desk to get lunch. Again, the most junior person on the desk is responsible for that. Alternatively, they will rely on the generosity of their interbank brokers to provide lunch. Regardless, the trader will generally eat at his desk staring at his screens and talking on the phones.

Traders are watching for market movement which will affect their positions and are waiting for client requests to come in from the sales force. They are intensely focused and often talk in short staccato sentences. They don't have time for long discussions on anything they feel is irrelevant to the markets. In the middle of sentences, they will "hop" off the phone if they need to make a market or if market prices move suddenly. At the end of the day (between 4 and 6 p.m.) depending on the financial product and location, they go through the process of **closing the books**. They ensure that all trades were put into the systems correctly. They either decide what the end of day price for their financial product will be or they confirm with the middle office that the prices shown on particular screens are accurate to use as end of day prices. They send out an overnight commentary to offices in other jurisdictions about what happened in the market that day. Finally, they send any important instructions to the overnight trader.

Interestingly, when put down in black and white, the job of a trader doesn't sound that exciting. This is a person who has to run to the bathroom in order not to miss any key market events. This is a person who has to cut off conversations in the middle of a sentence in case the markets move or a client needs something ASAP. This is a person who sits in front of computer screens for 12 to 14 hours a day, five days a week. Why is that exciting? The fact is that the energy and excitement of the trading floor are very appealing and in some cases addictive.

> A junior sales person on the trading floor in Toronto was responsible for sending around a market commentary to the rest of the large US bank about the Canadian market every evening. One day, the recipients of that email were in for a bit of a shock. She had accidently sent an email about her date the night before to the global email distribution list. Needless to say, that email was more widely read than the normal market commentary.

Conclusion

What different traders do in order to make a market depends on the exact request from the client and the type of trader that they are. The process is generally the same, but each market making request is different even within the same financial product. The key is that traders take a risk when they make a market and thus the process they follow is meant to minimize the risk as much as possible. The bid, offer and the bid–offer spread they determine is meant to compensate them for that risk. However, most transactions are competitive and thus traders often take more risk than they would like to by providing a tighter market.

This market making analysis shows the complexity of the role of the trader and the vast amount of information that he needs to process in order to make prices for client trades. This is a crucial role on the trading floor because getting the price wrong can cost the bank the client relationship or it can cost the bank a lot of money. If the bid–offer spread is too wide, the risk is that the client might be unhappy and stops trading with the bank for some period of time. If the bid–offer spread is too small, the risk is that the bank might lose money if the trader isn't able to hedge or close out his position and the market price moves against him. The trader has to find the exact point that works for everyone. He needs to be reading the market and the client situation carefully to determine what that point is. On every trading floor around the world, there are hundreds of traders making markets for clients in a similar way every day. Inevitably, some of them get it wrong every day as well.

Discussion Questions

When a bank loses money on a client trade, is it the fault of the trader or the sales person?

Why is the bid–offer spread an indication of the profitability to the bank?

Do banks deserve the bid–offer spread that they charge?

Why do market makers always have to have a view?

Please see www.terriduhon.co for answers and discussion.

CHAPTER 7

How Is Proprietary Trading Different from Market Making?

This chapter will differentiate between the two main roles a trader can play on a trading floor: proprietary trader and market maker. One popular definition of proprietary trading is playing with the bank's capital. But what most people don't understand is that market makers also "play with the bank's capital." So what is the difference between a proprietary trader and a market maker? The answer to that is pretty simple: the market maker must be prepared to buy or sell whenever a client needs to buy or sell. In other words, he must be prepared to put a price on a trade even if he doesn't want to. Hence, he makes markets. The proprietary trader, on the other hand, gets to decide when and if he wants to trade. He is a market taker. In essence, once you understand that market makers are slightly different versions of proprietary traders you will begin to understand a bank's approach to risk management. This chapter will again refer to the examples that were described in Chapter 4 and use them to show the key differences between proprietary trading and market making. This chapter will also answer questions such as: How does a market maker make money? Why do great proprietary traders at banks fail at hedge funds? Why does a trading desk need to be able to lose money?

Years ago, the head of the proprietary trading desk in Asia for a large international bank was a legend on that bank's trading floor. He would discuss his views on the financial markets with other senior managers in the bank on the weekly global call. His views always got relayed to everyone else on the trading floor particularly when he had a story to tell. None of his trading views seemed to have a relationship to the financial markets. In particular, tea and his grandmother featured heavily in his commentary. His financial market view would start with, "My grandmother bought US dollars today because she did not like the price she had to pay for tea, so I have bought US dollars." Irrespective of how he came to his view, he was consistently profitable for decades.

Historically, proprietary traders have sat on the bank's trading floor and traded all the same products that the bank's market makers traded. They were allocated capital (in other words money they could put at risk by taking positions in financial products) and were expected to make a return on that capital. From this perspective, they sound very similar to market makers. Ultimately, the difference is that a proprietary trader is not required, or "forced" as some would say, to make a market. They are not market makers: they are market takers. The key distinction is that a proprietary trader's job is to take risk and make money as a result and a market maker's job is to provide liquidity to clients and make money as a result.

They end up doing similar activities, but their risk positions should theoretically be very different. In other words, the market maker generally has stricter risk limits than the proprietary trader. The market maker is supposed to provide liquidity by taking risk then close out or hedge the position generally in the same day. The proprietary trader is supposed to take risk over longer periods than the market maker and is often expected to make more money.

Since the credit crisis, there has been a lot of discussion about major banks' proprietary trading activities. Many financial market commentators have concluded that bank's trading desks had all become proprietary traders and thus they had taken on too much risk within the banking system. The **Volcker rule** in the United States, which is part of the Dodd-Frank Act passed in the summer of 2010, prohibits banks in the United States from proprietary trading. This rule implies that if proprietary trading is removed from the major banks they will take less risk. To some extent this is an oversimplification of proprietary trading and a lack of understanding of market making. The fact is that market makers will continue to take risk and to have capital allocated to them on which they need to generate a return.

Proprietary Trading Desk Overview

The word "prop" stands for **proprietary trading**. In market jargon, we say that the bank is taking risk for itself. More specifically, the bank is allocating capital to a trading book strictly for the bank to profit from market price movements rather than for the purpose of client-related risk taking. The concept has been that a bank sits in a unique position in the financial markets and is able to see all the flows of client trades, client interests and possibly future trades. As a result a bank should be able to profit from this knowledge. So, if the bank knows that a client wants to do a large transaction that is likely to move the market prices, the bank can take advantage of that information and front run the client and make money off the back of a client trade. But this clearly sounds like foul play. So there must be a mechanism to stop this type of activity, and there is. Proprietary desks are not part of the market making desks. They are separated generally by an aisle. There is a sign that declares that they are a proprietary trading desk. In effect, the aisle and the sign act like a Chinese wall. The fact is that the proprietary desk is a client of the trading desk while at the same time taking advantage of the bank's research, technology and non-client information flow.

Everyone knows not to discuss client business with the proprietary desk, and vice versa; the proprietary desk is often reticent to tell the market makers what their views and strategies are. Although a simple aisle doesn't sound like a deterrent to information flow, it does work. To expand on this point, a sales person who has had a conversation with a client about a client's trading strategy is unlikely to tell anyone else about that conversation unless necessary. A market maker is equally unlikely to tell anyone else on the trading floor what his trading strategy is, with the exception of perhaps a few people on his team such as a junior trader who executes interbank trades or his boss. The information flow that the proprietary desk is trying to capitalize on is the flow of general financial market information such as the following conversation between a head of sales, head of trading and head of proprietary trading in fixed income:

> Head of Treasury Sales: My guys are hearing a lot of concern about the non-farm payroll.
> Head of Treasury Trading: I'm hearing the same thing from interbank brokers and I get the sense that the market is heavy on the offer.
> Head of Prop: Yeah, the research doesn't seem to have any consensus and I think the market is long and wrong.

To translate this conversation, non-farm payroll is being released soon. There is no financial market consensus on the research, which is something the proprietary desk will be able to see because it will receive the research from all the major banks. It is not giving details of different bank research to a competitor; it is merely giving a broad comparison of the research it has seen. The head of trading is also relaying that he is getting the sense that his counterparts at other major banks are long. He says they are **heavy on the offer**, which means there is more interest in the interbank market in selling treasuries than in buying them. The head of proprietary confirms this when he says the market is **long and wrong**. "Long and wrong" is a phrase used when a market participant is known to own a financial product and the market price of that financial product has declined (or is expected to decline). The market participant has lost (or will lose) money, which means that the implicit bet that the market participant made on market prices going up was (or might be) wrong.

This is a very generic conversation and no sensitive client information is being discussed, but these three individuals all have a unique position within a bank in that they are in a position to hear and assess a lot of information from different financial market participants. The head of sales may be covering a few large clients himself, or he could be simply managing the sales desk. In either case he will be having bilateral conversations with his sales force and key clients throughout the day and hearing a cross-section of clients' thoughts. The head of trading will be talking to all the interbank brokers all day and exchanging rumors and gossip in addition to seeing the entire client trade flow. At the same time, he is getting indicative pricing information from interbank brokers on the product he trades and will get indications from his interbank broker about the general feeling or mood of the other major banks. The head of proprietary will be speaking to his team, who are speaking to other major banks sales people all day long because they are not only a client of Megabank but also a client of all the other major banks. So they will be getting a sense of what other banks are thinking as well as what other banks' research departments are saying. Together, theoretically, these three individuals should be as well informed as anyone of what the financial market is thinking at any point in time. Figure 7.1 shows the main flows of information on the trading floor which primarily include the sales people and the market makers. Anyone else sitting on the trading floor will be unaware of most of this conversation especially with all the electronic communication and trading that occurs today.

Proprietary desks often trade more than one product. So while a market maker only trades one product, a proprietary trader will look across products

FIGURE 7.1   Key trading floor information flows.

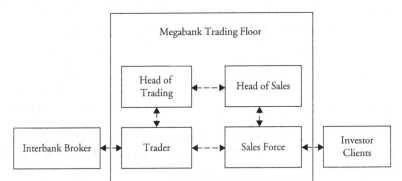

and often across asset classes. For example, one team of proprietary traders will trade interest rate and currency products, while another team might trade credit products. At the same time another team may also trade equity and commodity products. Yet, they all sit in the same area. This puts the proprietary traders in a unique position of being able to see information flows across financial market participants, across financial products and across asset classes. With this access to information flow as well as access to capital, they should be able to make money. Or this has been the theory.

Proprietary traders are often considered the same as hedge fund clients and often covered by the same sales force as they have similar investment strategies. These strategies are often called **arbitrage** strategies, which means that they have identified a financial market inefficiency and are in a unique position to take advantage of it. In the 1980s this was popular in the currency markets. There was less information flow globally and as a result there were often opportunities to buy at one price in one location and sell at another price in another location almost simultaneously and make money without taking risk. With the globalization of financial markets and the relatively inexpensive instant information flow available, this type of scenario is very rare now. It does happen in very illiquid markets but even then not very often. Today proprietary traders and hedge fund managers are not arbitraging the financial markets; they are executing macro or micro investment strategies. They may have a view that the US government has over borrowed in the treasury market and will create inflation in the long term, so they will sell 30-year US treasuries. This is an example of a macro view and strategy. They may have a view that Ford has turned around and is undervalued and so will buy Ford shares or Ford bonds to take advantage of that view. This is an example of a micro strategy. These are investment decisions made off the back of financial market analysis and research. The main goal of this type of trading is to maximize profit by taking.

> Often market makers and proprietary traders who are well known for making money in a particular financial market are hired by hedge funds to run an investment fund. What is often forgotten about these individuals is that they sit in a very privileged position on the bank's trading floor and they see a lot of information and trade flow. When they land in a hedge fund or start one on their own, they often end up not making as much money as they (and their investors) were expecting. They had significantly undervalued the information and trade flow from a bank's trading floor.

Proprietary Desk Liquidity

From a market maker's perspective, having a large active proprietary desk can be a valuable source of liquidity for hedging purposes. We will take the three examples from Chapter 4 and look at the possible involvement of a Megabank proprietary desk. In the PACAM treasury trade example (Figure 7.2), it's unlikely that there would necessarily be any proprietary trading desk involvement. It is not a particularly large or difficult trade to transact. The proprietary desk could easily have called the treasury market maker with the exact same request. Note that the proprietary desk would not usually work through a treasury sales person. It would often have a direct relationship with the market makers with whom it wanted to transact. This is not that unusual in the very active hedge fund investor base. Depending on the hedge fund or the proprietary desk, it may not want a sales person intermediating unless the sales person was particularly technical or plugged into the trading desk.

For example, at the point that the market maker says, "I sell $1 billion 5-year on-the-run treasuries for 100 and 17 thirty seconds to PACAM," he needs to know what his plan of action is going to be. It could be that he is happy to be short for a little while during the day and will buy treasuries opportunistically throughout the day to cover his short. It could be that the proprietary desk comes in and asks where he is willing to buy a large notional amount of treasuries and he is able to give it a good price, such as 100−16.5, which is what the screens are showing but not for the size that the

FIGURE 7.2 PACAM trade overview.

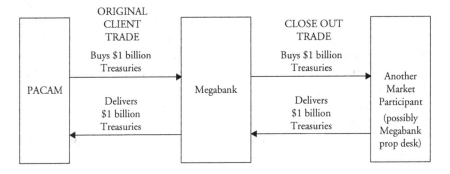

proprietary desk wants. This allows the market maker to make some money on his trade and to continue a good relationship with the proprietary desk, because it will be pleased to get such tight pricing on its trade (Box 7.1).

Box 7.1   Possible market maker profit on the PACAM treasury trade

Market maker sells $1 billion treasuries at 100−17 to PACAM.

$(100 + 17/32)\% \times \$1$ billion $= \$1.0053125$ billion of cash received on the sale

Market maker buys $1 billion treasuries at 100−16.5 from Megabank's proprietary desk.

$(100 + 16.5/32)\% \times \$1$ billion $= \$1.00515625$ billion of cash paid on the purchase
$\$1,005,312,500 - \$1,005,156,250 = \$156,250$ profit

There is no communication between the market maker and the proprietary trader about why the market maker is able to give the proprietary trader such tight pricing. The market maker will likely say something along the lines of "because you're such a good client, I'll show you 100−16.5." Remember that the proprietary trader has the same exact screens as the market makers so the proprietary trader knows exactly where the market is in the 5-year treasury. He will know whether this is a good price. But he can sometimes have more information than the market maker because he is having similar conversations with other banks. So if the Megabank market maker has missed a nuance in the marketplace, and there is another bank interested in buying in size at 16¾, then the proprietary trader will be furious with the treasury market maker and say something along the lines of, "Do you think I don't know where the market is? I know that there is a 16¾ bid in the market for size right now."

This will prompt some scrambling on the part of the market maker, who has two options. He can either try to do the trade at 16¾ or say that he's not that interested in buying right now. If he goes the first route, the proprietary desk now knows that the treasury market maker is very interested in buying, is likely short and wants to cover his short now that he knows there is another big bid in the treasury market. On the other hand, if the market maker says he's not that interested, he takes the risk that the market price moves because of this big bid in the treasury market and he loses money on the whole PACAM trade. What he decides to do is a function of his view on the financial market in general, his risk limits and his relationship with the proprietary trader.

The word **choice** is often thrown around on the trading floor by those who hold a privileged position in the financial markets or who are possibly overconfident in their trading ability. "Choice" means that a market maker is willing to buy or sell at the same price. Giving a client a market of choice means that the trader believes he can make money on the trade whether he buys or sells and he doesn't need a bid–offer spread in order to make money. "Choice" is a rare word to use on the trading floor but one that is sometimes used by the proprietary traders to indicate the incredible flow they see in the financial market and the money they can make as a result. When they use the word, they are effectively saying that they can be better market makers than anyone else. Another reason the word "choice" is used is that if a market maker makes a choice market for a client the client is conventionally obligated to trade in one direction or the other simply because he has been given the best market possible.

The Supermart bond issuance and related interest rate swap from Chapter 4, on the other hand, is a scenario where the proprietary trading desk could possibly be involved from the beginning. The interest rate swap desk needs to pay fixed on a large notional amount of interest rate swaps in order to hedge. Proprietary desks are an important source of liquidity in the marketplace because they are known to do large notional trades when they have a view. Thus, the market maker knows that if he has a large notional position that he needs to hedge he can often use his own proprietary desk to see whether the proprietary desk has an interest in part of the hedge.

The head of interest rate swap trading would say to the head of the prop desk something like: "This is highly confidential. We possibly have a client transaction coming up which will give us a large position in the interest rate swap trading book. Do you have any interest either way in an interest rate swap trade if this deal happens?"

The idea is that the market maker doesn't want to give away more information than he needs to, particularly given that there is theoretically a Chinese wall between the businesses. He is simply asking whether the proprietary desk has a current view in the interest rate swap market and whether it will be doing any transactions in the interest rate swap market over the next few weeks. The proprietary desk can then give either a yes or no to this question. A "no" means that the conversation doesn't go any further.

A "yes" can go in two directions: the proprietary desk is looking to either pay or receive the fixed rate in interest rate swaps. If the proprietary desk is looking to pay fixed then it is going in the same direction as the market maker, but if the proprietary desk is looking to receive fixed then perhaps a deal can be done. At the end of the day, these individuals work for the same bank. They should have an alignment of interest in ensuring that the client gets the best execution that Megabank can provide. And so it may come down to their having a frank conversation about the deal.

If it so happens that the proprietary desk is able to help facilitate a deal for a client by providing market liquidity, then it's a win–win situation. But if not, then this conversation must be treated as confidential and something that neither side will seek to profit from.

This is clearly not how it always works and has been one of the criticisms of the proprietary desk idea. There is rarely an alignment of interest between the proprietary traders and the market makers at the same bank. The proprietary traders are often incentivized simply to make the most profit possible on the capital they are allocated. So it is not in their interest to provide liquidity just for the sake of providing liquidity. Nor is it in their interest to do a trade at a price that suits a client if they think they can get a better price elsewhere. However, if it happens that the proprietary desk is looking to receive fixed on an interest rate swap during the same time period that the client is looking to execute its interest rate swap, there may be a brief window of alignment of interest.

The equity structured product example from Chapter 4 is similar to the PACAM treasury trade example from a notional perspective. The £200 million notional amount of the equity options trade embedded in the structured bond is relatively small such that it is not a position that the market maker would normally have a lot of difficulty in hedging. The issue is that this option is not necessarily quoted on the exchange or in the interbank market due to the 5-year maturity. To the extent that the market maker thinks the proprietary trader might be interested in the other side of the trade, they might have a quick conversation. Because there is no market for this trade, the proprietary trader can't affect the price of the equity option by front running and thus this is an easier conversation to have.

Everyone on the trading floor is obsessed with making markets. When financial markets are quiet, they are constantly looking for opportunities to make markets for entertainment. Once, at a large US bank in London, there were some desk moves scheduled on the trading floor, so some large plastic crates had been dumped on the trading floor for people to pack up their personal belongings on their desk to get ready for the move. It occurred to someone that the crate might just be too small for anyone to fit in it so a challenge was made. Within 30 minutes, there were ten people lined up around the box to see whether they could fit inside, with markets being made by the crowd of people standing around. Other classic scenarios are making markets around sports events. This makes the obvious link to "betting" which, although theoretically inaccurate, is another word often used to describe trading floor activity.

How Market Makers Are Similar to Proprietary Traders

The key distinction between market makers and proprietary traders is that the market maker makes a market and the proprietary trader is a market taker. The market maker is providing liquidity to the bank's clients while the proprietary trader is a client. The similarity is that they are both allocated capital on which they have to make a return, and every trade they do requires them to have a view on the financial market.

Take the PACAM treasury trade example in Box 7.2. The market maker has to take a view in order to make a market in the first place. He needs to decide whether this is a position he wants to hold or a position he wants to close out and in what timeframe. And, he also needs to decide how much money he needs to make on the trade if he closes out immediately compared to if he holds the position.

Box 7.2   PACAM trade overview

- On-the-run US treasury 5-years
- Coupon: 0.875%
- Maturity: 1/31/2117
- Megabank price quote: 100−16 at 100−17
- Market quote: 100−16.5 at 100−16.75 $300 million a side

PACAM says, "I lift the offer for $1 billion 5-year on-the-run treasuries at 100−17/32."

In the scenario where the market maker doesn't have a strong view on the financial market that day, he may not want to take any large positions either way because if the market price doesn't move he won't have an opportunity to make money. If he believes that the market prices will be relatively stable with low volatility for the day, then he is less focused on making money intraday and more focused on a longer-term view.

In theory, a market maker is supposed to be able to make a market and hedge at mid-market thus locking in the **bid to mid** or **offer to mid**. This is the difference between the trade price, either the bid or offer, and the mid-market price. The market maker has made the market of 100−16 at 17 for PACAM. This means that his mid-market price is 16.5. But the screens show a market of 100−16.5 at 16.75, which is a different mid-market of 16.625. So the market maker's mid-market price is different from the rest of the marketplace's. In Chapter 6, we identified that this market maker is axed to sell treasuries so he has skewed his mid-market price to show this.

The price line in Figure 7.3 represents the price of the 5-year treasuries where the price increases to the right and decreases to the left. The market maker can see a "market" on the screens but he makes a market which is different from that. Thus, the market mid and the Megabank mid are different, as shown on the price line in the figure.

Although the idea that a market maker can hedge at the mid-market price is a very common concept on trading floors, it is not realistic at all. Unfortunately, the "profit" that Megabank will assign on the trade is the difference between 16.5 (the market maker's mid-market) and 17 (the trade

FIGURE 7.3 Mid-market price calculation.

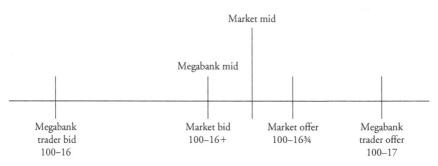

price with PACAM). Each client trade is assigned a "profit" using this calculation to distinguish between value added of the sales person in getting the client trade and the value added of the market maker in hedging or closing out the client trade. The sales person knows that the market maker's mid-market price is 16.5 and that the profit he can communicate to his boss on "his" trade is one-half of 1/32. On $1 billion, this amounts to $156,250. The problem for the market maker now is that the bank has effectively **recognized** this profit without actually realizing the profit by closing out the trade (Box 7.3), that is to say the sales person will book the theoretical profit as profit that the sales person brought to the bank prior to the market maker closing out the trade. Once the market maker closes out a trade, the exact profit (or loss) to the bank is then realized. For example, the sales person could say that he brought in $156,250 of profit to the bank but the market maker is only able to realize $100,000 of profit. That will show up as a loss on the market maker's part of $56,250.

Box 7.3   PACAM theoretical trade profit

PACAM trade profit and loss (P&L): not yet realized.
   Market maker sells $1 billion treasuries at 100−17 to PACAM.

   (100 + 17/32)% × $1 billion = $1.0053125 billion of cash received
      by Megabank

   Market maker says the mid-market is 100−16.5.

   (100 + 16.5/32)% × $1 billion = $1.00515625 billion
   = $1,005,312,500 − $1,005,156,250 = (theoretical) $156,250 trade
      profit

For the market maker, this poses a problem. This idea theoretically assumes that every trade he does with a client he can close out at mid-market prices. For the PACAM treasury trade, if he sells $1 billion at 17, he needs to buy $1 billion at 16.5. He knows that the interbank market for around $300 million is 16.5 at 16.75 so he could immediately trade $300 million at 16.75 by lifting the offer. The reason he would trade at 16.75 rather than 16.5 is that 16.75 is the offer side of the market. As a market maker to PACAM, he gets to buy on the bid and sell on the offer, but in the interbank market, if he wants to trade immediately, he is the market taker rather than the market maker. He has to lift the offer of another market maker or hit the bid of another market maker, in other words he has to buy at the higher price and sell at the lower price.

If he is not in a hurry and can take the risk that he doesn't get the price he wants on the size he wants, he can put himself on the bid. This means calling up the interbank broker and telling him that Megabank is a buyer at 16.5 for a few hundred million. But that decision has some risk associated with it. The market price may move without Megabank buying anything at 16.5. At the same time, in the scenario where he decides to lift the offer at 16.75 for $300 million, there is a possibility that the market price would move upwards and he may then be looking at buying the next $700 million at 17. If that's the case, Megabank has assumed that he has locked in a profit of ½ of 1/32 on $1 billion when in reality he has locked in ¼ of 1/32 on $300 million and 0 on the next $700 million (Box 7.4). (Note this is not taking into account the fact that he was already long $400 million, as mentioned in Chapter 6.)

Box 7.4   Different profit and loss scenarios

Market maker sells $1 billion treasuries at 100−17 to PACAM.

$(100 + 17/32)\% \times \$1 \text{ billion} = \$1.0053125 \text{ billion}$

Scenario 1

Market maker buys $300 million treasuries at 100−16.75 from the broker
   market.
$(100 + 16.75/32)\% \times \$300 \text{ million} = \$301,570,312.50$

Market maker buys $700 million treasuries at 100−17 from the broker market.

(100 + 17/32)% × $700 million = $703,718,750.00
= $1,005,312,500 − $301,570,312.50 − $703,718,750.00
= $23,437.50, which is far less than the theoretical $156,250 that the sales person has recognized as profit.

Scenario 2

• Market maker sits on the bid in the broker market at 16.5 and waits to get hit.
• Market maker also waits for client trades to come in.
• Market maker takes the risk that the market price moves up before he can hedge.

The Megabank market maker has the responsibility to at least make the profit that the bank assumes he is going to make and there is often the expectation that he will make more than that. The hedge strategy above in scenario 1 would not be an option as the profit is only $23,437.50 rather than the $156,250.00 profit he is expected to make as a minimum. From Megabank's perspective, this is not so unreasonable. Megabank is one of the top banks in the treasury market. It sees a good portion of the flow in treasury trades through its client base. In fact, this is one of the reasons that the trade price to mid-market is often allocated 50% to the market maker and 50% to the sales person. This is an acknowledgement that Megabank has a large franchise from which both the market maker and the sales person benefit.

Imagine the scenario where market prices are stable and 16 at 17 is the bid to offer all day; the treasury trader as the market maker to Megabank's clients will be able to buy at 16 and sell at 17 all day long. He has the potential to see billions of treasury trades pass through his books this way in benign financial markets. From Megabank's perspective, it is funneling this flow to him and with this flow comes a lot of financial market color on which he should be able to build a more informed view of what financial market sentiment is and how to position himself in the future and make profit over and above the trade price to mid. This implicitly makes the market maker a proprietary trader to some extent.

But that is a benign financial market scenario. There are few days when there are a lot of trades being done in a financial product and benign financial market conditions such that the market maker doesn't even need to come to work. He could just call in the bid and offer and sit at home while his trading book racked up profits. As this clearly doesn't happen, we need to look at the more realistic scenario, which is that market prices move constantly. It is rare for the market prices not to have intraday movement. So, the treasury market maker needs to have a view on the intraday movement as well as on the longer term. The reason he needs a view on both is that in the scenario where there is not enough liquidity in the treasury market to close out a position on the same day he needs to decide whether he is happy to keep the position overnight or even for the longer term. Keeping a position overnight entails a larger usage of capital so this should only be done if he thinks he can make more profit by keeping the position overnight.

> One junior market maker came to a more senior individual for advice one day. He was trading a small book on a larger trading desk for a big UK bank in London. His concern was that he couldn't figure out how to make money when he was forced to trade with clients. He said 50% of the time the client trades made money and 50% of the time they didn't. The advice he was given was to skew his bid to offer to ensure that he didn't win all client trades but that he won the client trades he wanted. He was also told to ensure that the sales people were aware of his axes and to get them working on them with clients. The junior market maker laughed and said that on his desk the way the market makers dealt with the sales people was just to shout at them when they brought "bad" trades to the desk.

The fact is that a market maker at Megabank is in an incredibly privileged position. He sees all the client flow and hears all the financial market color. At the same time, he has a reason to be in the financial market. This means that he is constantly making markets and taking positions as a result of client trading. This gives him a reason and a way to develop a view and really test the financial market depth with actual trades. He does have the constraint that he must at least lock in the profit from the client trades, but that is simply a minimum job requirement. Market makers at other banks who have much less client flow than Megabank look at the Megabank market makers with envy. They would love to see some of that flow, hear some of that financial market color and have the ability to be that active in the treasury market. They have a much bigger challenge, which is that if their sales person asks them for a price they are almost always in competition with a larger bank like Megabank. That means that if they want to win the business they must at least show the same price as Megabank. And, given that they likely have a weaker relationship with the client, they probably need to show a slightly better price to win the business. This is hard to do. If the market maker at a smaller firm sells $1 billion treasuries at 17, he is unlikely to see another client trade for $1 billion that day and possibly the other client trades he sees won't even add up to $1 billion that day. So he won't have client flow to try to trade out of his position. His only option to lock in a profit is via the interbank broker market. This means he has no choice but to put a bid in the interbank broker market at 16.5 and sit and wait to be able to cover his position.

Trading Book Accounting

Although not an obviously exciting topic, the accounting of the trading book (both the market maker and the proprietary trading book) has a lot to do with trading floor mentality. The accounting for trading books is a concept called **mark to market** (**MTM**). This means that if the trading book buys 1 share for $10 and the price for that share at the end of the day is $12, the trading book has a profit, also called P&L, of $2 for that day. Every day, the value of that share is calculated against that day's share price in the market and compared to the price the day before. Over time, if the trader then is able to buy another share at $12, and sell that same share for $14, that is a P&L of $2. At the end of the quarter, the only two trades were buying 1 share at $10 and making a bid−offer spread of $2 on another trade. Now, the price of the share that the trader owns is $15. So, the P&L in that trading book is $5 for the share the trader owns plus $2 for the bid−offer spread the trader made, for a total of $7. Every quarter banks publish their P&L for their trading books using this methodology. The next quarter, the trader doesn't do any other trades and still owns that 1 share. Now the share price is $5. This represents a P&L for the trading book of −$10 for that quarter. Table 7.1 summarizes this.

The criticism of this method is that it makes the profitability of the banks very volatile and a function of market prices rather than a function of their value add as financial market facilitators. The other criticism is that traders and sales people are paid bonuses on the mark to market of trading books rather than the locked-in profit or loss of client trades once they have been closed out or hedged.

TABLE 7.1   Sample Quarterly Mark to Market

Quarter	End of quarter share price	Bid−offer spread P&L	Outstanding shares	Total
1	$15	$2	1 share bought at $10($15 − $10) = $5	$7
2	$5	$0	1 share marked at $15($5 − $15) = −$10	−$10

A saying that is often repeated on the trading floor is "you're only as good as your last trade." This is almost a direct reference to the concept of mark to market. The intense focus by the sales person on "How much money did that trade make?" and from the trader "What was my P&L today?" results in a situation where the "star for the day" on the trading floor is the individual who made the most money that day and the "star" from the previous day is long forgotten.

Trader Capital Allocation

All of these trading decisions ultimately revolve around the risk limits (or capital) that traders (both market makers and proprietary traders) are given. Another way to think about a risk limit is that it is an amount of money that each trader can lose. If a bank consistently takes a certain amount of risk and thus can lose a certain amount of money, it is required to put capital aside to compensate for that possible loss. Today, after the credit crisis, this is even more important than before. A trading desk is assigned a particular amount of capital to put at risk each year based on what amount of risk was taken the previous year. Simply put, this is a specific amount of money that a trading desk can lose. Although the definition is "an amount of money that can be *lost*," the goal is for the trader to make a profit as a result of his ability to take risk.

A market making desk is assigned an amount of capital that the bank believes it needs in order to provide liquidity to the financial markets for the bank's clients. In other words, the market making desk is allowed to take risk in order to make markets for the bank's clients. But his job is to make a profit as a result of taking that risk. The profit expectations are over and above locking in the bid to mid or offer to mid from client trades (as illustrated in Boxes 7.3 and 7.4). The point of having capital allocated to the trading desk effectively acts like a trading or risk limit. The capital is assigned based on what a reasonable position in the market making book is and what a reasonable market price move against that position is on a daily basis.

The same applies to a proprietary trading desk but for different reasons. It will be assigned capital in order to take risk solely based on the trader's market views. The amount of capital will be allocated based on the risk and return on the proprietary trading book the year before.

A simple way to think about capital is that it comes from retained earnings. The bank is effectively re-investing its profits into its risk taking businesses. This means that these businesses need to be profitable. They have to make returns on their investments. The treasury trading book needs to have a profit on the capital not just that market makers use but that they have been allocated. This profit is obviously over and above the cost of running the treasury sales and trading business. For example, the treasury trading book might have been allocated $3 million of capital but it is only possibly using $2 million on the PACAM trade if the market makers keep the entire $1 billion position open overnight. The amount of capital usage is determined by the risk management methodology applied, which is explained in Chapters 12, 13 and 14.

Because a market making book primarily takes risk as a result of providing liquidity to clients, the trader is often able to buy at a lower price and sell at a higher price on the same day. This locks in profit without using very much capital because the positions aren't always held overnight and are more rarely held over longer periods of time. The longer the position is held on average, the more risk to market price moves and thus the more capital the trading book should hold. Because market makers use the capital for the short period of time the position is open, the capital is then "re-cycled" and used for the next client trade. This results in a situation where trading books with very little capital usage have very high P&Ls each year. For example, a trading book which is allocated $2 million of capital could make $500 million in P&L each year.

Conclusion

We can see that a proprietary trader and a market maker have a lot in common. The big picture for both of them is that they need to understand the financial market sentiment and take a view on the market prices in both the short and long terms. The driver for both of them is that they need to make a return on the capital they use. Here they sound similar. However, the key difference is that the market maker must take positions when the client decides to trade with him whether it is the direction he wants to be in or not. He then has to ensure that the bid–offer spread is appropriate to compensate him for the risk he is taking. The proprietary trader, on the other hand, only trades when he has a view and a strategy and he thinks the price is right.

To say that trading floors shouldn't be taking risk at all is a misunderstanding of the role that the trading floors have in the financial markets. In order to provide the liquidity and access to financial markets for their clients, trading floors need to take risk. Granted, this risk needs to be managed properly and should not be taken without proper consideration for the right hedge or close out strategy, but market makers need this ability. What is misunderstood is the implicit pressure on the market maker to make money over and above the trade price to mid-market on client trades. That "profit" is often assigned to the sales person as a result of bringing the client to the table. The trader is thus implicitly encouraged to take more risk than perhaps necessary because the truism in financial markets is that there is no return without risk.

Discussion Questions

What might be the concern of shareholders in banks who have large proprietary trading businesses?

Why is proprietary trading similar to trading for a hedge fund?

Do traders want to be proprietary traders or hedge fund traders?

Why are market makers forced to trade with clients?

Please see www.terriduhon.co for answers and discussion.

CHAPTER 8

What Is the Relationship Between Sales and Trading?

This chapter explores the sometimes explosive relationship between the sales person and the trader. This relationship is never straightforward, as they may not always be or seem to be playing on the same team. The various flashpoints they will encounter are almost always over one of two things: the client or the profit. The client issue is a difficult one to find the right balance for. The sales person can sometimes become too close to the client and thus want to get the best deal possible for the client, to the detriment of the bank. The trader can lose sight of the value of the relationship and want to make too much money. The other question is profit. How much does the sales person get paid for the trade his client has just done is a much debated point and brings up the thorny subject of bankers' bonuses. This chapter will explore different scenarios where these controversial situations can occur by referring back to the examples from Chapter 4. This chapter will also answer questions such as: Who owns the client? What is the value of the franchise? What makes a good sales person? What makes a good trader? Why don't traders talk directly to clients?

A trader on the fixed income trading floor for a large US bank in London had a shrewd reputation. He was known for not always showing his hand. This meant that when financial markets were very illiquid he was often vague about where the mid-market price was. At the end of the day, sales people liked him because his understanding of financial market dynamics was excellent. He also consistently made money. A sales person described him to a new hire as "a bandit, but he's our bandit." He was explaining the fact that when a trader makes money it benefits the whole business.

The relationship between the sales person and the trader on the trading floor is a source of friction which can be summed up as to whether the two people believe they are on the same team. The issue is almost always over one of two things: the client or the profit. The client issue is a difficult one to find the right balance for. The sales person can sometimes become too close to the client and thus want to get the best deal possible for the client, to the detriment of the bank. At the same time, the trader can lose sight of the value of the relationship and want to make too much money. This is a delicate balance that must be struck. To some extent it is the natural tension that in general makes the trade a fair trade for both sides. The sales person can see that the better the deal his client gets, the more the client will trust the sales person and want to do business with him. This is the long-term, volume viewpoint. On the other hand, the trader knows that there is a minimum amount of money that the bank needs to be paid to take on certain risk. He will sometimes do a **loss leading** trade for the benefit of the client relationship, but this is rare. Mostly, he wants every trade to be profitable.

Take the PACAM treasury trade example from Chapter 4. If the sales person pushes the trader to give a better price to the client, this means tightening his bid–offer spread. This would have been a tough market for the trader to make because it would have been hard for the trader to make any profit on the trade and may have even resulted in a loss. The sales person would have argued that PACAM is one of Megabank's biggest clients. "We need to show them that we appreciate them by giving them great prices. We're in competition so we can't look bad." If the trader succumbed to that logic he might have shown a tighter price than he originally did (Box 8.1). Now, he doesn't know if he will be able to lock in any profit on that trade.

Box 8.1   Unfair scenario to the trader

- PACAM wants a market for $1 billion on-the-run treasuries.
- Original Megabank price quote for $1 billion: 100−16 at 100−17.
- Tighter market at the urging of the sales person: 100−16.25 at 100−16.75.

A treasury trade isn't a trade in which a client should ever feel that he got a bad price, because it is such a liquid market with so many market makers and electronic trading systems. The client should always be able to see where the treasury market prices are from several different sources. A structure that is more complex or tailored, on the other hand, is one for which there aren't electronic trading systems, nor are there many market makers (Box 8.2).

Box 8.2   Unfair scenario to the client

It is harder for the client to see prices on tailored or structured products, because they are not quoted on any screens. The client may not be asking another bank to price up the structure, because it is too complex or it is not public information.

Example:

- Retail investors in the equity structured product example
- Supermart's cross-currency swap in the original scenario from Chapter 4.

In both examples, Megabank could potentially build in a lot more profit than necessary to cover the risk being taken.

The other source of friction is profit. How much the sales person gets paid for the trade his client has just done introduces that most contentious of issues: bankers' bonuses. As previous chapters showed, every trade that the bank does for its client gives the bank a risk position. Simply looking at the difference from trade price to mid-market price and saying that this is profit the sales person generated is not fair to the trader because it is not a given that he can lock in that profit, as discussed in Chapter 7. However, he wouldn't be trading if the bank didn't have the relationship, so it is common to assign the term **sales points** to some portion of the profit that comes from trade price to mid-market. This means that the trader often takes extra risk in order to try to make profits in the trading book over and above the sales points that have come from client trades.

In the PACAM treasury trade example, the trader's mid-market price was 100−16.5. When PACAM traded at 100−17, the mid to offer theoretical profitability was $156,250 (see Chapter 7, Box 7.3). This is theoretical because, until this amount is locked in by a close out trade, Megabank is not guaranteed to make this money.

The sales person will want to assign the entire $156,250 of theoretical profit to his sales book profits. These are his sales points for this trade despite the fact that the profit is not guaranteed until the trader is able to close out the position. Different banks will have different rules about how sales points are calculated but they are most commonly calculated as some portion of the mid-market to trade price, so either bid to mid-market or offer to mid-market.

One way to think about sales points is like commission on the trade. But the calculation of that commission isn't locked-in profit. The profit of the trade can change over time depending on how the market prices move and how the trader closes out or hedges the trade. In some cases, exotic derivatives in particular, the trader has to manage the risk of the trade over the life of the trade as market prices change. The best example of this was during the 2008−2009 credit crisis. There were sales people and traders who were paid bonuses based on the theoretical profit and loss (P&L) of trades between 2004 and 2007 that years later caused the loss of billions of dollars for some banks.

Another issue is that the concept of commission can lead to questionable business practice on the part of sales people and clients where the sales person promises to pay a portion of the commission to the client if the client does certain trades. Obviously, this is highly illegal but has been known to happen.

At the end of the day, the relationship between the sales person and the trader should be an open one because they are on the same team. The sales person should try to sell positions that the trader is axed to hedge or close out. The sales person brings flow trades to the trader and the sales person is a good source of financial market color for the trader. On the other hand, the trader is a good source of trade ideas and financial market color for the sales person. The more money the trader makes, the more the sales person is likely to be paid. The trader can also help strategize on the right price to show the client. But all of this really requires some level of trust between the two roles.

A sales person in New York had just joined a large US bank and was being introduced to the head of trading at that bank. The new sales person introduced himself and said, "I trade with the OPEC countries." The head of trading corrected him: "Against." The sales person said. "Excuse me?" The head of trading said, "Against. You trade *against* the OPEC countries."

A Day in the Life

The sales person's day generally starts at around the same time as the trader's, around 6:30 a.m., and commences with the morning meeting. This is not significantly different from the morning meeting for the traders and they are often done together. While a recap of the previous day's client business might be discussed, including any post-mortems of client trades lost, from the sales person's perspective, the crux of this meeting is about financial market color for the day. What is the story that sales people are telling to their clients today? This story can come from a number of different people within the bank.

- There could be a senior sales person who is well respected for his views on the financial market who gives his thoughts on the financial market every now and then.
- There could be a member of the research team who introduces a new piece of research. He'll hand out a printed copy and point to the highlights. Then he'll email it out to the sales people, who then forward it to their clients. This could be an economic piece on the global economy, it could be more focused on a particular region or it could be a trade idea. Whatever new research piece that is coming out in the asset class and products that the sales team covers could be introduced.
- There could be a trader who comes every now and then to talk about the trading views on the financial market, or a trader could come in and talk about specific axes the trading desk has. Similar to the research piece, this could be a trader from any of the products that the sales team covers.
- The members of the sales team may all be required to identify good trade ideas and present them to the broader team.
- There may not be a physical meeting but a trader and a strategist speaking over the **hoot 'n' holler**. The hoot 'n' holler is the broadcast system to the entire trading floor. When the hoot 'n' holler is used, the whole trading floor is silent while everybody listens and takes notes.

There is no set formula for the morning meeting but generally it gives sales people a reason to talk to their clients that day.

For example, a senior sales person has just produced a financial market commentary. He is well respected for his views and well known in the financial marketplace as a result. He often produces a parable which relates the financial market behavior to a recent story, such as a presidential election. These commentaries come out once a week or so and are distributed via email to many different financial market participants both internally and externally. He may read out the commentary at the sales meeting ahead of sending it out via email. These sales people are rare but valuable.

The sales people then look through all the emails and bloombergs they received between last night and this morning. The key messages are trader financial market commentary, trader axes, new research reports and runs. Trader financial market commentary is generally sent out from each trader to his main sales force either each night or each morning. It gives a picture of what flows were seen in a particular financial market the day before and what is expected the next day.

Sample trader commentary from the Megabank interest rate swap trader:

> The market yesterday was relatively quiet. Not much flow in the interbank broker market and only a handful of client trades. The client trades all indicated that they were hedging ahead of the unemployment number coming out today. Our economists think the number will be higher than expected, which would likely push rates lower. I don't think it will move the market that much as I don't think the market has a big position at the moment. I'm still axed to pay 3-years and receive 5-years.

This commentary is giving some simple color on an interest rate swap market. It's hard to interpret this commentary without the context of the current economic situation and without understanding the normal dynamics of this particular market. But one interpretation of this commentary could be that the market prices have been relatively stable for a while and are expected to continue to be that way given that the interbank market doesn't have a big position in one direction or the other. Clients are also indicating that the business they are doing is hedging ahead of the number, which still supports the idea of the interbank market being market neutral. The Megabank research team has published its view that the number will be higher than expected, which would cause the financial market to worry about the state of the economy. This should push rates lower. The trader is also axed to pay the fixed leg on 3-year interest rate swaps and receive the fixed leg on 5-year interest rate swaps.

This trader commentary isn't particularly interesting and is probably similar to what other traders are saying to their sales force, so the members of the sales team will be unlikely to forward it to their clients. It is something to discuss with their clients rather than bother them with an email about.

Sample Megabank research commentary:

> As a big number is coming out today, the research team has produced a short economic commentary. This commentary summarizes the different financial market opinions on what the number might be today. These different opinions come from public research reports that are written by other banks, other financial companies or other independent research firms. The Megabank number will be highlighted and there will be an explanation as to why our number is different from the consensus.

This research commentary is a good summary of the current expectations and something clients will likely appreciate receiving, so the sales force will likely forward it to their clients.

Finally, the sales force is looking for **runs**. These are current bids and offers on the key products that the sales people deal with. The traders would have just sent them out in the morning to let the sales force know where the market prices are this morning (Box 8.3) if they are not already showing on an internal electronic trading system. There might be a short commentary as well if the run is different from the end of day prices the day before and a repeat of the trader's axes.

Box 8.3   Megabank interest rate swap run

2yr 0.66%/0.67%
3yr 0.75%/0.755%
4yr 0.88%/0.89%
5yr 1.05%/1.07%
7yr 1.22%/1.23%
10yr 1.50%/1.52%

Axed to pay 3-years and receive 5-years.

The sales force will all operate differently, depending on their style and their clients. Some sales people will cut and paste the runs for the different products they cover, for example US dollar interest rate swaps, treasuries and agencies. They will insert their own financial market commentary, which might be a combination of everything they have read and heard that morning. They will attach the senior sales person's parable as well as the Megabank market commentary on the unemployment number. They will send all this in one email to all their clients. Other sales people won't bother pulling it all together and will just forward all the emails and bloombergs to their clients.

Because most institutional investors who are active traders will be covered by multiple banks, a sales person knows that the client will receive something similar from every other bank. The client is not necessarily just going to delete all this information, because it is not always the same. The runs are especially important as they tell the client where the market price is in the products they trade as well as the axes for each different bank. Some of the commentary will be valuable as well. The client will determine over time which commentary and research it considers most insightful and will read those regularly.

Once that is done, the sales person then picks up the phone and starts calling all his clients to have a chat about the unemployment number. The most common questions sales people ask are "What are you thinking?" and "Anything I can help you with?" A common question from the clients to the sales person is "Any interesting axes?"

The sales person's day is a busy one. He needs to be able to answer the phone and have a technical conversation about the market with his clients any time they call. He needs to develop trade ideas to show his clients. He needs to keep abreast of market developments by watching the same screens that the traders are watching. He needs to develop relationships with clients in order to try to do more business with them and be able to recommend applicable trade ideas to them. This is the sales person's job. Whenever the question of why traders don't often talk to clients comes up, it's easy to answer. It's because they are not the best relationship managers nor do they have time for it. They are entirely focused on making markets and managing their risk position. This makes them curt and often difficult to deal with during the trading day.

The end of the day for the sales person on the trading floor is similar to the trader's end of day. The sales person ensures that all his trades have been booked properly. He ensures that all his sales points are entered correctly into the system. He double-checks that he has confirmed all the details of each trade with his clients. Finally, he looks at any admin he needs to do. This is generally around getting new clients on board or issues with old trades with his clients that need to be sorted out.

Unfortunately, this doesn't mean it's time to go home. The after-hours relationship management is as important as the business-hours relationship management on the part of the sales person. Drinks, dinner and/or a show are often on the cards for the evening. Because sales people cover multiple clients and are constantly looking to deepen the relationship or increase it to embrace more people, both junior and senior, they can be out every night. Also, don't forget that weekends are often used for client events such as playing golf or going to a big game. A sales person's job never stops.

Know Your Client

Most banks have existing relationships with a lot of clients. A new sales person out of university will often be assigned to work as the junior sales (also called coverage) person to a few different senior sales people. Over time, that junior sales person will either be handed smaller clients to manage themselves or a more senior sales person will move on, leaving a gap for the junior sales person to fill. However, there are always new clients to develop. This could be a bank looking to expand its coverage into a new region, a new client type or a new asset class. But often this is just new entities that need access to the financial markets.

This means that part of the job of the sales person is to set up new accounts for the bank. Once contact has been made between the sales person and the new client, the administrative process of setting up trading lines begins. Banks don't trade with clients unless the bank has gone through a full know your client (KYC) process, originally mentioned in Chapter 3. This is primarily to ensure that the client is not involved in any sort of money laundering. This is a legal and compliance process which needs the coordination of the sales person who liaises with the new client to coordinate the meetings and the financial information transfers that need to occur.

CUTTING ADMINISTRATIVE CORNERS WITH A NEW CLIENT

Getting new clients set up within the bank is often considered a huge administrative pain for the sales person. As a result, sales people sometimes try to cut corners and wheedle their way into trading with a client before the process has been fully completed. The sales person "promises" to finish the process as long as he can get approval for this "one big trade." The conversation is one we can all imagine. "Look, this is a huge new client. We could make millions with the client. We need to be able to show them that we can step up to the plate and do this trade that they need today. After that I promise we'll go through all the hoops." When this happens, it's inevitable that the process doesn't get completed properly. There are many cases for which this sort of haphazard approach to client management got the bank into trouble.

Then the bank needs to figure out what financial products the client will want to trade and what kind of trading limits the bank will allow the client. This is primarily handled by the credit risk officer for that type of client. (The credit risk officer role is discussed in Chapter 14.) Some clients are very complex series of different legal entities, which means that they don't just trade as ABC Asset Management; they trade as ABC Super Fund I or ABC Income Fund B, for example. This means setting up trading limits for each different fund. This is a huge amount of work on the part of the sales person. He needs to coordinate with different areas of the bank in order to make this process happen. There is not another person within the bank who will make this process happen. This is the sales person's job. He is responsible for getting this new client over the administrative hurdles and getting trades done with them. He needs to:

- Identify the senior trading floor individual who will sign off on the new client process. This is normally the head of sales. This is also where the financial products and the possible trade sizes are identified.
- Kick off meeting, including credit risk management, legal, compliance, sales, documentation and middle office. The senior individual will authorize each of these teams to devote resources to fulfill the new client process.
- Credit risk officer and compliance officer liaise with the new client to get all the relevant financial statements necessary to determine the risk limits for different financial products and address all compliance issues.
- The legal and documentation team then puts in place all the documentation necessary to trade the relevant financial products for which approval has been given by the credit risk officer.
- Middle office sets up the client in the bank's systems as a new trading counterparty.

Regardless of whether this is a new client to the bank, the sales person should know what his client's general strategy is and how his client operates (Box 8.4). If a client is an asset manager, the sales person should know what its assets under management are, how much is allocated to fixed income vs. equities vs. other and what its general strategies are. This information comes from doing some research, going out to meet the key individuals in their offices and getting to know their team. Often getting to know a client happens in a more social setting, which is no different from any other client relationship around the world.

Box 8.4   Getting to know the client

Sample PACAM fixed income fund

- PACAM's fixed income STABILITY fund invests 100% in government bonds from the United States and Europe.
- Its target maturity is five years.
- It goes long and short and often sits on a large amount of cash.
- It has recently hit $100 billion of AUM (assets under management).
- It often trades in $1 billion sizes.

Sample PACAM equity fund

- PACAM's equity GROWTH fund invests 100% in US small and medium-sized companies.
- Its target return is 6% per annum.
- It goes long and short and often sits on a large amount of cash.
- It has recently hit $200 billion of AUM.

Sales people often think that they own a client. Particularly after they have gone through a new client process with a client, they see the client as their own as opposed to the bank's. When they move to work for a new bank, they talk about taking relationships with them. What the sales person misses is that the process of getting a client set up within a bank embeds the client into that bank. There are now contact points throughout the bank and there are often other sales people in other asset classes who begin to trade with that client as well. While the client values the relationship with the individual sales person, the client values the relationship across the bank more. So ultimately the ownership, if the bank has managed it properly, is with the bank.

Managing the Client Relationship

Understanding client strategies and modus operandi is crucial for the sales person to be able to interpret the requests that come in from the client. This is how the sales person can help the trader to better understand the context of the request from the client. In the PACAM treasury trade example from Chapter 4, the US treasury sales person at Megabank gets a call from his client, PACAM. PACAM asks the sales person, "Where is the market, in size, for the 5-year on-the-run treasuries?" The sales person should be able to make some assumptions about what PACAM is doing. Those assumptions will help the trader to make a market.

One thing that everyone on the trading floor knows is that time is crucial. The market prices are continually moving, so a request from a client like this needs to be dealt with as soon as possible. The first thing the sales person needs to do is to let the trader know what's going on. The sales person will put PACAM on hold to open a line to the treasury trader and say, "I need a firm market for PACAM for $1 billion on-the-run 5-year treasuries. I don't know if they are interested in buying or selling but we're likely in comp. You know how they are. I'll get as much info as I can and revert."

The sales person has made a lot of assumptions in passing this information to the trader. He has assumed that PACAM needs a firm market, the notional amount is $1 billion and that PACAM will put Megabank in competition with other banks. The only way the sales person could have made these assumptions is by having covered PACAM and the specific individual at PACAM for several years. What this implies is that, while different firms have a general approach to trading, ultimately there is a person who needs to execute the trade and his style of execution may be different from another person's at the same firm.

The two extremes of execution style could be classified as "relationship" and "competition." Some clients rely on relationship to get the best execution. They look carefully at what the different runs are from the different banks. They get to know the sales people really well and decide which sales people they will work the most with. They will let the sales person know what they are doing when they are looking to execute a trade. They may not tell them the full strategy, but they will likely say which direction they are going and in what size. They will do price checks on trades but won't always put the banks in comp.

On the other hand is the competition execution style. This is the client who doesn't trust any of his sales people and feels that the best execution will always come from putting the banks in competition. This client never tells the sales person what direction he is trading and what his size is until the sales person needs to know. Clients often fall somewhere in between and it is a function of individual styles and individual sales people and the pricing that the trader generally gives (Table 8.1).

In the PACAM trade, the sales person knows the style of the client and will try to confirm that while the trader is making a price. The sales person says, "The trader is getting me a market right now. Do you want firm prices

TABLE 8.1   Client Extremes

Relationship Clients	Competition Clients
Develop personal relationships with sales people at different banks	Rarely develop personal relationships with sales people
Exchange market views and discuss different trade ideas	Rarely exchange market views and never discuss trade ideas
Often ask for a one-way market and they double-check prices on electronic trading systems	Always ask for two-way markets
Rarely trade in competition	Always trade in competition
See the bank as part of their team	See banks as merely providing a service
Are happy for a bank to make money on their trades	Want to ensure that banks make the least amount of money possible on their trades

or is this indicative? Should I assume $1 billion? Are we in comp? Any other color you can give me?" The sales person knows that he will be unlikely to get much information from the client, but he needs to try. The client immediately says, "I need firm prices. I'll be trading around $1 billion and you're in comp. If I don't hear from you within 30 seconds, I'll trade away."

The sales person has left the line open to the treasury trader while he spoke to PACAM. The sales person puts the client on hold and says to the trader, "No other color. I need firm prices, around $1 billion and we're in comp. He'll trade away within 30 seconds if we don't get a price in now."

This is a difficult situation for a trader to manage but, as the sales person said, "You know how they are." This means that the execution style of this client is well known and something the sales person and the trader have discussed. The trader has to make a market for the client. The trader knows that the market needs to be competitive or he may be dropped from the list of banks that PACAM calls. In that case, he would miss the flow and possibly damage the relationship with PACAM. PACAM doesn't only trade treasuries with Megabank; it also trades equities and various derivatives across the globe.

When PACAM gets the quotes shown in Box 8.5, it can see that Unibank is showing the tightest bid to offer. As PACAM wants to buy treasuries, Globobank and Megabank are showing the best offer. PACAM can go back to Megabank and Globobank and ask for tighter prices or he can trade on what he's been shown. Different clients will approach this situation in different ways.

Box 8.5   Quote comps for PACAM treasury trade

- Electronic trading system: 100−16+ at 100−16¾ $300 million a side
- Megabank: 100−16 at 100−17 $1 billion
- Unibank: 100−16.5 at 100−17¼ $1 billion
- Globobank: 100−16 at 100−17 $1 billion

Remember, as discussed in Chapter 4, clients often like to ask for two-way markets to ensure that the bank doesn't front run them. Traders dislike giving two-way markets because, in a way, it's double the work. Determining a trader's bid is as much work as determining a trader's offer. To determine the bid the trader is asking himself, "Where am I comfortable buying?" The answer to that doesn't give the answer to "Where am I comfortable selling?"

Both the sales person and the trader will feel that they are simply providing a service for the sake of a larger global relationship with PACAM. They don't feel that they are necessarily adding any value or even getting any value. Both the sales person and the trader have tried to develop a better relationship with this client in a variety of ways from inviting him to social events or by trying to give him more detailed and interesting financial market commentary, but to no avail. As a result, the trader and the sales person will feel like they are a team working to some extent against this client as that is the type of relationship that the client has created.

The other extreme is the client who develops strong relationships with a few banks and spends the day chatting with those sales people and exchanging views on the financial market and general strategy ideas. This is a situation where a sales person can feel the need to step up for the client and will often put pressure on the trader to show a better price. The trader may or may not understand why the sales person wants to do this. Regardless, the trader's focus is on profits. If the trader takes risk, he needs to make a minimum return in order to do that.

A sales person will also often try to bring the traders out to visit clients both formally in their offices as well as informally. It is hard for a trader to be away from his desk and so meetings at the client's offices during trading hours are rare. It is also rare for a client to be allowed onto a trading floor for anything other than a brief walk through or a meeting in a closed room off to the side. This relationship is unlikely to be a strong relationship because of the constraints around the trader's time, but the trader should recognize the value of the color that the sales person receives from the client and will want to enhance the relationship if possible.

Ultimately, we have to ask whether it is good or bad for a client to exchange too much information with a bank. In other words, what is the bank doing with this information and can the bank be trusted? Clearly on large trades which have the potential to move the market price there is an issue of front running, which needs to be managed, but on smaller trades it is hard to see how a bank could use that information against the client. As long as the client is aware of where the market price is from other sources and does not rely upon one bank to provide it with market prices, it is hard for the client to lose out. There are some clients who feel that their job is to get the best execution possible, which means leaving the least amount of money on the table possible. In other words, they don't feel that the banks deserve large bid–offer spreads for the service that they provide, while others feel that banks provide a valuable service and are happy to allow them a reasonable bid–offer spread. Remember that the bid–offer spread is how the bank gets compensated for the risk the bank takes in providing liquidity so it is slightly strange that a client doesn't want the bank to be compensated for this risk.

The bid–offer spread is another way of expressing the market liquidity of a product and the potential profitability to a bank of a trade. In general, the larger the size of the trade, the wider the bid–offer spread is. However, the reverse is true once the trade size breaches a minimum threshold. Below a certain size in any financial market, the operational cost of doing a trade must be taken into account and the bid–offer spread is wider to reflect a minimum profit that the bank must make. For derivatives and fixed income products, the maturity of the product is also a factor. The longer the maturity, the wider the bid–offer spread.

At the same time, the client may feel that its strategy is proprietary and so it is wary of letting anyone know. That is a fair point to some extent. Some clients feel that they have found some strategy or some arbitrage from which they will only benefit if others don't see it. Of course, this works in two ways. There are some investors who are happy for the financial market to know what their strategy is because they got in early and the more investors that follow the same strategy the more the market prices will move in their favor (Table 8.2).

An on-the-run treasury trade is an example of a trade that is very transparent. There are several electronic trading screens and most banks will publish their bids and offers on their trading screens for clients to see. It is generally a very liquid and transparent marketplace. So the friction between the sales person and the trader and between the client and the bank is less common. A more complex and less transparent financial product, though, has the ability to create more friction. Ultimately, it comes down to trust. In a financial product that is not transparent, do you believe that the trader (if

TABLE 8.2 Example of Trade Strategy that Was Public

Market Participant	Trade
Berkshire Hathaway	Warren Buffet publicly declared that he was investing in bank stocks during the 2008–2009 credit crisis
PIMCO	Bill Gross publicly declared that he was investing in US treasuries during the 2008–2009 credit crisis
Speculators	It was common knowledge that speculators were selling Greek debt during the Greek crisis in 2010

you are a sales person) or the bank (if you are the client) is showing you a fair market price?

An exotic equity derivative is a good example. Exotic derivatives are unlikely to have visible market quotes anywhere. So in the scenario where a sales person had a client, Archery, who wanted an exotic derivative, there would be a slightly different discussion.

The client would most likely not ask for a two-way market, nor would it be likely to trade in size. Exotic derivatives are generally put together for a client for a reason. A client has a specific view or something specific that he wants to hedge. He works with the sales person to determine the right structure that suits him. The size and the direction of the trade are generally known ahead of time. The sales person will likely have been having ongoing communication with the trader as the trade idea develops with the client.

Let's take the example of the following equity derivative: an option on the FTSE 100 which pays out 50% if the FTSE 100 reaches 8,000 in five years (Box 8.6).

Box 8.6   Exotic equity option structure

- Option notional = £10 million
- Underlying: FTSE 100
- Strike: 8,000
- Maturity: 5 years
- Payout: If FTSE 100 is at or above 8,000 at the maturity date, the option buyer receives £5 million; otherwise, the option buyer receives £0.

   The question to the sales person from the client is, "What is the option price for this trade?"

The sales person may be asked by the client to tweak certain features of the transaction and will ask for price updates regularly. The client may say, "We want the payout to be in 4.5 years. Can you price that up?" Or "We want a 60% payout. Can you price that up?" The client may have a specific amount of money he can spend on buying this option and/or he has a return target. In this example, the client is trying to fine-tune his investment in this option to minimize what he spends on the option and to maximize the return. He may have communicated all of this to the sales person. The sales person will end up calling up the trader every time the client wants an update. If this goes on too long, and the trade is not that large, thus the profit won't be that large, the trader will become irritated and feel that the sales person isn't properly managing the client. This will lead to some friction.

Sales person:	Archery wants another tweak on this trade. Can you change the maturity to 4.5 years?
Trader:	What's going on? Is the client going to trade this or not?
Sales person:	They are doing this in combination with another trade so there are a lot of moving parts.
Trader:	OK, here's the new price.

The next day

Sales person:	Archery wants to go back to the 5-year maturity but with a 60% payout. Can you price that?
Trader:	Are they ever going to trade this?
Sales person:	When they're ready.

The next day

Sales person:	Archery wants to go back to the original trade with a 50% payout. Can you refresh that price?
Trader:	This is such a waste of time. Are we in comp? Are we even sure they are going to trade with us?
Sales person:	Just give me the price.

If the trade is small, the trader may say there is a minimum amount of money that Megabank needs to make to even process the trade so the profit that he prices into the trade may look too large to the sales person. Often clients in these types of trades aren't asking to see both sides of the market and they understand that asking another bank to price check may not be that welcome from another bank because of the work involved. So the client is either able to estimate the price itself using its own internal models or it trusts that the bank will do a fair deal. This type of situation may lead to some friction where the client discovers that the profit that the bank priced in looks really high and comes back to the sales person and complains. If the sales person was aware that the profit would be high, he would have understood why the profit was high, but if he wasn't aware, this would lead to some friction.

Sales person:	Where's the mid on this trade? You gave me a price of 25% but not a mid.
Trader:	The mid is probably around 22%, but I'm not making a two-way on this.
Sales person:	We can't show a bid to offer of 6%. That's way too wide. You need to tighten it.
Trader:	There is no market in this product. I'm taking the risk so I'm telling you what the price is.

It sometimes occurs that in highly tailored transactions there is not even a market standard model so different banks will propose very different prices for the same product. If the client sees this, the client could be irritated with the bank that showed the worst price and the sales person may or may not be aware of this possibility, so again this could lead to some friction.

Sales person:	He's seeing 24% away.
Trader:	I thought you said it wasn't in comp?
Sales person:	It's his prerogative to check our price. We look ridiculous now. I told him we were giving him the best prices we could.
Trader:	This is exotic. I have no idea how the other bank is coming up with their price so if the client wants to trade away he can.
Sales person:	I'm not losing this trade. You're going to need to step up.
Trader:	You're not taking the risk. I am. I'm telling you the price of 25% is a good one. I know different banks have different models for this.

The key issue is that in highly tailored and exotic trades the market maker is making a lot of assumptions about what the fair price is and about what a fair bid–offer spread should be. This is one of the hardest jobs a market maker has because if there is any competition at all it is easy to look way off-market. The more communication between the trader and the sales person in these situations, the less likely it is that friction will result and the better managed the client is.

> A senior sales person in New York was acting as a mentor to a junior sales person. One day, the junior sales person had executed a trade with one of his clients but the client had made a mistake and asked to change the price of the trade by 0.01%. The trader didn't want to move. The junior sales person asked the senior sales person if he could go talk to him. The senior trader on the desk heard the senior sales person asking one of the traders to make this change and got involved. The senior trader started asking the senior sales person, "Do you know what you are asking him to do? Do you know how much this is costing?" Unfortunately, the senior sales person hadn't done his homework on the trade so had no idea what the cost of 0.01% actually was. This infuriated the senior trader, who started shouting. The lesson learned was "know the numbers." Never ask for something from a trader without knowing what the financial impact will be.

Sales Person Stereotypes

While there are some stereotypes that can be made about clients, some stereotypes can also be made about sales people. The two most common stereotypes are the technical sales person and the relationship sales person. Both of these sales people are equally effective but in different ways and in different markets. Most people on the trading floor are familiar with broad macroeconomics as well as the key mechanics of the product on which they work. It would be odd to have a sales person who didn't know how to at least estimate the profit on a trade they had just done with a client. It would be odd for a sales person not to understand what employment numbers meant and how they might affect financial market prices. It would also be odd for a sales person not to understand the significance of earnings being released by major corporates and the impact that that could potentially have on market prices. But some sales people are simply more interested in the more complex and technical discussions than others.

For example, a sales person in equity derivatives might be comfortable with the trader's pricing models and might be able to update pricing on his own instead of constantly bothering the trader. The sales person will have agreed with the trader ahead of time that he will be doing this and will agree what methodology he will use to update prices. He will also double-check his prices with the trader every now and then. Of course, if he is close to trading, he will need to confirm exact pricing with the trader. This is a more technical sales person. He has learned how to use the trader's pricing model. He has demonstrated that he understands the methodology. He is comfortable having the conversation directly with the client and tweaking the structure rather than needing to bring in a structurer or a trader. This is a particular skillset which is very valuable, particularly in derivative products.

On the other hand, there are sales people who are not particularly technical in this way and are more than happy to bring in a structurer or a trader to model and re-price the structure every time a tweak is needed. These sales people are often very skilled in either originating or closing a deal. These are more classic sales skills.

Despite the number of women that work on the trading floor today, it is still an old boy's club. There was a very technical sales person in New York who covered hedge funds. She was also very keen on sports. She had good relationships with the more technical clients and good relationships with the clients who were less technical, primarily because she could talk sports. However, one day, she got a call from the head of the sales desk. He had received a call from one of her clients who wanted a new coverage person. The head of sales was embarrassed because he knew what a good sales person she was and, in particular, he didn't want to have to explain that the client wanted to be covered by a man because he wanted to be taken out to strip clubs.

The skillset required to be a sales person is significantly different from the skillset required to be a trader. A sales role is primarily about relationship management, while the role of the trader is about risk management. One might even say that the role of the trader is about having an iron stomach. In other words, the trader has to take the risk that he makes or loses money on every trade he does for clients. Not everyone can live with that stress. Many market participants would agree that traders as a result get paid more than sales people. However, at the end of the day, the sales person has a skillset that can be used in any company and in any industry, while a trader has very limited career options outside of the trading floor. People often say that the career progression of the trader is to ultimately become a proprietary trader or work in a hedge fund, but that is the top of the pyramid. Also, as previously discussed, not all market makers are good prop traders.

Conclusion

The trading floor is a complex and volatile place. Market prices are constantly moving and most client requests are urgent ones. They want to trade before the market price moves against them. At the same time, the traders have taken on risk by virtue of providing liquidity to clients, so they are busy trying to hedge or close out their positions and manage that risk while sales people are asking for updated market prices or discussing financial market color with them.

Amongst all that, a sales person and a trader have to forge a relationship within the context of the natural tension between the bank and the client. Ultimately, that tension keeps a fair balance between the bank and the client as well as between the trader and the sales person. At the end of the day, the most successful trader–sales person relationships are the ones built on mutual respect and the idea that they are working on the same team while at the same time doing the right thing for the client. Based on some of the revelations that came to light post the 2008–2009 credit crisis about bank relationships with clients, unfortunately it is not always clear that banks even know what the "right thing" is anymore.

Discussion Questions

Is the relationship management or the risk taking more important to a bank?

Why aren't sales points real money?

Why do traders and sales people often have difficult relationships?

Please see www.terriduhon.co for answers and discussion.

CHAPTER 9

What Role Does the Research Analyst Play?

This chapter explores the world of the research analyst on the trading floor. Some trading floors use the term "sales, trading and research" and others merely "sales and trading." Why is a distinction being made? Some banks talk about "revenue generators" vs. everyone else and research can fall inside or outside that space. What is the purpose of the research team? How can one bank consider them revenue generators and other banks not? In particular this chapter will explore what role they play on the trading floor and where their key relationships are. This chapter will also answer questions such as: What is a desk analyst? Who reads the research? Is it biased? Are there conflicts of interest?

One junior research analyst at a large German bank in New York was well known on the trading floor for being incredibly technical. He would spend his time poring over the numbers and writing models to make projections for how a company would perform. As a junior research analyst he didn't cover any particular sector but worked with different research analysts as they needed. One day, he was talking to an investor about a particular company and explaining the numbers. The investor interrupted and said, "That's all very interesting, but what business are they in?" The research analyst was stumped. He knew the financials like the back of his hand but not what the company actually did. He seemed to have a vague idea but couldn't articulate it. The investor said, "The financials all look great, but is this a business that will be around forever?" The research analyst had been so focused on the numbers of the company itself that he hadn't looked at the industry and given some thought to the viability of the business model. The company was a small publisher.

Some trading floors use the terminology "sales, trading and research" and others merely "sales and trading." At the same time, some banks talk about **revenue generators** and **cost centers** and research can fall inside or outside that space. This highlights the difficult role of the research team on the trading floor. Researchers don't cover clients, they don't take risk and they don't create products. They create ideas. Their role is to analyze companies or financial markets and publish reports giving their views. This research is made available to the bank's clients via a combination of email distribution (including bloombergs) and client access to the bank's proprietary section of its website.

Researchers sometimes sit on the trading floor but, similar to the proprietary traders, are supposed to be on the other side of the Chinese wall. Ideally, their research is meant to be the independent views of the individual writing the report and not the views of the bank itself. This means that they are able to say that a company's stock is overvalued and should be sold even at the same time that the bank is working on a big equity issuance for that company. Equally, the bank's traders may have a position in the debt of a company and want to sell it so they can't influence research to publish a report that encourages investors to buy it. That would be considered a conflict of interest.

Research is considered a valuable part of the service that a bank provides to its clients. Researchers are often asked to visit clients and discuss their views on the financial markets or on particular companies by the sales force. They build up reputations for themselves over time and develop a following of investors who rely on their views. A bank wants to have researchers that its clients are interested in following. It helps to make the relationship stronger. Every year different financial publications or industry organizations compile rankings and awards for researchers. These awards and rankings are compiled by surveying the investor base. These top research analysts are highly sought after in the job market and are often poached by the investors who are looking to beef up their asset management team.

Banks are not the only places that have research teams. Asset management firms have research teams to help the asset manager decide where and how to invest. They often produce research reports or investment strategy

TABLE 9.1 Research Classifications

Research Teams	Activities
Analysts	Equity or credit analysts Analyze individual entities
Economists	Regional or global Analyze macroeconomics
Strategists	Product or asset class specific

reports which are not published or made available to the investors in that asset management business. This is called "proprietary strategic research" and is used only to make investment decisions. The research within an asset management business is similar to that of a bank, with one exception. The research within an asset management business is used for the asset managers to make investment decisions themselves, whereas the research within a bank is published, made available for the bank's clients to use to make investment decisions. There are also independent research businesses which only produce research. As that is their main business, they charge a fee for this. Access to that research is restricted to their clients only.

Generally we can say that a bank has three broad areas of research (Table 9.1). The first are the research analysts. They cover the issuers. The equity analysts focus on equity issuers and the credit analysts focus on the debt issuers. The second are the economists. They are looking at the state of the economy globally and by jurisdiction. The third are the strategists. They focus on financial products such as interest rate swaps or equity derivatives. They all make investment recommendations.

The Role of a Credit or Equity Analyst

Credit and equity analysts are generally divided by sector or industry. This is an acknowledgment that different types of businesses operate with different financial targets. A research analyst who analyzes utilities will not necessarily be able to write a report about banks without doing a lot of homework. A generic and broad breakdown of research analysts would be:

- financial services, which includes banks, insurance companies, pension funds and asset managers
- retail, which includes supermarkets and clothing chains

- utilities, which includes electricity, gas and water providers
- telecommunications, media and technology (also called TMT), which includes telephone companies, Internet providers, television companies, media companies and publishers
- industrials (also called cyclicals), which includes chemical companies, manufacturing and paper and packaging
- oil and gas, which includes oil companies, refineries and pipelines
- mining and metals.

Even within these categories there are further breakdowns and specializations. The challenge is that within each different category there are possibly hundreds of companies whose shares or debt trade in the public markets. One research analyst can only cover so many companies in detail. In fact in general they cover between five and 10 companies in detail. Rather than have hundreds of research analysts employed, the bank picks a few key companies in each category on which the research analyst will focus and the research analyst only gives a general view on the rest of the category (Box 9.1) and statistics that are published for each category. They show the key statistics the research analyst thinks are important for that category across all the companies in that category.

Box 9.1   Banking sector example

US bank analyst might cover

- JPMorgan Chase
- Citibank
- Bank of America

European bank analyst might cover

- Deutsche Bank
- Barclays Capital
- UBS

These six banks all have similar global trading platforms, retail businesses, investment banks and lending businesses. But they are headquartered in different regions and they are all huge entities, so two analysts will cover them as a result.

Banks choose the key companies their research analysts focus on based on who their clients are. If a bank operates primarily within the smaller and medium-sized entity space, it means that the new issues that the bank generally sells to its investors are primarily smaller and medium-sized issuers. That bank will focus on the smaller and medium-sized entities. Another bank might have a regional client base of primarily German issuers on which it focuses. The major banks are under pressure to produce research sometimes for hundreds of issuers. The banks ultimately service their key clients and that drives the decision of who their research analysts cover.

A research analyst's job can be broken down into three main activities:

- The first is to do fundamental analysis on a company. This means that the analyst:
  - is looking at the financials of the company: the balance sheet, the cashflow statement and the income statement.
  - reads and analyzes all the public information available about the company, including what the company publishes as well as any other public information sources such as financial media reports.
  - attends company announcements and the annual general meeting held for shareholders and potential shareholders.
  - is often given time by the management of the company to ask questions about strategy and growth prospects. The management within public companies understands the value of having the research analysts understand the strategy and the business. Management will even schedule road shows to meet research analysts and present their earnings or a new strategy.
- The second activity is to understand the competitive landscape of the company. This means to understand how the company measures up to its competitors and where it stands within the industry.
- The third is to understand the impact of macro forces on the industry and how that will shape the company's growth prospects.

Research analysts then use this information to form a view on the company and make an investment recommendation. The analysis, the view and the investment recommendation are then published.

An investment recommendation is generally referred to as **buy, sell or hold**. The idea is that a research analyst will recommend one of three things. A buy recommendation for a stock or bond, which may encourage investors who don't own a particular stock or bond to buy it (Box 9.2). A sell recommendation may encourage investors who own a particular stock or bond to sell it. A hold recommendation is considered neutral. If an investor doesn't already own a particular stock or bond they won't buy it but if they do own it they won't sell it.

Box 9.2   Example of buy recommendation

Explore Commodities (EXP, listed on the Australian stock exchange) is focused on the exploration, evaluation and development of a multi-commodity resource portfolio in Australia. We maintain our BUY recommendation on the stock and 50¢ price target. Current price 10¢.

Box 9.2 is a recommendation to buy a stock issued by the (fictional) company Explore Commodities. The ticker is EXP. A **ticker** is the abbreviated reference to a company whose shares are traded on a stock exchange. The recommendation includes a summary of what the company does and the target price that the research analyst expects the shares to reach. The current price is 10 cents so if the price hits the target, it would mean a five times return for the investor.

Over and above publishing this research, a research analyst's job is to forge relationships. They forge relationships with the companies they analyze. They meet the management. They visit the company and see its operations. (This is where the analyst **kicks the tires**, in other words does due diligence on the company. This is a reference to a new car buyer kicking the tires.) They also forge relationships with the sales people and their investor clients. They visit clients to discuss their new research report and give their views on an industry. They are part of the relationship management for issuers and investors.

The exact analysis and recommendation slightly differs between equity and credit analysts. That difference in focus is a function of the key difference between equity and debt and how investors view those products. Very generally, equity investors are looking for an increase in the value of their investment. They want to buy a share for 10 cents and hold it while it appreciates to 50 cents over a target period of time. Equity investors are looking for growth. The equity analyst is looking to determine how the company is going to grow and increase value for the shareholder.

A fixed income investor on the other hand is possibly looking for some price appreciation, but mostly he is looking for stable income (Table 9.2).

TABLE 9.2 Difference between Equity and Fixed Income Investor

Fixed Income Investor	Equity Investor
Invests $100 in a 5-year Supermart bond with a 4% coupon	Invests $100 in the equity of Supermart
His extreme risk is that Supermart defaults and he doesn't get all his money back	His extreme risk is that Supermart performs terribly and the shares aren't worth anything
His downside is that interest rates go up and he is only earning 4% per annum when he could be earning higher	His downside is that the equity markets don't perform that well and his $100 is now worth $80, for example
His upside is that interest rates go down and he is earning 4% per annum when he could be earning lower	His upside is that the equity markets perform very well and his $100 is now worth $200, for example

He is looking to invest in a bond and receive a coupon in return and get all his money back at maturity. The credit analyst is looking to identify whether the company will be able to pay back the money it has borrowed. He is really looking at whether the company will remain stable over the life of the debt in order to easily pay the coupons over time and the principal back at maturity. So, the credit and the equity analyst look at the same data of the company itself (e.g. the full set of financial statements), but they are producing different results.

Very generally we say that equity investments are about growth and fixed income investments are about stable income. For every generalization there is the exception; mature or blue chip stocks, for example, are less about growth and more about stable dividend, or in other words income. They are often called "income stocks" and are a key investment strategy for pension funds. In fixed income, there are distressed companies whose bonds trade at a huge discount such as a price of 40% instead of closer to 100% and they are similar to equity investments because the investors are not looking for the coupon income: they are looking for a price appreciation.

Equity analysts focus on the equity markets. As mentioned in the earlier chapters of this book, the majority of the focus on the financial markets is on the equity markets. There are hours and hours of commentary and reams and reams of written material on the equity markets. The equity analysts as a result play a very important role in that space. They not only produce some of the reams of written material, which is often quoted in news commentary, but also are often asked to provide live commentary on specific stocks and stock markets in general. The bank benefits from this exposure and generally encourages as much of this as possible for its equity research department.

Credit analysts focus on the debt markets. They are very similar to the equity research teams, with the big exception that they include government entities as a research sector because, while governments don't issue equity, they are large issuers of debt. The credit analyst will also give a trade recommendation similar to the buy, sell or hold recommendation of an equity analyst. However, there are several different products in which an investor can take exposure to a company in the fixed income market as opposed to the equity market because issuers usually issue several different bonds and loans but only one share (Box 9.3).

Box 9.3   Credit analyst recommendation

Pay4calls is a payphone company in the United States with payphones in every major city with populations above one million. While the financials of the company are very stable, we are concerned about the viability of this business model for the long term. We recommend selling the 10-year bonds and buying its 2-year bonds. Short-term BUY, long-term SELL.

Possible M&A activity within a sector will create speculation and similar investment strategies across equity and debt instruments. If there has been a lot of M&A activity in the regional bank sector where larger companies are buying up smaller companies in order to gain a greater market share, both the equity analyst and the credit analyst will recommend buying equity and debt in the smaller companies in that sector.

Due diligence is a crucial part of any investment process. This is normally when an investor visits the company in which they are about to invest and kicks the tires. Once, a large Italian bank was doing a road show to investors in Europe. The Italian bank was looking to sell part of its loan portfolio. The Italian bank would always start its presentation with the statement that it was the oldest bank in Italy. Then it would go on to explain its business model to potential investors. Eventually, one of the investors in London stopped the presentation as soon as the statement was made about the age of the bank and immediately asked with a furrowed brow, "Exactly how old are these loans?" The rest of the road show excluded the point about being the oldest bank in Italy.

Conflict of Interest

One of the big issues around the research analyst role has been the conflict of interest issue. This was a high-profile issue in the late 1990s when there were some questions raised about the fact that a research analyst at a bank had been paid off the back of the fees that the bank made on an initial public offering (IPO) for a client. The research analyst was very well known and his research was well distributed. He had written a buy recommendation for the shares of the IPO. The conflict of interest issue was considered significant in this case due to the very large bonus he was paid which had been attributed to the high-profile IPO. At the time this was an open secret in the financial markets. Every bank about to issue an IPO published buy recommendations for those shares. It was implicitly part of the deal. Today, it is not supposed to be part of the deal and the independence of the equity analysts is <u>supposed</u> to be an important element of their role.

Another conflict of interest issue is front running. When a research analyst is about to publish research that recommends a buy or a sell of a particular stock or bond the trader at the bank should not be positioned to profit from this.

Front running

- Equity analyst is about to publish a buy recommendation for a stock he's had on hold for a year.
- Before he publishes the research, he tells the equity trader to buy some of the stock.
- The trader buys some of the stock at $40 a share.
- The equity analyst publishes his recommendation and the share price rises to $45 off of investors reacting to the report.
- The trader is able to sell his shares at $45 a share and make a $5/share profit.

The Chinese wall is pretty strong between the research analysts and the traders on the trading floor. The traders are careful about what they say to equity and credit analysts particularly if they know the bank is involved in either a debt or equity issuance for a client. At the same time, sales people and traders have regular conversations with the research analysts. They are often solicited for their views by sales people in order to pass on to their clients or by traders who are looking for more color on a particular stock or bond. And as mentioned above, the more well-known research analysts are often invited to meet with clients and present their views.

There is an old story in the financial markets about due diligence. A research analyst for a large bank was doing some due diligence on an oil company. He had decided to visit the company because the financials for the company didn't feel right to him. There was something wrong but he couldn't figure out what it was. He called up the company and asked to visit. They said that was fine. They were always interested in meeting with research analysts. He visited the company and walked around. He looked at the operations and the various assets of the company. One of the assets was a store of oil held in huge tanks. He was brought over to take a look and the equivalent of a dipstick was pulled out of one of the tankers to show him that they were full of oil. Eventually, the research analyst went back to his desk and concluded that everything was fine. He wrote his research report explaining his due diligence visit and giving the company a hold recommendation. Shortly after that, the company went bust. They had been cooking the books and it turns out that those tanks of oil were filled with water and had just enough oil floating on the top to coat the dipstick.

The Economists and Strategists

In addition to the equity and credit analysts who focus on analyzing individual companies, there are the economists and the strategists. The **economists** will give macro investment strategies based on their view of macroeconomics. An example of a macro strategy is to overweight equities and underweight fixed income, and to avoid autos. A **strategist** will give specific investment strategies about financial instruments. An example of a recommendation from a strategist is to buy 2-year equity options and sell 3-month equity options.

The conflict of interest issue still exists for economists and strategists in that their job is not to help the traders distribute the risk on their books. If a trader has a large position which he wants to get rid of, he can't ask the macro strategist to write a report about it. With this in mind, there is a much more open relationship between the traders and the macro strategists as they discuss and debate macro views and trading strategies. Often the traders will suggest trade ideas to the strategist that they have come up with. Remember that a trader is constantly required to take a view on the financial market and the products that he trades in order to make markets for clients.

At the same time, many trading strategies are not only within one product but are often cross product and in some cases are cross asset class. A few examples of different trading strategies are below.

A Fixed Income Trading Strategy

> We expect the ECB to ease for the next several years. We see a short end rally while the long end is unlikely to move significantly for the next year. We recommend buying 2-years and selling 10-years in German government bonds (bunds).

This strategy is about the economic policy of the European Central Bank (ECB). Although Europe doesn't issue "European bonds," the German bunds are considered a proxy for a "European bond." Everyone in the financial markets is aware of and has views on what different governments are doing with their economic policies. It is a constant source of discussion on the trading floors because of the impact it has on the economy and on the financial markets in general. "Easing" means that the government will continue to keep interest rates low to encourage people and entities to borrow money and invest in the economy, which encourages growth. One way to do this is to lend money to European banks in maturities of less than two years in order to encourage more lending. To do this the ECB needs to borrow money in longer maturities, such as 10 years. The result is less supply in two years and more supply in 10 years. The recommendation is to buy 2s and sell 10s.

This type of trade strategy would be something that the majority of institutional investors with a fixed income allocation would consider and possibly implement. This is taking a long and a short position in European government bonds. This strategy would not be considered complex or exotic.

Implementing the fixed income strategy

- Buy €10 million 2-year German bunds at 100.24%
- Sell €10 million 10-year German bunds at 101.46%

Ideal scenario six months later

- 2-year price has increased to 102%
- 10-year price has stayed the same
  Investor profit: $(102\% - 100.24\%) = 1.76\%$ on €10 million
  $= €176k$

Source: This a simplified calculation.

An Equity Trading Strategy

> We expect the US economy to start to show improvement toward the second half of the year. The first half of the year the S&P500 will be range bound and will rally toward the end of the year. Maintain defensive positioning then position for the rally in late summer.

The term "range bound" simply means that while the S&P500 stock index might see some price moves it is unlikely to be significantly different from where it is currently trading today. This strategy would normally include the expected range. The phrase "year-end rally" means that the S&P500 stock index will go higher in the fall so investors should start positioning for the rally around the end of the summer. This means that investors who have this same view should start to build up their long position in US equities in the summer.

Defensive means that the investors may not want to be too long at the moment. While the expectation is for the S&P to be range bound, there is no reason for investors to take excessive risk. The word "maintain" implies that this research report is referring to a previous report which recommended a defensive position. "Defensive" can also mean specific sectors such as utilities, which are considered defensive sectors. These are sectors which investors go long even when other financial market prices aren't expected to improve.

This strategy is a strategy that would be considered or implemented by the majority of institutional investors with an equity allocation in their funds. This strategy is about a choice between investing in the financial markets and holding cash which many investors choose in periods of uncertainty. This means they are not invested in anything while they watch the market price moves and determine their strategy. They will increase the amount they hold in cash and decrease the amount they have invested in equities.

Implementing the equity trade strategy

- Initial cash vs. equity position is 10% cash and 90% long equities.
- Defensive position might be 20% cash and 80% long equities.
- In late summer, the investor can rebalance this to 5% cash and 95% equities if he really believes in the possibility of a year-end rally or share price increase.

Often, the main feature of the trading floor morning meetings is a presentation from one of the research analysts. For government bond traders, for example, it might be an economist, who highlights key data being released that day and reviews the research team's macroeconomic view and the likely market price impact. For equity traders, for example, it might be an equity strategist, who looks at asset management allocations globally and has recently produced a report about equity vs. fixed income allocations.

A trader at a large US bank was talking to another trader at a large Swiss bank. They were both based in New York. They were discussing the financial markets. They disagreed on the financial market direction and made a bet about it. The loser had to shine the shoes of the winner. That Friday, when the financial markets opened, the trader from the Swiss bank showed up at the offices of the US bank with a shoeshine box that he had bought from a shoe shiner on Wall Street. He sat down and shined the shoes of his rival trader. While traders are compulsive gamblers, they do honor their bets.

Desk Analysts

Research analysts are a key resource for both clients and market makers. As mentioned several times, traders need to have a view on the financial market and on their product in particular in order to make markets. Thus, traders are very well versed in the bank's internal research views and recommendations. They use the research to help them assess financial market events and create their own view of the financial market. If the traders at a bank consider that the views of a particular research analyst are very valuable, they will often offer that person a job as a **desk analyst**. That is a research analyst specifically dedicated to working with the trading desk and helping the traders form views on future price moves. This avoids the issue of conflict of interest, because the desk analyst does not publish research (Table 9.3).

To some extent this is a very similar role to moving to an investment fund. They no longer publish their research but their research is used in a similar way to how it would be used with an investment fund. Depending on the research analyst, this can be the ideal career move. Sometimes there are research analysts who would like to have a more direct involvement in the financial markets, and being a desk analyst or working for an asset manager is one way

TABLE 9.3 Desk Analyst vs. Publishing Analyst

Desk Analyst	Publishing Analyst
Produces trade strategies that are for the eyes of the traders on the desk only	Produces research reports which are for distribution to the bank's clients
Rarely, if ever, goes out to meet investor clients	Helps build relationships with investor clients and, as a result, when he produces a new research piece this analyst visits as many investor clients as possible to present the results
Sits on the trading desk with the traders and does not have a conflict of interest as long as the research is not published and distributed	Often doesn't sit on the trading floor, in order to avoid issues of conflict of interest

to do this. In that role, the desk analyst not only gets to continue to analyze the financial markets but also gets to help implement trading strategies.

Obviously, sitting on a trading desk is not exactly the same as working for an asset manager because a market maker's primary role is not to take proprietary trading positions. However, they do have to take a position when a client requests it and so knowing how to price that request and what the hedging strategy should be requires a view on the financial market.

Conclusion

The research function is one that exists in a broad range of financial companies from banks to asset managers to hedge funds. Broadly speaking, their role is to give a view or an opinion on future market price moves in different financial products. A bank's research department is made up of a broad range of abilities and focuses. There are research departments who focus on every asset class, some who focus on individual issuers and some on macro market trends. There are economists who are very technical and others who are more qualitative. There are trained accountants whose expertise is working through the details of the company's financial reports. There are quantitative researchers whose expertise is analyzing esoteric options markets to look for relative value. This produces a huge and diverse amount of research from some of the major global banks.

While a research analyst's job on the face of it is to publish research, he is actually a key resource in the relationship management of the bank's clients. All researchers ultimately build relationships with the bank's investor clients while equity and credit analysts forge relationships with issuer clients as well. At the same time they must all be aware of the conflict of interest issues and the views they express must be derived independently of any position the bank's traders have or wish to take.

Discussion Questions

Why are research teams sometimes called "cost centers"? Is this a fair description?

Is research valuable if it doesn't have a trade recommendation associated with it?

Why do banks produce trade strategy research reports?

What investors in particular benefit from research reports?

Please see www.terriduhon.co for answers and discussion.

CHAPTER 10

What's So Special About Trading Derivatives?

This chapter will distinguish between cash traders and derivatives traders. A cash trader is the general term for a bond or equity trader, in other words a non-derivatives trader. Simply put, the cash trader buys a product, for example a stock or a bond, from one client and then sells the same product to another client or another bank. At the end of that process, the cash trader is left with no residual risk. The derivatives trader, on the other hand, does not have the luxury of no residual risk. A derivatives trader enters into a contract with a client and then tries to replicate the equal but opposite contract with another client or bank. This is generally impossible to do as most clients want something tailored. Even if it were possible, there would be residual risk in the form of cashflows between the bank and the two different entities, which can go on for years. This introduces the concepts of operational risk and counterparty risk. This chapter will continue with the examples started in Chapter 4 and highlight the differences between cash trading and derivatives trading. This chapter will also answer questions such as: Why do cash traders have position mis-matches? Where does counterparty credit risk come from? Is trading derivatives harder than trading cash products?

In the 1980s, there was an extreme divide between the corporate finance business and the global financial markets business. The corporate finance teams were exclusively university graduates from the top universities around the world. The markets people were not university educated but they could do a deal when they saw one. They were known for being rowdy and considered slightly uncouth by the university crowd, but they were respected for being extremely commercial, in other words they could make markets and make money. As derivatives became more popular and the banks started hiring university graduates particularly with math and science degrees to work in those areas, the trading floor environment changed a bit with some entertaining clashes between the old guard and the new. In particular, the old guard on the trading floor referred to this author as "MIT" for the first year as they marveled that it now apparently took a math degree from MIT to do a job they had been doing successfully for years. However, trading floors are the ultimate meritocracy. Make money and you are respected, university degree or not.

The difficulty of interpreting financial market dynamics, making a market and managing the ensuing risk is compounded by the complexities and nuances of individual products. One of the big distinctions that we can make in the financial market is between cash products and derivative products. Cash products are generally thought of as stocks and bonds. This means that a client wants to buy or sell something today and the cash is exchanged against the delivery of that product almost simultaneously either on the same day or within a few days. On the other hand a derivatives trade can have cashflows between the two parties for years. Also, cash products have very little residual risk in a trading book when they are closed out, while derivatives trading books inevitably have residual risk even when they are hedged because there are often cashflows due from one party to another for years. Table 10.1 lists the main differences between cash and derivative products.

One interesting point to note is the exception to the key differences listed in Table 10.1. Exchange traded derivatives are more similar to cash products than they are to over the counter derivatives. The key difference is that cash is not necessarily only exchanged within a few days of the trade: there are still cashflows that need to be exchanged in the future. This chapter will focus on the over the counter derivatives as they make up the bulk of derivatives traded as well as the focus of the bank's trading floor. Remember that of the approximately $700 trillion derivatives contracts outstanding, only around 10% are traded on exchanges (source www.bis.org).

TABLE 10.1 Key Differences between Cash Products and Derivative Products

Cash financial products	Derivative financial products
Stocks and bonds	Forwards, options and swaps
Cash is exchanged for product within a few days	Bilateral contract which represents a series of cashflows in the future
Traders who have positions close out those positions by buying or selling the same product	Traders who have positions hedge those positions by trading another bilateral contract with another counterparty
There is no residual risk once a position has been closed out	There is residual risk for the life of the contract

Bond Intermediation

It is not entirely fair to say that cash trading is as easy as buying from one client and selling the exact same product to another. While the treasury market is considered one of the most liquid financial markets in the world, not all treasuries are the same. The US government regularly issues specific maturities which as soon as they are issued are called "on-the-runs." Typically, they issue according to the schedule outlined in Table 10.2.

As soon as a new treasury is issued, the previous on-the-runs are now off-the-runs. The further and further away from being an on-the-run a treasury is, the less liquidity there is in that bond. When a client says it wants a price in a 2-year, 3-year, 5-year, 7-year, 10-year or 30-year treasury, unless the client specifies otherwise, everyone will assume it is asking for the on-the-run.

The 5-year treasury trader at Megabank could get the phone call that ABC Asset Manager is looking to liquidate some of its older treasuries as it is reallocating its investment portfolio with a heavier equity portion. The treasury trader at Megabank is asked for a bid on an old 30-year that now has five years left to mature.

TABLE 10.2 US Treasury Issuance Calendar

Maturity	Issuance calendar
T-bills (4-week, 13-week, 26-week, 52-week)	These are treasury bonds with a maturity of less than 1 year. There are new issues every week
2-year, 3-year, 5-year, 7-year, 10-year notes and 30-year treasury bonds	These are issued every month

Comparing 30-year and 5-year on-the-run treasuries

Old 30-year treasury

- Issue date: May 15th 1987
- Maturity date: May 15th 2017
- Original issue size: $14.017 billion
- Coupon: 8.75%

5-year on-the-run treasury

- Issue date: Jan 31st 2012
- Maturity date: Jan 31st 2017
- Original issue size: $35.659 billion
- Coupon: 0.875%

The treasury trader has never traded this particular bond before so needs to first look up the details of the bond issue. He's going to want to confirm the coupon, the maturity date and the total size originally issued. He'll speak to the other treasury traders to see whether any of them have ever traded this particular bond before. He'll check with the treasury sales team to see whether there are any clients that might have traded it before. He is really looking for any color on this bond he can find. He needs to know if there's anything about this bond in particular that would make the price different from what the theoretical market price should be. For example, it is possible that this bond is almost entirely owned by one investor and as a result it never trades. Or that this bond has been mostly redeemed by the US government such that there are very few left. These are things to consider and be aware of.

Then, the trader needs to work out what the theoretical market price should be. He figures this out from the fact that the fair price of all treasuries is a function of the current yield. Remember that the current yield of the on-the-run 5-year is 0.77% despite the fact that the coupon is 0.875%. (This calculation is from Chapter 5, Figure 5.2.) To price the old 30-year, we need to know what the current yield on this old 30-year should be. Because treasuries are so liquid and so frequently issued, there are treasuries with maturities from 0 to 30 years that are actively traded. We know what those yields are. For a bond with a maturity that falls between two points, it is easy to **interpolate** the yield. That interpolation will get a yield and that yield will be used to derive a price. Notice that as the maturity of the old 30-year is closer to the on-the-run 5-year than the on-the-run 7-year, the yield of the old-30 is also closer to the yield of the on-the-run 5-year (Box 10.1).

Box 10.1   Interpolation

5-year on-the-run

- Maturity date: Jan 31st 2017
- Current yield: 0.77% (This is the yield that corresponds to the current market price which is easily available on the electronic trading systems.)

Old 30-year treasury

- Maturity date: May 15th 2017
- Interpolated yield: 0.84% (This is the yield that we calculate by interpolating between the yields for the maturities on either side of this bond. We use this yield to determine the price for the bond. Because the yield is so low, and the coupon 8.75% is so high, the price of this bond will be higher than 100%.)

7-year on-the-run

- Maturity date: Jan 31st 2019
- Current yield: 1.27% (This is the yield that corresponds to the current market price which is easily available on the electronic trading systems.)

The treasury trader does some research and some price analysis. He determines that there isn't a lot of trading in this particular bond because it is primarily owned by a handful of asset managers who aren't active traders. They are buy-and-hold investors and they have held these bonds for a long time. Because of when these bonds were issued, the coupon on these bonds is high compared to the 5-year coupons today. The coupon is 8.75% compared to the coupon of the 5-year on-the-runs at 0.875%. This represents significant income generation for these funds.

The trader puts a price on the bond and agrees to buy it from ABC Asset Manager. Now he owns this old 30-year bond which has very little liquidity. He will now need to figure out how to sell the bond on. Because it has little liquidity, it is unlikely to see much trading in the interbank broker market. However, Megabank has several clients that already own this particular bond so he needs to see whether any of them will be interested in buying the $50 million that he just bought. In the meantime, he wants to close out his position. In this case he'll need to hedge the position using another financial product rather than close out the position on the financial product he has. The obvious hedge is to use the liquid on-the-run 5-year to do that. The trader sells $50 million of the on-the-run 5-year. Box 10.2 shows the trader's position.

Box 10.2   Trader position

- Long $50 million old 30-year
- Short $50 million on-the-run 5-year

Now the treasury trader has a position mis-match. The question is how much is this a concern for him? He has priced the old 30-year bond off the back of the price of the on-the-run 5-year. His analysis of the market price dynamics indicates that they should be correlated. Ideally, this means that when the price of the old 30-year goes down the price of the on-the-run 5-year goes down by the same amount. Because he is long the old 30-year, when the price goes down he will lose money, but because he is short the on-the-run 5-year, when the price goes down he will make money.

The Megabank trader made a decision to buy the old 30-year before he knew that he could find a buyer on the other side. He made a decision to take the risk in order to provide liquidity to a client. He knows that his approach to pricing and hedging was entirely market standard so he is not anticipating that he has much risk on his books. The problem is that he is not sure how long it will take to close out his position. He is hedged, but not perfectly — as perfectly would mean the old 30-year isn't on his books anymore.

Prior to the credit crisis, this would have been a relatively easy decision to make, but today this type of risk will be subject to more scrutiny and will require the trader to estimate how long he will have this position on his books. Also he needs to ensure that he puts a price that compensates him for the extra capital he will have to allocate to this position. Thus, his bid–offer spread is a crucial decision.

Derivative Intermediation

In the interest rate swap market, an interest rate swap trader will get a request from Archery Fund. "Where is your market in 5-year interest rate swaps for a few hundred million?" The trader makes a market of 1.05% at 1.07%. This means that he will pay a fixed rate of 1.05% for the next five years or he will receive 1.07% for the next five years in exchange for Libor. Archery Fund has decided to pay fixed on the interest rate swap, so it lifts the offer and agrees to pay Megabank 1.07% per annum in exchange for Libor. Now, Megabank has a contract with Archery Fund for the next five years. Table 10.3 lists the cashflows.

TABLE 10.3 The Interest Rate Swap Cashflows

	Megabank pays	Megabank receives
Start Date	0	0
End year 1	(Libor = 0.93%)*	1.07%
End year 2	(Libor = ?)*	1.07%
End year 3	(Libor = ?)*	1.07%
End year 4	(Libor = ?)*	1.07%
End year 5	(Libor = ?)*	1.07%

Note that when the interest rate swap is traded, we know what the first Libor will be. It is the Libor that was set the morning of the trade date at 11 a.m. in London. We don't yet know what the other Libor rates will be.
* Numbers in parenthesis are payments.

Megabank wants to hedge this trade. This means that it wants to do the opposite transaction. It is receiving fixed from Archery Fund and now needs to pay fixed to another **counterparty**. (Counterparty is the term we use for the two parties in a derivatives contract.) Depending on the client flow that Megabank sees and the market price moves that the interest rate trader anticipates, the trader may decide to hedge some of this trade in the interbank market. He knows that there is interest from another bank in receiving a fixed rate of 1.06% on a few hundred million so he contacts the interbank broker and agrees to pay the fixed rate. The other bank turns out to be Unibank. Now Megabank's cashflows have changed. (See Figure 10.1 and Table 10.4.)

One question that should occur to readers is why Archery didn't trade directly with Unibank. If Unibank were interested in receiving fixed and Archery were interested in paying fixed then they should have just traded with each other, right? Not necessarily. The primary reason for this may have been that Archery didn't ask all the banks for a quote. It may have better

FIGURE 10.1 The hedged cashflows.

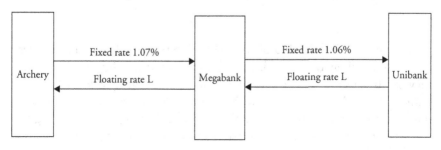

TABLE 10.4 Megabank Cashflows

	Megabank receives from Archery	Megabank pays to Archery	Megabank pays to Unibank	Megabank receives from Unibank
End year 1	1.07%	(Libor = 0.93%)*	(1.06%)*	Libor = 0.93%
End year 2	1.07%	(Libor = ?)*	(1.06%)*	Libor = ?
End year 3	1.07%	(Libor = ?)*	(1.06%)*	Libor = ?
End year 4	1.07%	(Libor = ?)*	(1.06%)*	Libor = ?
End year 5	1.07%	(Libor = ?)*	(1.06%)*	Libor = ?

*Numbers in parenthesis are payments.

relationships with some banks than others and may not have trading lines in place to deal with all the banks. **Trading lines** mean that the counterparties have signed documents allowing them to trade derivatives with each other.

Megabank's profit is the difference between the two sets of cashflows. The Libor cashflows cancel each other out, so Megabank's profit is the difference between the two fixed cashflows. The one caveat is that Megabank will also have to pay an interbank broker fee for doing a trade in the interbank broker market. The interbank broker market acts like a dating service. But when there is a marriage, the broker wants a fee. The conversation might happen along the following lines:

Megabank trader: Where is your market for 5-years?
   Interbank broker: We've got a market of 1.05 to 1.07, but I can probably get one of my guys to meet in the middle. What side are you on?
   Megabank trader: I'm on the bid, but I'm looking to do a quick deal for a few hundred. If you don't have interest immediately, I'm off.
   Interbank broker: Let me come back.

Traders and interbank brokers have an interesting relationship. Traders often don't entirely trust their interbank brokers and are cautious about what they say because it will be interpreted and passed on as general financial market color. A conversation with an interbank broker can be used to influence the market sentiment or market prices. Obviously, influencing the market is not the same as crying wolf, but indicating that Megabank is a buyer (on the bid) in size for a particular product will elicit a range of reactions: traders who might be happy to hit the bid in size as they may have a position they need to move all the way to traders who back off on the offer in the hopes of seeing the market price move wider. There is no guarantee that the market price will react one way or another. Note that this relationship is not significantly different from the relationship between Megabank and its clients.

In the above dialogue, the Megabank trader is basically saying, "If you can trade now, great. Otherwise, there is no trade to do." The interbank broker can interpret this as meaning that Megabank will go to another interbank broker to do the trade or that Megabank possibly has a client with whom it can hedge. It doesn't really matter: the interbank broker only knows that if there is a deal to do he wants to be the one to do it. He immediately speaks to the other interbank broker in his office that has the relationship with the bank that is possibly on the other side. Box 10.3 outlines Megabank's profit on the swap.

Box 10.3   Megabank swap profit

- Swap notional $400 million
- Difference on fixed cashflows of 0.01% between Archery and Unibank trades
- Floating leg cancels out

    0.01% × $400 million = $40,000/annum

The risks that Megabank has for the next five years are counterparty credit risk as well as operational risk. The operational risk is clear. There are cashflows for the next five years that need to be calculated, paid, received and monitored. This is mostly an automated process today but that doesn't mean that things don't still go wrong.

This is a simple example of the financial market intermediation that Megabank provides to its clients. With the exception of the profit, or the 0.01% between the fixed legs of the interest rate swap, the cashflows are exactly the same.

If we take the Supermart example in Figure 10.2, we see a similar situation. Megabank is receiving fixed from Supermart of 3.15% for five years and paying Libor + 2.04% in return. Megabank will hedge that risk by

FIGURE 10.2 Supermart interest rate swap hedge cashflows.

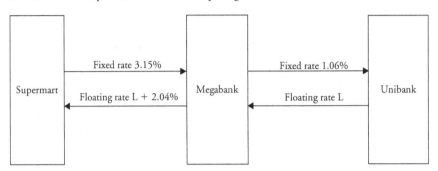

paying fixed and receiving Libor on a market standard interest rate swap. Megabank's hedging options are primarily in the standardized interbank broker market, although it may have enough client flow to hedge some of this with clients. If Megabank decides to do a similar hedge as in Figure 10.1, the cashflows are shown in Figure 10.2.

Here, the cashflows don't really match. If Megabank has done the trade on the same day, the cashflows will occur on the same day and they net to the same amount, but still the cashflows aren't exactly the same. There is 2.04% added to each cashflow with Supermart. (See Box 10.4.)

Box 10.4   Cashflow netting: Simple calculation

- Fixed flows: Megabank receives 3.15% (from Supermart) and pays 1.06% (on the hedge)
  - Net: Megabank receives 2.09%
- Floating flows: Megabank receives Libor (on the hedge) and pays Libor + 2.04% (to Supermart)
  - Net: Megabank pays 2.04%
- Net net: Megabank receives 0.05% each year on the trade notional.

Remember that the Supermart trade was for a $7.5 billion notional so the bid–offer spread is wider, thus the profitability is higher.

Take this scenario one step further and assume that Megabank isn't able to hedge until the next day. One day later it does a trade with Unibank with the cashflows shown in Table 10.5.

TABLE 10.5 Cashflows with One Day Mismatch

	Megabank receives from Supermart	Megabank pays to Supermart	Megabank pays to Unibank	Megabank receives from Unibank
Start Date	0	0	0	0
End year 1	3.15%	(Libor (0.97%) + 2.04% = 3.01%)*	(1.06%)*	Libor = ?
End year 2	3.15%	(Libor + 2.04%)*	(1.06%)*	Libor plus 1 day
End year 3	3.15%	(Libor + 2.04%)*	(1.06%)*	Libor plus 1 day
End year 4	3.15%	(Libor + 2.04%)*	(1.06%)*	Libor plus 1 day
End year 5	3.15%	(Libor + 2.04%)*	(1.06%)*	Libor plus 1 day

*Numbers in parenthesis are payments.

These cashflows look almost exactly the same as the previous scenario's, with one big difference. Libor is set every day based on the banks' willingness to lend to each other. There is no guarantee that Libor on one day will be the same as Libor on the following day. This is now a risk that Megabank needs to manage. It manages this by finding a bank that has the opposite risk, but this will take time and management.

This scenario shows that when a client request is for a tailored product the liquidity providing role that the bank plays is particularly important. In fact, it could be said that over and above providing liquidity the bank is intermediating between tailored trades and standardized trades. The client often doesn't have the expertise to manage this type of risk and thus needs a bank to manage it on its behalf. If Supermart were only able to trade the standardized products, it would end up with cashflow mismatches between its bond and its interest rate swap, which although justifiable are generally not that easy for most people to explain (Figure 10.3).

Often corporates do very basic derivatives hedges and still end up with a lot of questions over why and how they got into a particular trade and express anger at the banks for transacting with them in the first place. A bank needs to be very careful that what it is offering its clients is exactly what those clients want, is a product that is commonly used for the specified purpose and is understood by its clients. At the end of the day it is almost impossible for a bank to confirm that a client totally understands the risks but the bank can establish guidelines for its sales people to follow which gives reasonable comfort that the bank has done the right thing by the client.

FIGURE 10.3 Supermart hedging with market standard product.

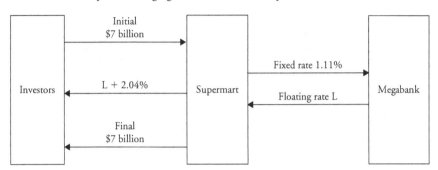

Supermart originally did the interest rate swap with Megabank because it borrowed money with a floating coupon and it was concerned about interest rates going higher. Two years later, the scenario occurs that interest rates have reduced even further. Supermart can see that Libor (L) is now 0.10%. Supermart could have been paying L + 2.04% on its bond and instead it is paying 3.15% to Megabank (Figure 10.2).

If Libor is now 0.10%, then Supermart's coupon payments on its bond would be 2.14% per annum, as long as Libor stays at 0.10%. Instead, they are paying 3.15% to Megabank, which is a difference of 1.01%. On $7.5 billion, this is over $75 million per year for the remaining three years. While questions could be raised over this internally at Supermart, the fact is that Supermart had a view on interest rates that didn't turn out. Supermart decided to hedge according to the view it had at the time it issued the bond.

A junior trader on a derivatives desk was very busy one day with client requests and market prices moving. One of the trades the trader was working on was a cross-currency position that a client wanted to unwind. The client had put on a trade a few years ago, and the value of the trade was positive to the client. The client wanted to realize its profits. Unfortunately, it was a very active trading day so the junior trader modeled up the trade himself. He wasn't able to get anyone else to check his model. He executed the unwind with the client and it turned out that his model was wrong. He overpaid the client by $250,000. This was his first year on the trading desk. He was sure he was going to get fired. The head trader took him aside and told him that everybody gets to make an expensive mistake once. This was his.

Counterparty Credit Risk

Counterparty credit risk exists in any financial transaction which has an exchange of cashflows between the two counterparties to the transaction in the future. The risk is that one of the counterparties defaults at some point in the future and is no longer able to make the payments it is obligated to pay. When trading stocks, bonds and currency, the risk is considered very small because cash is generally exchanged within days of the transaction (Box 10.5). When trading derivatives, the risk is larger because there could be cashflows out to 30 or 50 years in some cases.

Box 10.5   PACAM treasury trade settlement

- Treasury trades exchange cash for treasuries on the day after the trade. We call this T + 1.
- If the PACAM trade was agreed on Monday, the trade would settle on Tuesday.
- If the PACAM trade was agreed on Friday, the trade would settle on Monday.
- The settle is:
  - Megabank delivers $1 billion of 5-year treasuries to PACAM
  - PACAM pays $1,005,312,500 (this is the trade notional of $1 billion times the trade price of 100–17).
  - There are no more cashflows between PACAM and Megabank on this trade.

If PACAM were unable to deliver the cash for the treasuries to Megabank on the next day as detailed in Box 10.5, the trade would fail. If the market price of the treasuries changes from 100–17 to 100–05 the next day and the trade failed, Megabank would have a problem. The Megabank trader thought he sold treasuries at 100–17 on Monday morning. He wanted to close out the position, so he bought some treasuries at 100–16.5 on Monday afternoon. But on Tuesday it turns out he didn't sell the treasuries to PACAM because PACAM didn't have the cash to settle the trade. Now Megabank is long treasuries at 100–16.5 and the market price has moved dramatically on Tuesday to 100–05. Megabank has a loss (Box 10.6).

Box 10.6   Megabank loss post PACAM default

- Megabank sold $1 billion treasuries at 100−17 on Monday.
- Megabank closed out the position by buying $1 billion treasuries at 100−16.5 on Monday.
- PACAM fails to deliver the cash on Tuesday.
- On Tuesday, after the fail, Megabank has to close out the original close out trade by selling $1 billion treasuries at 100−05, which is the current market price.
- Cost: 100−16.5 minus 100−05 = 11.5/32nd of 1% of $1 billion = $3.5 million LOSS.

Derivatives, on the other hand, are not considered cash products. Here we are talking about swaps, forwards and options (Table 10.6). They are contracts which have an exchange of cashflows between the two counterparties in the future.

In the Archery trade (Figure 10.1), the interest rate swap trade done at 1.07% was a fair market rate for a 5-year interest rate swap. Two years after the trade was executed, there are still three years of cashflows left to exchange. Focusing only on the Archery trade, Table 10.7 shows the cashflows still left to exchange.

These cashflows look like a simple 3-year interest rate swap. Today, (two years after the trade was executed) the market price of 3-year interest rate swaps is 0.89%. We can see that Megabank is receiving a higher amount on the fixed leg of the old 5-year swap and has what is called a positive mark to market. Mark to market is the process of calculating the

TABLE 10.6   Future Cashflows for the Three Different Derivatives

Product	Cashflows
Swaps	There is no initial exchange of principal but an exchange of cashflows for 1 year out to 30 years. Most common are 2 to 10 years
Options	There is an initial exchange of the option premium, then a final exchange of the option payout at maturity, which can be 1 week to 10 years. Most option maturities are 3 months to 1 year
Forwards	There is no initial exchange of cashflows but a final exchange at the maturity, which can be 3 months to 10 years. Most common are 3 months to 2 years

TABLE 10.7 The Remaining Cashflows for the Last Three Years of the Interest Rate Swap

	Megabank pays	Megabank receives
End year 3	(Libor = 0.5%)*	1.07%
End year 4	(Libor = ?)*	1.07%
End year 5	(Libor = ?)*	1.07%

*Numbers in parenthesis are payments.

current market price or current market valuation of a financial product. Mark to market for a stock or a bond is simply looking at the current market price of that stock or bond today compared to where the stock or bond was originally traded. The mark to market is a profit or loss calculation using current market prices. It is a little more complex for a derivative but the concept is the same. We can calculate that mark to market (Box 10.7).

Box 10.7   Megabank mark to market calculation

- Swap notional $400 million
- Difference on fixed cashflows of 0.18%:
  1.07% (original trade fixed rate) − 0.89% (current 3-year interest rate swap fixed rate)
  0.18% × $400 million = $720,000/annum
- Over three years this is a gain of $2.16 million.

This is a simplified calculation.

Derivatives are often called a "zero sum game." This means that if one counterparty makes money another counterparty loses money. So, if Megabank has a positive mark to market (also called a **valuation**) of the interest rate swap of $2.16 million, then Archery will have a negative mark to market of an equal but opposite amount. Megabank has a hedged position, though, so while the trade with Archery has a positive mark to market the trade with Unibank has a negative mark to market of *almost* equal and opposite amounts. The difference is that Megabank has net made a profit on these two trades (Box 10.8).

Box 10.8   Megabank net valuation

Mark to market calculation

- Archery trade: difference on fixed cashflows of 0.18% (1.07% − 0.89%), POSITIVE mark to market

    0.18% × $400 million = $720,000/annum

    - Over 3 years this is a gain of $2.16 million
- Unibank trade: difference on fixed cashflows of −0.17% (0.89% − 1.06%), NEGATIVE mark to market

    −0.17% × $400 million = −$680,000/annum

    - Over three years this is a loss of $2.04 million

      Net: $2.16 million − $2.04 million = $120,000

    Megabank still has the profit from the 0.01% difference for the remaining three years of $120,000.

    This is a simplified calculation.

The net result is that Megabank has equal and opposite positions (ignoring the profit Megabank made between the two trades) and is considered hedged (also called market neutral) in this scenario (Figure 10.1). The risk it does have is counterparty credit risk. This comes about if one of the counterparties defaults and is no longer able to make the payments in the interest rate swap to Megabank. Megabank will not be able to replace the exact same cashflows.

Megabank has hedged the trade with Archery by doing another swap with Unibank. This is called market neutral because as interest rate swap market prices move Megabank will lose money on one side but make money on the other side. The remaining risk to Megabank is that either Archery or Unibank has a default and can't continue to make the remaining payments on the interest rate swap that are due.

For example, if Archery defaults two years after the trade is done, Megabank will be able to do a trade where it receives 0.89% fixed for the remaining three years, because 0.89% is the current market price for 3-year swaps but this is not the same as receiving 1.07% for three years (Figure 10.4). This is called "counterparty credit risk." This is the risk that the counterparty defaults when the trade is **in the money**. (This is when the mark to market is positive to the bank as opposed to **out of the money**,

FIGURE 10.4 Megabank new hedge position.

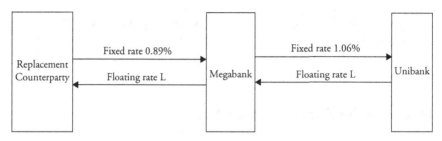

which is a negative mark to market.) These are huge risks for banks to manage and they require a lot of analysis and capital to manage properly.

When Archery has a default, Megabank is still paying a fixed rate to Unibank of 1.06% for the remaining three years of the swap. Megabank has risk on this position and so has to hedge. The hedge Megabank can do is a 3-year swap at the current market price, which is 0.89% (Figure 10.4). The Megabank loss is the difference between paying 1.06% and receiving 0.89%. However, because interest rates can go up as well as down, it could also be the case that Archery had a default when interest rates have gone up to 1.50%, for example. If that is the case, when Megabank hedges the Unibank trade for the remaining three years with a fixed rate of 1.50%, Megabank will *make* money. This is not a free lunch for Megabank. This money will be owed to the administrator of the Archery bankruptcy.

While both cash products and derivative products have counterparty credit risk, the bulk of this risk derives from the derivatives trading books because settlement in cash trades is generally within a few days. It is easier to identify counterparties who are within days of a default than it is to identify counterparties who default in a few years' time. Banks don't generally trade with counterparties who are so distressed that it is likely that they will default within a few days.

Cash traders and derivatives traders have a natural rivalry on the trading floor similar to the rivalry between the bankers and the market individuals. It's a friendly rivalry which goes along the following lines: cash traders think the derivatives traders are nerdy geeks who are only interested in their models, and derivatives traders think the cash traders are monkeys because anyone can buy or sell a cash product. Neither of the accusations is true, of course, but it's fun to have a friendly rivalry. According to one derivatives person in London, his view of the cash traders was that they seemed to spend all day at the pub and then went home at 3 p.m.

Illiquid Derivatives Intermediation

The equity option that is embedded in the equity structured product example from Chapter 4 is considered a standardized equity option. Normally, we say that in the case of a standardized derivative making a market is about understanding financial market dynamics and knowing at what price a hedge can be executed. However, while this option is standardized, it is not liquid, which means there is not a price that is being quoted in the interbank market for this option.

If there is not a visible traded market in a product, then that product's price must be a function of another more liquid or more standardized product. The idea is that if a relationship exists between the tailored derivative and the standardized derivative then we can price and hedge the tailored derivative. To some extent this is what we did in the old 30-year trade. The trader determined that there was a relationship between the on-the-run 5-years, the more liquid product, and the old 30-year, the illiquid product, and as a result was able to price, trade and hedge the old 30-year.

There are billions of short-dated FTSE 100 options that trade every day. **Short-dated** means a maturity between three months and one year. A 5-year FTSE 100 option maturity is much harder to price because it doesn't trade on an exchange and it is rarely quoted in the interbank broker market. This makes it very illiquid and thus harder to hedge but not impossible. When a derivative is very illiquid and there is not a market price for that derivative, the trader needs to determine first how he will hedge the derivative. The cost of that hedge will then determine how the trader will price the derivative. Table 10.8 compares illiquid options with standardized ones.

An equity index option price is theoretically a function of the price of the index and the price of other more liquid options on the same equity index. Thus, the hedge for this option is for the trader to do some equity index trades and some shorter-dated equity options trades. The trader will use a model to determine what amount of each of those products he will use to hedge.

It is very common for banks to price and trade products that don't trade in exchanges or in interbank broker markets. They do this because a client

TABLE 10.8 Illiquid vs. Standardized Option

Illiquid Option	Standardized Option
Maturity greater than two years Note this depends on which equity index is being quoted	Maturity less than two years Note this depends on which equity index is being quoted
Not quoted on an exchange	Quoted on an exchange for benchmark maturities
Not quoted in the interbank broker market	Quoted on the interbank broker market for non-benchmark maturities
Priced primarily as a function of the hedges	Priced based primarily on supply and demand

has requested it or because they know there is client demand for it, as in the equity structured product example from Chapter 4. However, a bank will have this trade and its imperfect hedges on their trading books for the life of the trade because there is no way for them to perfectly hedge the trade.

If the Megabank equity trader could hedge this product exactly, he would have a similar result of our first interest rate swap scenario. He would have a trade with the structured bond on the one hand and a trade with a bank on the other. He would still be sitting in the middle of the two trades for the next five years (Figure 10.5). This would still entail operation and counterparty credit risk, which would need to be considered and managed.

It is unlikely that this equity option trade could be hedged as illustrated in Figure 10.5 with another bank because another bank's trader would likely put the same price that the Megabank trader would put on it. In which case, what would Megabank's added value be? If Megabank wants to simply pass the risk on to another bank, then the profitability of the equity portion of the trade will be passed directly to another bank. The structuring team would not want to do a transaction in which the Megabank trader would give up some profitability to another bank.

Megabank wants to price and hedge this risk itself in order to retain more profit. This means that it needs to know what standard liquid products there are in the equity markets to use for pricing and hedging. It then needs to figure out what relationship the illiquid equity option has to the standard equity options which trade. Because the equity options market is relatively well developed, there are some market standard relationships and models that exist that help Megabank to think about the price and the hedge for this option. As the option is a function of both the standard option products as

FIGURE 10.5   Megabank sitting in the middle of a perfect hedge.

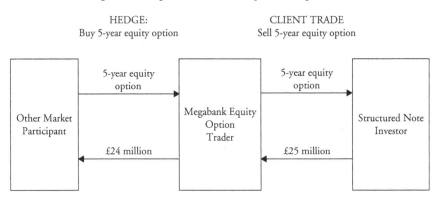

well as the FTSE 100 index, the hedge will be a combination of both of these products.

This leaves Megabank with a position that needs to be considered and possibly re-hedged every day. Products such as options are complex products to manage in the long run because the hedge relationship changes over time, as do market prices. The more technical term for this is that the relationship between the financial product and the hedge is **non-linear**. Most financial relationships are non-linear but options in particular have this feature and are thus more complex to price, trade and manage over time. Of course, if it were possible to buy one option and sell the exact same option to another counterparty that level of complexity goes away. But, the value added of Megabank as a liquidity provider is that Megabank can offer products that are tailored to what clients need or want. Megabank then has the ability to manage that tailored risk against the more liquid standardized products.

The issue that this brings up is the issue of model risk and capital usage. Capital usage is clear. It takes more capital to hold positions that are not perfectly hedged and to re-balance hedges throughout the life of the trade. The amount of capital to allocate is a function of how comfortable Megabank is with the model risk. In other words, how good is the hedge that the model determines? We generally say the model is as good as the assumptions we put into it.

Conclusion

Different products and different markets create different complexities for a bank. One broad distinction we can make is between cash products and derivative products. The key differences to highlight are counterparty credit risk and operational risk. While both products have these risks, they are minimal in cash products and monumental in derivative products.

Another distinction we can make is between liquid and illiquid products. The more liquid the product, the less the trader struggles to price and hedge his position. The less liquid, the more the trader is relying upon a model to help him determine what the right price and hedge might be. This is the same across cash and derivative products. The one distinction to make is that over and above illiquid is the issue of tailoring in the derivatives world. The more tailored the financial product is, the more complex the pricing model is and thus the more complex the hedging strategy is.

While we say that banks provide liquidity to their clients, this description is too simplified for some financial products, tailored derivatives and illiquid products in particular. Banks often provide liquidity in derivatives by intermediating between tailored derivatives for clients and standardized derivatives which banks use to hedge. Banks provide liquidity in illiquid products, such as the 30-year treasury or the 5-year equity index option, by intermediating between the illiquid product and the liquid products which they use to hedge. Note that tailored derivatives are also by definition illiquid products because they are often designed for one client only.

A broad generalization can be made: the more liquid the product, the tighter the bid–offer spread, the easier to hedge, the less risk to the bank and so the less money to be made by the bank. And of course the opposite is also true. If we focus on the last point – the more risk to the bank, the more money to be made by the bank – we see the key relationship that is often forgotten between risk and return. A bank takes more risk in derivative products, illiquid products and tailored products and as a result should make more money on those trades. However, because the risk can be difficult to quantify, sometimes the bank ends up with more risk than it bargained for.

Discussion Questions

Is trading derivatives harder than trading cash products?
Why don't cash products have significant counterparty credit risk?
Why does a bank take more risk in an illiquid market?
Why is the size of the bid–offer spread an indication of an illiquid market? What else can it be an indication of?

Please see www.terriduhon.co for answers and discussion.

CHAPTER 11

Where Does Structuring Fit?

This chapter will explore the obscure world of the structurer. This is a difficult position to capture because it can involve so many different responsibilities depending on the asset class and the bank. The role of a structurer, on the whole, only comes into play in tailored derivatives or structured products. The structurer sits between the trading desk and the sales person and takes a bunch of constraints (what the client wants to do, what the trader wants to do, the legal framework, rating requirements, tax framework and accounting framework) and tries to find a product that fits and still makes money for the bank. This chapter will use the equity structured product example from Chapter 4 to expand on the role of a structurer and his ability to take a bunch of moving parts and create a product at the end. This chapter will also answer questions such as: What makes a deal happen? Who is more technical: the trader or the structurer?

In the harsh trading floor environment, there are individuals who are identified as highly valuable but also a little more sensitive than others. Contrary to the immediate assumption that these individuals might be bullied, they are often protected from the more aggressive behavior of the trading floor. One such individual, let's call him Kevin, was an incredibly nice and incredibly smart structurer on the trading floor of a US bank. He would help anyone who asked and would slowly explain certain products or risks to them as necessary. He was also incredibly gentle in his overall behavior. One day, the structuring team was trying to get a deal done and was frantic as a result. One individual asked Kevin to fix a problem with a spreadsheet. Kevin didn't do it quickly enough to suit that individual and Kevin received a barrage of shouting as a result. The stress was too much and Kevin burst into tears. The head of the desk had a fit. He unleashed a barrage of his own at the individual responsible, which ended with the words: "No one makes Kevin cry!"

The role of a structurer, on the whole, only comes into play in tailored derivatives or structured products. Sometimes these products are driven by the client; at other times they are originally driven by the potential profit the bank sees in the product. In either case, the structurer is responsible for pulling together all the different pieces and determining whether a deal can actually be done. In some cases the constraints are overwhelming and don't always lead to a deal being done. The structurer can negotiate with the different parties to find a compromise in some cases, but in others a deal often doesn't happen, despite what can be months of work. The big problem is that a change in one area can affect another area, which then needs to be re-negotiated or re-configured. The process that a structurer follows is an iterative one in which the structurer's goal is to get a deal done. Sometimes, by the time the deal finally happens, the deal has changed so much that the original driver is no longer applicable.

Most structured products are not this complicated. The equity structured product example used in Chapter 4 is an example of a common and relatively simple structured product (it is reproduced later in this chapter as Figure 11.1). The process of getting a deal like that done can be a long one, primarily due to a complex compliance procedure to sell to retail. But generally that is a matter of time and effort rather than struggling to get all the pieces to fit together.

The Deal Origination

Tailored derivatives or structured products are often driven by a particular need on the part of the client. Tailored derivatives are often traded with clients such as corporates who have specific financial risk to manage, such as long-term currency risk or an interest rate mismatch. The banks provide a very important role in intermediating between the tailored derivative and the standard derivative product. In these cases the client rather than the bank is generally the driver of the transaction because it is a specific risk that the client needs to manage.

TABLE 11.1 Structured Product Bond Compared to a Standard Bond

Structured Product	Standard Bond
Coupon is 5% per annum as long as Gold price is above $1,500/oz OR Coupon is 2% unless the S&P500 goes below 1,000, in which case the coupon is 1%	2% fixed rate per annum (fixed coupon) OR Libor + 1% per annum (floating coupon)
Arranged by a bank for an investor	Arranged by a bank for an issuer
Not traded by any bank other than the arranging bank	Traded by several other banks

Structured product is a term generally associated with a bond which has a tailored derivative embedded in it that is created by a bank specifically for an investment profile which a client desires (Table 11.1). In the case of institutional investors, the origination of the structured product could work both ways. The institutional investor may do a **reverse enquiry**, which is when the investor asks the bank to create something for him. Or the bank puts together a presentation with a structured product idea and sells it to an investor. In the case of retail investors, the origination of the structured product is almost always driven by the bank putting a product together and selling to the retail investors. The difference is that often a structured product sold to institutional investors may be put together for one investor only, whereas the structured product put together for retail may go to hundreds of different retail investors.

When the bank drives the product origination, the seed is that someone on the trading floor has an idea of a product that suits a particular financial market view. This could be a sales person whose client has just expressed a particular view or a trader who has this view himself or a structurer who is looking for new ideas. So the following conversation could occur:

Equity structurer: I've been looking at the FTSE 100 and thinking about financial market sentiment right now. I think retail investors are still interested in guarantee structures. They are nervous about their pensions right now and there isn't a lot of return with deposits now that interest rates are so low. Also, this market has to improve over the next five years. The FTSE 100 is 5,000 today; if we give the investor a real kicker if the FTSE 100 hits something like 8,000 in five years' time, I think we can sell it.

Equity options trader: OK. That makes sense. How much can you spend? I'll think about what option might be the most interesting.

Equity structurer: I can spend about 17% up front, but I need to get some updated funding prices.

The question "How much can you spend?" is a direct reference to the cost of the zero coupon bond that Megabank will issue for this structured product. From Chapter 4, we know that Megabank will borrow £166 million and pay back £200 million at maturity in five years' time. If we sell the bond for £200 million to investors and only spend £166 million on the zero coupon bond, which is 83% of the notional, then we can spend the other 17% on buying an equity option.

The equity options trader knows that 17% up front will include the profitability to Megabank, so whatever option he chooses needs to have a price below 17% so that Megabank can make a profit. He also knows that for a 5-year retail product Megabank does not allow a profit higher than 5%, so the option mid-market needs to be 12% or higher.

This situation is relatively common. It is in everyone's interest on the trading floor to do more business. So, everyone will be interested to hear about a new idea. The structurer in particular needs to continually think about new ideas because if there isn't any reverse enquiry business at the moment he doesn't have much to do and at the end of the day won't get paid that much. The equity options trader is happy to help out because he gets to do a trade and make some profit as a result. He is generally especially interested in putting together a few ideas for which option might suit because he will try to choose an option that suits his current position. He will also try to pick an option that isn't too exotic and thus won't add too much risk to his book.

The structurer is trying to understand financial market sentiment so that he can identify what might incentivize investors to buy Megabank's product. Clearly, he can look at what other banks are selling to their retail investors. But there may not be another product being sold to retail at the moment or the product that's popular with retail is one that Megabank has decided it doesn't want to do for some reason.

Working on the trading floor can be an intense experience. It is normally a minimum of 12 hours a day five days a week. Most people eat lunch at their desk and very rarely leave the office during the day. There are no dividers between desks, so people are in constant communication with other people on the same desk. One structuring team had worked together for years. The members of the team sat next to each other every day and rarely left the office for meetings. One night, there was a team dinner in London and the discussion was around partners and marriage. In the discussion, one team member turned to another and asked, "So are you ever going to get serious with your girlfriend?" Everyone was aware that this person had been dating someone for a while but weren't even aware of her name at that point. The response was, "We're getting married next week." There was amazement around the table. After sitting next to each other for the vast majority of the waking hours in the week, the rest of the team wasn't even aware that one of their members was getting married in a matter of days.

Deal Negotiation

While the equity options trader is looking for an ideal options structure, the structurer goes to talk to the funding team. Even if the equity trader had originally come up with the idea, the role of the structurer is to make a deal happen if there is one to do. So he needs to do the legwork to pull all the pieces together. Because this is not the first structured bond that Megabank is selling to retail, there isn't any reason for the structurer to physically go to the funding department. He should already know the person he needs to speak to. He can either send a junior structurer to the funding department to get some updates which will allow the junior to start to develop a relationship with the funding department or he just makes a quick call or sends an email. Regardless, the information exchange is along the following lines:

Equity structurer: We're looking at another guaranteed bond in UK pounds. I need to get some updated prices from you. Any axes or any restrictions I should know about?

Funding desk: I've emailed you our current pricing grid (Box 11.1). We're axed to fund in the 5- to 10-year maturity. We're not keen on the 2- or 3-year maturity right now. If you do anything under 400, you can use the prices I've sent and anything over that we need to discuss. We've decided that anything under 50 is a no-go.

Box 11.1   Funding desk's current pricing grid

Megabank's fixed coupon borrowing curve

   2 years: 2.80%
   3 years: 3.40%
   5 years: 4.00%
   7 years: 4.25%
   10 years: 5.40%

The equity structurer has not told the funding desk what product he's looking to do in detail. The funding desk doesn't need that information. All the funding desk needs to know is that another deal is on the way that will entail Megabank borrowing some money. Based on the current pricing grid, the funding desk will borrow between £50 million and £400 million at 4% per annum for five years. However, the structure needs a zero coupon bond so he needs to figure out what the cashflows would be for a 5-year zero coupon bond where Megabank effectively pays 4% per annum. From Chapter 4, Table 4.9, we know that this translates into borrowing 83% up front and re-paying 100% at maturity in five years' time.

The structurer then confirms with the equity options trader that he can spend up to 17% up front, including the profitability to Megabank. The equity options trader then comes back with the idea shown in Box 11.2.

Box 11.2   Equity options trader's option idea

The FTSE 100 is at 5,000 today.

The option notional is £200 million.

The investor pays 13% of the notional amount of the trade as the cost of the option. This is equal to a cost of £26 million for the option.

At the maturity of the option, if the FTSE is at or above 7,000, the investor receives a 50% payout from the bank. If the FTSE is below 7,000, the investor receives nothing.

Example:

- FTSE 100 at maturity: 7,000
- FTSE 100 return: 40% (5,000 to 7,000)
- Investor receives a payout of 50% or £100 million.

The structurer and the trader have a discussion and they decide to go with it. The structurer now needs to speak to the head of retail distribution and determine whether the head of retail distribution thinks his team can distribute this product. He didn't go to this person before because he didn't know what the numbers were. He merely had an idea. He needed to have some concrete returns to pitch to the head of distribution. The conversation goes along the following lines:

Structurer: I've put together this structured product which is guaranteed and gives investors a 50% payout in five years' time if the FTSE 100 is above 7,000. It's a zero coupon, and we'll provide secondary market making to investors over the life of the product. What do you think?

Head of retail distribution: Well, I think this is the right time to do this trade. We haven't had a lot of product to distribute in the last few years and most clients have a very conservative risk profile. In this low interest rate environment I think this will be appealing. How soon do you think you can get this ready?

With the support of the head of distribution, the structurer has now ticked all the business head boxes and needs to go through the retail distribution compliance process. He puts together a "term sheet," which will have all the key details of the transaction as well as all the risk factors and disclaimers, and sends it to the compliance department. Compliance reviews it and decides that with a few tweaks to the document the transaction can be approved.

This whole process has taken one or two weeks. The initial conversations with the trader, the funding and distribution teams could have been done in one or two days. The compliance process will likely have taken up to a week or more depending on how complex the structure is and whether something like this has been done before. In the meantime, the structurer has been agreeing indicative timelines with the head of retail distribution for educating the retail sales force, distributing the term sheets to potential investors and the commencement and closure of the subscription process.

As soon as the structurer gets the approval from compliance, he gets updated pricing from the equity options trader as well as the funding desk. Unfortunately, he gets some surprising news from the equity options desk. Equity options are suddenly more expensive. The structure he was talking about now costs 20% rather than 13% because market prices have moved.

So he goes straight to the equity options trader and they discuss what they can do. They decide to tweak the option structure a bit. Instead of the original idea, they will pay the investor whatever the return on the FTSE 100 is above 5,000. This will allow them to do a deal and it still sounds attractive to the retail investor. The structurer now needs to go and confirm this with the head of retail distribution, who isn't so sure about the trade anymore. To him, it sounds like a major change (Table 11.2).

The structurer goes back to the equity options trader to see what else they can do. The structurer asks the equity options trader to price up some other options. The structurer is trying to find a compromise. The trader prices up some alternatives but they are all too expensive. The structurer asks the trader to come up with some other alternatives and at the same time the structurer goes back to the funding desk to see whether there is any movement on the funding side. He will also go back to the head of retail distribution and ask him to really think about what deal needs to get done.

This process could iterate for weeks while each side moves a little and ultimately everyone is happy that the right deal is going to be done. While that is happening, the market prices continue to move. This makes these deals constantly moving targets. Both Megabank's funding prices and the

TABLE 11.2 Summary of Change

Original Equity Options Proposal	New Equity Options Proposal
The FTSE 100 is at 5,000 today	The FTSE 100 is at 5,000 today
The investor pays 13% (this is now 20%) of the notional amount of the trade as the cost of the option. The investor pays the bank £26 million (this is now £40 million) for the option on a £200 million structured product	The investor pays 12.5% of the notional amount of the trade as the cost of the option. The investor pays the bank £25 million for the option on a £200 million structured product
At the maturity of the option, if the FTSE is at or above 7,000, the investor receives a 50% payout from the bank. If the FTSE is below 7,000, the investor receives nothing	At the maturity of the option, if the FTSE is at or above 5,000, the investor receives the exact return of the FTSE as the payout from the bank. If the FTSE is below 5,000, the investor receives nothing
Example: FTSE 100 at maturity: 7,000 FTSE 100 return: (7,000 − 5,000)/5,000 = 40% Investor receives a payout of 50% or £100 million	Example: FTSE 100 at maturity: 7,000 FTSE 100 return: (7,000 − 5,000)/5,000 = 40% Investor receives a payout of 40% or £100 million

price of the option will be moving. If it turns out that the deal simply won't work, then the deal simply won't work. But this deal originally had enough profit to justify it and interest from the head of retail distribution, so the structurer wants to see whether he can make it happen. In the midst of all this, the structurer can decide to reduce the amount of profits to Megabank in an effort to get a deal done. Megabank will have a minimum profitability to do any trade. The structurer can discuss the profitability with the head of structuring and decide whether he can move on that.

> Finally, in this scenario, the structurer manages to convince the head of retail distribution that this new structure makes sense. He says: "The previous structure only paid out if the FTSE 100 went above 7,000. Given the market environment, there is a chance that this won't happen. This current structure pays out for any move above 5,000. We have to expect some price appreciation over the next five years . . . we just don't know how much. The investors will get some return in this new structure. The other structure had a payoff which sounded big but was by no means definite. Also, the other structure is much more exotic than the current one. That means we as a bank take slightly less risk to get this deal done." Figure 11.1 illustrates the full trade.

The structurer then gets final approval from the compliance department and confirms that the deal is a go with the options trader and the funding desk. They have been made aware that they will be asked to hold the prices for the next few weeks while the retail sales team is given training in the product, the term sheets are sent to potential investors and the phone calls are made.

These trades are interesting because there is a generally acknowledged maximum amount of profit that can be made per annum on trades that are

FIGURE 11.1 Structure overview.

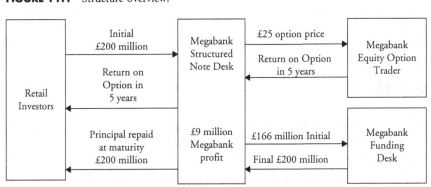

distributed to retail. Megabank has decided that 1% per annum is a good rule of thumb. This ensures that different parts of the bank are not being too greedy and trying to make more money on the trade than appropriate. What does this really mean? There is not a visible market for these products so it is hard to determine whether the bank is making a fair price on them. These products are also going to retail, which will not know how to analyze the price and determine whether it has been given a fair product. In a country where these products are very common, the pressure will be on a bank to make its products more attractive than other banks'. This will put some pressure on the profitability of the transactions and ensure some amount of fair pricing to the retail investor. In a country where there is less competition, the retail investor ultimately relies upon the financial regulator to ensure that he is getting a fair deal. Unfortunately, this is a subjective concept, so it is hard to set a guideline. While the investor is taking some risk, so is the bank and it needs to be compensated for this.

One of the benefits of working on the trading floor compared to working in corporate finance is that trading floor hours are generally restricted to 12-hour or maybe 14-hour days five days a week. This is in contrast to the corporate finance new hires, who are famous for pulling all-nighters and working weekends on a regular basis. However, every now and then there is a transaction that requires a little more work (from the structuring team in particular). One structuring team on the trading floor in New York had spent the night working on closing a large deal and was exhausted by 6 a.m. when people started to arrive on the trading floor for work the next morning. The structuring team decided to take turns sleeping 30 minutes on the couch in one of the offices on the trading floor. Unfortunately, this was quickly rejected when one of the senior managers on the floor said it was unprofessional to have people sleeping in view of possible visitors to the trading floor. The structurers were stunned. They had just spent the whole night working and needed to continue through the day but weren't allowed to take a nap.

Deal Closing

While the retail distribution team is building up an order book, the structurer is working on putting the rest of the deal together. This primarily entails liaising with the legal team, both internal and external, to get the final set of documents together and approved by all connected parties.

The starting point for the set of documents is most likely a previous deal that has been done that is similar. The structurer can easily go through a previous set of documents and update it to reflect the current deal. Then he sends an email with this draft to all relevant parties for them to review. This means that the equity options trader will need to check the terms of the equity option and confirm that they are documented properly. The funding desk will need to check the terms of the borrowing and confirm that they are correct. The accounting and tax teams will confirm that there are no issues with the structure from their perspectives. The internal legal department will need to check that the framework of the document is correct and the external legal department will also work through the entire document and make sure every issue has been considered.

Many snags might occur in this area. For example, the equity options trader may notice that the terms that the structurer put in for the equity option are missing some key definitions and need to be added. The funding desk may have made some updates to the funding documentation; these will have to be added. The legal department has updated the risk and disclaimer section and that needs to be updated. The tax law has changed and requires the tax lawyers to add a few paragraphs and delete some old paragraphs. These changes may be managed by the structurer or by the internal or external lawyers. It depends on precedent within the bank and the team.

A final set of documents will be circulated to all the previous parties as well as the head of retail distribution. At this point there shouldn't be any major changes. All the interested parties give their official approval of the documentation and wait for the final notional amount of the deal to be confirmed. When the subscription process is over, the head of retail distribution will confirm the notional amount with the structurer, who will send that information to the equity options trader and the funding department and confirm that the deal has been done. He will also send that information to all the other interested parties. The lawyers will update the documentation, send out one final draft in case there are any outstanding issues and then circulate the final set of documents for signature. The key signatures are the equity options trader's and the funding department's. Once those signatures are made, the final set of documents is circulated and filed electronically.

The deal is not yet officially done, although the documentation is signed, but the equity trader and the funding desk now assume they have risk which they need to manage. The reason the deal is not officially done is that the cash still needs to change hands and the ownership of the structured bond by the retail investors needs to be recognized. At that point the deal is officially done. However, this is a 5-year deal, and at any point the retail investors may want to sell their investment back to Megabank, so while everyone at Megabank is happy that a deal has gotten done, they all know that they could get a call at any point in the next five years which will require some work on their part to buy back the product they just sold.

The retail investor has bought a bond with an initial price of 100%. But over time, the value of that bond will change as the funding rate for Megabank changes or as the value of the equity option changes. If a retail investor comes back in a year and asks to sell his investment back to Megabank, the equity options trader will then need to buy back the option and the funding desk will need to give back the money they borrowed.

Secondary market pricing for the equity structured product

Imagine a scenario where the equity option had gone up in price by 20% in two years. The funding desk would return the cash it borrowed plus interest for two years, which would be approximately £176 million, and the value of the option would be £40 million. The value of the structured bond would now be £216 million. This means that, instead of 100%, the bond would be worth 108% of its original value. Alternatively, the situation could easily be the other way, such that the equity option had very little value, for example 4%, and the value of the bond would now be £184 million, so the bond would be 92% of its original value. This is the risk that the investor takes because the principal is only guaranteed in five years' time. Thus, before the 5-year maturity, the bond price will fluctuate based on market prices for the zero coupon bond that Megabank issued and the equity option (Table 11.3).

TABLE 11.3 Profit Analysis Two Years after the Structured Bond Is Issued

Scenario 1	Scenario 2
• Value of the zero coupon bond: £176 million	• Value of the zero coupon bond: £176 million
• Value of the option: £40 million	• Value of the option: £8 million
• Together: £216	• Together: £184
• Price in percentage terms: 108%	• Price in percentage terms: 92%
If an investor wants to sell the structured bond back to Megabank, Megabank might make a price of 108% and the investor makes money on his investment	If an investor wants to sell the structured bond back to Megabank, Megabank might make a price of 92% and the investor loses money on his investment

After working on the trading floor for 10 years, this author spent years working as an expert witness in financial litigation. Time and time again, the key issue concerned the documentation in a tailored or structured product. The exact terms of the transaction were often not clear, ambiguous and/or inconsistent. This resulted in hundreds of millions, and sometimes billions, of surprise losses on the part of the investor and sometimes on the part of the arranging bank. What became clear in every situation was that neither the arranging bank nor the investor had properly read through the documentation to understand the risks involved.

Conclusion

A structurer is often considered a very technical role. Structurers need to be able to model cashflows and to calculate different risk return profiles for the investors. They often need to be able to use the trader's models so that they can estimate the price of the products whenever they need to update the structure rather than bothering the trader repeatedly. However, that is a very basic requirement for the structuring role. At the end of the day a successful structurer is not necessarily the most technical person, although he absolutely needs to understand and communicate the more technical points. A successful structurer is the person who can make a deal happen.

Making a deal happen means he needs to understand the constraints of the different constituents to the deal he is working on. He needs to know not only what the constraints are but also whether there is any possible flexibility in them. He needs to understand the ramifications of moving different pieces of the puzzle. This is a combination of a deep understanding of the market in which he works and a deep understanding of the models he uses. Finally, a good structurer needs to understand how the documentation works for the product he is creating. He needs to be absolutely meticulous about this point because this is where it always goes wrong in the more complex products.

The 2008–2009 credit crisis has often been attributed to structured products. These particular structured products were so complex that often neither the bank that arranged them nor the investor that often requested them could properly understand what the risks were. While the banks have been vilified for their role in this, people have been reticent to place blame on the investors. This highlights the question of what responsibility a bank as intermediator should take in providing structured investment products to its clients.

Discussion Questions

Do structurers need to be technical?

Is structuring a role which is conducive to creating complex products for the sake of it?

Are structurers more like sales people or more like traders?

Are structured products dangerous?

Please see www.terriduhon.co for answers and discussion.

CHAPTER 12

Where Are the Quants?

This chapter is all about the individual who seems to have the most mystery on the trading floor: the quantitative analyst, also known as "the quant." Listening to the stories, most people would believe that quants come from Area 52 and are parachuted in on complex issues only. Other stories have the quant secretly running the bank. So what role do they actually play? Their role is primarily one of building the models which most traders use to price their derivatives. The secret is that they are not the experts on how the financial markets work and the traders rarely understand the inner workings of the model. So how can the model be accurate at all? This is where the relationship between the quant and the trader becomes crucial. The examples from Chapter 4 will again be used to illustrate the relationships, roles and responsibilities regarding the decision-making behind complex trades. This chapter will also explore the two theories of "Garbage in, garbage out" and "You tell me the price and I'll build you a model that says that" and answers the question: Does the trader just hit F9?

One trader on a structured trading desk was working with a quant to price a new type of trade. The trade was similar to one that they had done before, but not similar enough that they could use the same model or assumptions. After several rounds of discussions, the quant finally said, "You tell me the price and I'll build you a model that calculates that price." The trader was taken aback. Wasn't there a fundamental price for this risk? The quant said, "The price is wherever you think you can sell it."

Quantitative analysts (also called quantitative researchers or, simply, **quants**) get press every now and then about their "secret" role in financial markets. They, or their models, are sometimes blamed for adverse events when the media find a particular product to be too complicated. As a result, the word "quant" brings to mind Long Term Capital Management and "flash crash." Some news programs have even declared that financial markets are run by the quants. In reality, quants don't run financial markets. They do, however, play a very valuable role on the trading floor despite the fact that they often don't sit anywhere near it. They are in the same building but on another floor. Given that their role can be loosely described as creating or refining pricing or valuation models, it makes sense that they would spend the majority of their time in a quieter environment.

However, the fact that they are not sitting on the trading floor gives a hint to the limit of their power, as it were. They are experts at financial modeling theory. They are not experts on supply and demand within the financial markets, which ultimately determines the market price of a financial product. The traders hold this expertise. Thus, any financial model which is supposed to be used to value financial products needs the trader's input when it is being built and designed.

Pricing Models and What They Do

To understand the role of the quant, we need to understand what these models are doing. To do this, we'll break down the world of models into pricing models and risk management models. **Pricing models** are what traders use to price, hedge and value their trades, although note that these models aren't always necessary for highly liquid products, in particular those which trade on exchanges. **Risk management models** are used to identify risk and set trading limits in the trading books. These are used for all financial products, whether they are highly liquid or not.

In general we can break down the world of financial products into three types. There is no official term for this breakdown and it is unlikely that this breakdown is market standard, but it is a clear way to think about financial products. **Category 1** comprises liquid, standardized products which have observable market prices (Box 12.1). Exactly what products are on this list will change only slightly over time. A category 1 product can become illiquid and sometimes may not have bids and offers. But this is often during extreme market events where liquidity across all financial products has reduced. However, in normal circumstances, these liquid products do not need models to price them. They have observable market prices. The rule is that the fair value of a financial product is where it can be bought or sold in the financial market. If a product has a market price, a model isn't necessary to price it or hedge it.

Box 12.1   Category 1 financial products

- Exchange traded products (ETPs): publicly traded shares, equity indices, some equity index derivatives, some government bonds, some commodity derivatives, some interest rate derivatives and some foreign exchange derivatives.
- Over the counter products (OTCs): most government bonds, e.g. US treasuries, most corporate bonds, as well as most OTC derivative products such as benchmark maturity standardized interest rate swaps, benchmark standardized interest rate options, benchmark currency forwards and options, benchmark single-name credit default swaps and credit default swap indices, benchmark equity index options and forwards and some benchmark commodity derivatives.

These financial products don't need a model for the trader to put a price on them and agree to trade them, because the market price is visible and the product is liquid.

Category 2 comprises products that are not liquid or standardized but are so similar to a liquid or standardized product that they are priced as a function of the liquid or standardized product (Box 12.2). In other words, the model only uses observable market prices as inputs. These are products such as the old 30-year bond mentioned in Chapter 10 or the interest rate swap done with Supermart in Chapter 4. The old 30-year bond didn't have an observable price in the financial market, because it was not liquid. But the product itself is standard and the approach to pricing it is market standard. We know that any treasury bond can be priced off the observable treasury bonds that trade more frequently. So the model uses the known information about the old 30-year bond, such as the coupon and the maturity date, and then uses the observable prices on the liquid treasury bonds and calculates the right price for the old 30-year bond. These models are also used to calculate the right hedge, because, as is often said on the trading floor, all prices are a function of the hedge.

Box 12.2   Category 2 financial products

- Example: Supermart interest rate swap: the cashflows are not the same as the market standard product but they are easy to price off the market standard product.
- Example: Old 30-year bond: the bond is not the same as the on-the-run 5-year bond, but the cashflows are similar enough to price off the on-the-run 5-year.

These products need a model which uses Category 1 prices as inputs.

Category 3 is one which is non-standard and illiquid and can only be priced by making some big assumptions. The 5-year FTSE 100 option that we used in Chapter 11 (Box 11.2) falls into this category. The product itself is relatively standardized, but the maturity and the payout makes it exotic (Box 12.3). These products need a model which uses Category 1 prices as inputs but the exact relationship to Category 1 products is not as market standard as for Category 2 financial products.

Box 12.3   Exotic equity option structure

- Option notional: £200 million
- Underlying: FTSE 100
- Strike: 7,000
- Maturity: 5 years
- Payout: If FTSE 100 is at or above 7,000 at the maturity date, the option buyer receives £100 million; otherwise, the option buyer receives £0.

From this categorization, we can understand why almost every trader needs a model on his computer to price and hedge trades. Some traders will rarely use a model to make a market and hedge, such as a treasury trader, while others will only use models to make a market and hedge, such as an exotic equity options trader. Then there is a full range of products and traders in between.

At the end of the trading day (around 4 p.m.), the traders must close their books. This is a process of marking their books to market (MTM) or **marking their books to model** (mark to model, **MTMdl**). (Chapter 7 introduced the mark to market accounting that trading books are required to use.) This means that all outstanding trades on the trading book need to be valued at the end of day (EOD) market prices if they exist or using models based on end of day market prices of underlying components. The price of all financial products is either visible in the market or is determined based on visible financial product prices. This is a process where a middle office person uses an agreed methodology to put a final market price on all liquid and observable financial products every day. Then, those liquid and observable prices are put into the models to calculate the end of day prices on all of the other financial products that are outstanding in the trading book. The models which are used for pricing and hedging are also used to value trading book positions.

For example, in the treasury trading book, imagine the scenario where the treasury desk is originally long $400 million of the 5-years, sells $1 billion to PACAM and buys $700 million from the proprietary trading desk (Box 12.4).

Box 12.4   Treasury trading book position

- Trader owns $400 million at 100−16
- Trader sells $1 billion at 100−17
- Trader buys $700 million at 100−16+
- Net position: Long $100 million

The agreed methodology for the middle office person in charge of closing the books at the end of day is that he looks at the screens of the electronic trading systems at exactly 4 p.m. He will see bids and offers on those screens. He will put the bids and offers for each benchmark treasury and any treasury that Megabank owns into a spreadsheet and calculate the average mid-market point for each. That mid-market price point will be the end of day mark for the treasury book that night (Box 12.5).

TABLE 12.1 Calculating End of Day Position and Profit (or Loss)

Position	Size and price	Net position	End of day value
Opening Position	Long $400 million at 100−16	Long $400 million	+$125,000
PACAM	Sell $1 billion at 100−17	Short $600 million	$0
MB Proprietary Desk	Buy $700 million at 100−16.5	Long $100 million	+$109,375
Closing Position		Long $100 million at 100−17	+$234,375 in total

---

Box 12.5 Calculating the end of day mark

- Screen 1: 100−16+/17+
- Screen 2: 100−16¾/17¼
- Screen 3: 100−16+/17+
- Mid-market: 100−17

The model in which the middle office person has input the bids and offers will also calculate the profit for the treasury trading book that day (Table 12.1). The profit (or loss) is the difference between the value of the trading book last night and the value of the trading book tonight. For example, if there were only one bond in the trading book and last night it was valued at 100 and today it is valued at 101, then the profit is 1. Or if a bond was bought during the day at 99 and the end of day valuation is 100, then the profit on that bond for the day is 1.

Traders are always in need of new technology. They always want more screens, faster computers, better models. There is an unbelievable amount of money spent on technology and infrastructure around the trading floor. In the 1990s, the real need was processing power. One exotic trader at an American bank wanted some new Sun computer stations for his trading team because they were trading very complex products and they needed their computers to price their products faster. At the time, there was a budget constraint and the trader was told he couldn't have the new computers. He went into an immediate rage. He grabbed his financial calculator and stormed over to where the currency traders were sitting and he stormed up and down the aisle screaming, "I can trade currency on my calculator: why do they get six computers on each desk and I can't get two new Sun stations? Monkeys can trade currency. I NEED NEW SUN STATIONS!" While the rest of the trading floor thought this was highly entertaining, the currency traders were obviously less entertained.

Risk Management Models and What They Do

Risk management models are different from pricing models. Risk management models are used to help the bank quantify risk and allocate capital. They are also used to set up risk limits and risk monitoring systems as well as to help traders better understand and manage the risks in their trading books. Big picture, the question that risk management models are meant to answer is "How much can we lose?" Trading books take risk by providing a service to their clients. Traders make markets and end up buying or selling something which they can't always immediately or perfectly hedge. What risk management models do is to help the bank figure out, based on different historical analysis and different possible market scenarios, how much money a trading book can lose at different times.

There are regulations about how banks calculate risk and assign capital. These regulations require in some cases and suggest in others the exact methodology for this. However, the financial markets and their approach to risk are constantly evolving, which means that the regulations constantly evolve as well. The banks interact regularly with the regulators and discuss, debate and suggest changes to current regulatory methodology. However, the basic idea remains relatively constant: "How much can we lose?"

This is a very complex business primarily because the positions in the trading books globally change every day. One book which was short one day can be long the next. From day to day, there is not necessarily an expected pattern because a trading book is a function of the client demand. So each trading book needs to be assessed at the end of each day. (See Table 12.2.)

On an individual trading book level, the question is slightly simpler than on a global bank level. Looking at the treasury trading book, for example: one of the main risks is movement in treasury prices. So, if the

TABLE 12.2 Bank Trading Book Positions

Trading Book	Position/Closing Price Day 1	Position/Closing Price Day 2	Position/Closing Price Day 3
5-year Treasuries	+$100 million/ 100−16	+$150 million/ 100−17	−$100 million/ 100−18
US Equities	+$20 million/$50	−$20 million/$45	−$1 million/$45

treasury book is long, the risk is that treasury prices will fall. We generally assume that prices go up as often as they go down so really the question is more about treasury prices moving (or more specifically treasury price volatility) because we will do the same calculation whether the treasury desk is long or short. We need to look at historical treasury price movements and figure out how likely it is that treasury prices move in one day and how much they normally move by. We then need to figure out some worst-case scenarios for treasury price moves in one day. Again, historical data is very valuable. For example, we could ask "What have been the five worst one-day price moves in history and how likely are those moves to happen again?"

What we want to know is the answer to the question "How much money can we lose?" So, we pick a percentage, like 95%. What we want to know is, "What is the worst that can happen 95% of the time?" Looking at Box 12.6, we see that if we calculate the loss on our treasury position with a 0.2% price move, we will know our worst-case scenario 95% of the time. Another way to say it is that treasuries have only a 5% chance of moving more than 0.2% in one day. A 5% chance of something happening is the same as saying that a loss this big will happen every 1 in 20 days. The term **1 in 20** is often used to talk about risk in the financial markets. Another term used is **tail risk**, and more recently **black swan** risk. They all mean the same thing. Officially, the term is **value at risk** (or VaR). Ninety-five percent is a commonly used confidence interval to calculate VaR. It is a number the banks have gotten comfortable with from a risk management perspective.

Box 12.6   Historical worst 5-year treasury price moves in one day

- price move of 12% or more 1% of the time
- price move of 7% or more 2% of the time

- price move of 4% or more 3% of the time
- price move of 1% or more 4% of the time
- price move of 0.2% or more 5% of the time

These are example numbers only.

If the worst move 95% of the time is 0.2%, based on the data from Box 12.6, then we can calculate a value at risk of $200,000 which is 0.2% times the current 5-year treasury position of $100 million. What this analysis tells us is that, 95% of the time, we should not lose more than $200,000 in the treasury trading book with a $100 million 5-year position in one day. This analysis is redone every night for every book, because trading book positions can change every day based on client and trader activity.

This analysis is more than just number crunching. It is also about making some rational decisions about what scenarios need to be considered. Is the period after the Lehman Brothers bankruptcy something we need to consider as an event that could occur again or was it a one-off event? Is a reasonable period to consider one day or one week? These are the types of questions that need to be considered, discussed and decided, and on which the quants often take the lead.

Clearly, with derivatives books and more structured or illiquid products, these calculations become much more complex. Also, looking across the bank as a whole is a more complex analysis but it must be done, and in order to do it there needs to be a model that can analyze the data and calculate the required calculations every day.

Value at risk is a term that became famous because of the 4:15 report at JPMorgan in the Nineties. Every day at 4:15 p.m. in New York, every trading book globally would report their VaR to the CEO of JPMorgan. He would look at the VaR in every trading book and the combined number across the firm globally. Every day, he had a good idea how much money JPMorgan could lose in the next 24 hours. He would question big changes and highlight any trading books that were consistently low or high compared to their risk limits. This approach became popular across the banking industry and VaR became a market standard.

Financial Market Evolution

The financial market is continually evolving. There are new products and ideas that are always being conceived which are designed to hedge or value a particular type of risk or which are being designed with a particular investment profile in mind. Often these are derivations of existing products but they still need their own model to price them and calculate the risk for risk management purposes. In other cases, the product may be a new asset class for the financial markets, such as insurance derivatives. Inevitably, there is some theory somewhere which is the starting point for how the product might be modeled, but this means that the work of quants is never done. They are constantly working on new models for new products, or tailored products or even refining existing models.

Products themselves go through a natural evolution in which certain assumptions or theories get tested and proved or disproved by the marketplace. VaR is a good example of this. VaR became very popular during the Nineties and the Noughties as a key risk measure for banks, followed by a period of being very unpopular post the 2008–2009 credit crunch. Nowadays, stress testing is en vogue. The popularity of the VaR model was the relative simplicity of it, while the criticisms were about the false sense of security it gave senior managers. The fact is that VaR is still a very useful number, but it is only one measure of risk and should not be relied upon as the only measure of risk.

When a new product is created, new models need to follow it. The credit default swap was a new product in the late Eighties and early Nineties, and it is a product that has grown exponentially in terms of use and has evolved in terms of the different **credit derivatives** that exist (e.g. the credit derivative indices and credit derivative options). The approach to the modeling of new products is a function of the risk environment within each bank. Some banks are more cautious than others and will take a longer time to approve new products and their models. Ultimately, all new products need to go through a new product approval process, which includes the testing of the model as well.

Once a model has been approved theoretically, it can then be used by a trader making a price for a client. If a product is so new that there are very few other market participants, then there is initially very little testing of the model that can be done in a practical implementation. This means that if a trader puts a price on a credit derivative and trades it with a client and there is not another credit derivative that trades for weeks or months, then it is hard for the bank to know if the price is "correct." There has only been one price point, which is the one trade with the client. Over time, as more clients become interested and more banks trade credit derivatives, there are more price points in the financial market and the trader and the quants can observe how the market forces of supply and demand view their "theoretical" pricing model.

> F9 is the button on computer keyboards that re-calculates Excel spreadsheet models, which is how many tailored and structured products get priced. Often quants will set the spreadsheet such that it doesn't automatically re-calculate while the user (trader, structurer, sales person) is inputting data. The reason for this is that some calculations take a long time. If a trader is putting in data to a spreadsheet and it starts re-calculating after each number is inserted, it could take an hour to actually calculate one price. After the trader puts all the data in, he hits the F9 button to start the calculation. The joke on the trading floor is that there are people on the trading floor who are happy to hit F9 and not think about how the model works. The result is that when the model spits out a price they don't know what the number means or if it makes sense.

Quants' Relationship with the Trading Floor

Although quants often sit off the trading floor, they are often seen on the trading floor sitting with traders to discuss different issues. Some of those might be issues with assumptions that have been used in models or they need to discuss financial market dynamics. This relationship is a very important relationship for risk management purposes in a bank. The traders are often not nearly as quantitative as the quants. This means they often don't understand a lot of the mathematical terms used to price the products they trade. Terms like "monte carlo," "path dependent," "Gaussian distribution" and "closed form solution" are used frequently when discussing different pricing models but, while they might be able to describe broadly what these terms mean and why they are used, traders would be very unlikely to sit down and build a model using a monte carlo method, for example. The only reason they are familiar with the terms is probably because a quant described the concept to them in the first place. Quants can often been seen drawing diagrams for traders or trying to simplify a mathematical concept to make it useful.

TABLE 12.3 The Important Trader–Quant Relationship

Trader skillset	Quant skillset
Understand market dynamics	Understand theoretical financial modeling
Understand the supply and demand for a financial product	Understand how to manipulate models
Understand what the price means	Understand what are assumptions and what are not
Provide the commercial framework to the discussion	Provide a link to the academic community

Contrary to popular belief, most traders are not mathematicians themselves. Often there are analytical backgrounds for the more structured derivatives traders but they are not a requirement. There is very little need for a trader to sit down and work out a formula or build a model. It is not his skillset. His skillset is to read and understand financial market dynamics, make prices for clients and manage the resulting risk. The quant, on the other hand, needs to be able to build models and think about the theory, the methodology and the approach. Then, as a team, a quant and a trader can determine the right assumptions and discuss the financial market dynamics (Table 12.3).

Some products are so exotic and tailored that a quant will often sit full-time on the trading floor with the traders in order to be available for pricing more exotic products. This does not necessarily mean that the quant is the market maker. What it means is that the quant will have a lot more exposure to the financial market dynamics and have a better insight to the market making process. A **desk quant's** job will be to assist the traders in tweaking the model.

At the same time as the quants have a strong relationship with traders on the trading floor they also have a strong relationship with the academic community. The advancement of theories around pricing and risk management is a combination of both academic theoretical research and practical experience on the trading floor. The quants bridge that gap.

After the Orange County bankruptcy, all banks had to unwind (tear up) all the derivatives trades they had done with Orange County. Part of the legal process was that trades had to be valued using the same set of market data. They were very complex trades and required some complex models to value them. The models weren't connected to a central system that could price them all at the same time because they were so tailored. However, each model needed to be calculated using the same set of inputs at the same time. There was a whole structuring team working on this unwind. Each person had one model open and the head of the structuring desk decided to stand on top of his desk and call out to everyone to input the live market prices all at the same time. So he stood up and called out a count of three. The complexity of these trades and models is slightly frightening given the computing power that we have in the world today. The fact that models can become so complex and are not even connected to a central pricing system is concerning. While this is a story about derivatives trades in the mid-Nineties, technology has moved on, but so has the complexity of some derivatives trades.

Conclusion

The idea that there is a back room in banks where a team of quants sits and develops models to arbitrage the financial market is mostly a myth. There are always attempts to use a complex model by a small team of quants who believe that they understand the market better than anyone else and as a result are able to arbitrage the market. But those attempts happen as often within banks as outside of banks and, while some might be successful on a small scale, they are rarely successful on a large scale.

Quants are active members of the front office trading team primarily in the structured and tailored products. They are also heavily involved in risk management across all products. They are responsible for developing and maintaining the models used to price and risk manage financial products globally. They interact heavily with structured product and derivatives teams due to the tailored nature of those markets but they are also involved in more standardized and liquid products for risk management purposes.

The role of the quant is probably one of the most difficult to fill well. They don't fit the standard personality stereotype of an academic. Most academics are known for their work on theoretical models and concepts. Quants need to be able to bridge the gap between the theoretical and the practical and that skillset is unique in the financial markets.

Finally, because financial risk is complicated, quantifying it is a challenge for everyone. Even if all a bank traded were government bonds, as this chapter shows, it is still a complex and subjective process to quantify the risk. While the models may seem impossible to understand, they serve a crucial role in the risk management of banks, and the value of a quant should never be underestimated as a result.

Discussion Questions

Why don't quants run financial markets?

Are models too complex?

Why are there derivatives traders who don't know how the model works?

Why aren't quants traders?

Please see www.terriduhon.co for answers and discussion.

CHAPTER 13

What Are the Risks?

This chapter gives an overview of the different risks that traders take. These are generally broken down into market risk, credit risk, liquidity risk, funding risk and the often forgotten operational risk and reputational risk. They can mean different things in different banks but, broadly speaking, these are the big ones. However, a trader generally focuses on market risk, that is the risk that the price of what he owns will move in the market unless he is trading a credit product, in which case he will also focus on credit risk. He rarely considers the other risks, unfortunately. This chapter will use each of the three trades from Chapter 4 and walk through the key risks in each. This chapter will also answer questions such as: What risks aren't quantified? What risks are hard coded into financial companies? Where is the risk? What risk decisions are institutionalized? What risks are never considered?

Trading financial products is about identifying the risk and quantifying it. This means that when a trader says he'll buy something at 10 he believes that he can sell it for 11. He has quantified the risk he is taking via putting a price where he is prepared to buy. Because a lot of financial products aren't that straightforward, there are loads of discussions around trading floors which include the following questions: "What am I missing? Where's the risk? This looks like a win–win situation to me." In other words, "There is no way this is risk free. That is simply not how finance works."

Financial risk is generally broken down into market risk, credit risk, liquidity risk, funding risk, operational risk and reputational risk (Box 13.1). This sounds like a lot of different issues for a bank to consider and, frankly, it is a lot. That may be why it always seems to go wrong. There is not one of these risks that is necessarily bigger than the other. If they are not assessed regularly and managed properly, any one of them could cause a huge loss in a bank with the worst-case scenario being that the bank has to declare bankruptcy. Because of the role that banks play in the global economy, a bank going bankrupt, particularly a major bank, can cause a lot of market uncertainty, for example the Lehman Brothers bankruptcy. While the losses as a result of the Lehman bankruptcy were ultimately sustainable by the financial markets, the uncertainty of what a Lehman bankruptcy meant was the concern. Regulators as a result are very focused on the risk management of banks with a particular emphasis on what happens on the trading floors.

Box 13.1   Risk classifications on the trading floor

- Market risk
- Credit risk
- Liquidity risk
- Funding risk
- Operational risk
- Reputational risk

The various reports written by regulators all acknowledge that the financial community in general needed more comprehensive risk management practices. They stated that the banks which were best managed during the 2008–2009 credit crisis had management teams that took a global approach to risk across trading books and asset classes. They also exercised critical judgment and discipline in managing their risk globally.

This book has continually reinforced the idea that a bank's role is to facilitate its client's access to the financial markets. This boils down to market makers providing liquidity and taking risk because of client trades and then judiciously hedging that risk. While trading books will have residual positions because there are not always perfect hedges and the market maker has or will have to exercise judgment in executing his hedges, the point is not to deliberately put on positions that can't be hedged. In other words, a market maker is not a proprietary trader, nor is he a hedge fund manager. However, during the build-up to the 2008–2009 credit crisis, there were many banks who had convinced themselves that some of the structures that they originated, structured and distributed were good investments. We generically refer to this as **drinking the koolaid**. Many of the trading floors retained that risk rather than distributing it. There were several large banks which had severe losses as a result of retaining that risk. Had the senior management taken a disciplined approach to managing their risk, they would never have agreed to turning trading books into investment books and some of the product they originated would never have been done in the first place.

> Bank training programs for their new hires in global financial markets are fascinating for who they don't train as much as for who they train. The training programs are often exclusively for sales, trading, structuring and research new hires. None of the other trading floor roles get this training. In particular, middle and back office doesn't get this training and focus. Middle office is sometimes the business unit where risk management sits, which is an incredible statement on the part of the banks. This more than anything creates an elitist star system on the trading floor and a gaping hole in the knowledge base of the middle office professionals who need to understand financial products and markets in order to help control risk.

Market Risk

Market risk is the risk that market prices move. Sample positions for the 5-year treasury trading book from Chapter 12 are given in Box 13.2.

Box 13.2   Calculating a 5-year treasury trading book end of day position

---

- Trader owns $400 million at 100–16 at the start of the day
- Trader sells $1 billion at 100–17 to PACAM
- Trader buys $700 million at 100–16+ from the prop trading desk
- Net position: Long $100 million at the end of the day

> **Calculating value at risk for one day on today's position**
> - Current end of day position: +$100 million
> - 1 day 95% price change possible: 0.2%
> - Value at risk: $200,000

The classic assessment of market risk is value at risk, or VaR, introduced in Chapter 12. This is a calculation to figure out what the most likely worst-case scenario is over a particular period. For example, a 95% VaR tells us the maximum we expect to lose 95% of the time. A trading book such as the one in Box 13.2 is said to have a 1 day 95% VaR of $0.2 million based on the current position and risk management methodology. This means that there is only a 5% chance that this portfolio could make or lose *more* than $0.2 million in a day. VaR is calculated on the end of day position. Intraday, this trading book may have been long $400 million at one point and then short $600 million at another, but the only number we really care about is the end of day because that position is being carried overnight and can't be closed out until the next day, when market prices could have already moved (Box 13.3).

> **Box 13.3   Overnight market price moves**
>
> At the end of trading in New York, Asian markets open. US treasuries are traded in Asia but not with the same volume as in the United States.
>
> The US Treasury trader in Asia will continue to make markets on US treasuries for Megabank's Asian clients.
>
> However, market prices on US treasuries will not remain stable overnight if there is a major market shock. Market news out of Tokyo, Hong Kong or Singapore can affect the US Treasury market. When Europe opens, news out of Europe can do the same.

The VaR calculation is done on the end of day trading book position. This calculation should be done every day on every trading book in every bank. We know that is not necessarily the case because not every bank in the world has the best risk management practices but, ideally, they should be doing this calculation.

Looking at the numbers in Table 13.1, the senior management within this bank would be able to see the long or short position in each book and the total

TABLE 13.1 Sample Global VaR Calculation

Book	Treasuries	US equities	Euro government bonds	Euro equities	Japanese government bonds	Japanese equities	Total	Total taking into account diversity
VaR	$0.2 million	$1 million	$0.6 million	$0.8 million	$0.05 million	$0.2 million	$2.85 million	$1.8 million
Position	+$100 million	+$20 million	+€80 million	+€30 million	+JPY4 billion	+JPY1 billion	NA	NA

VaR position at the end of each trading day. We can't add up the longs and shorts across these books as that number doesn't have much meaning. A cumulative VaR position does have meaning. However, we don't just add up the VaR across the bank's trading books. There is some benefit from diversification. As mentioned before, when equities prices go up, bond prices often go down. So instead of seeing a total VaR of $2.85 million, we see a total VaR of $1.8 million. This number says that there is only a 5% probability that Megabank will lose more than $1.8 million in one day. To put this number into context, many major banks have VaR numbers globally of a few hundred million at any point in time. This is because they could have literally a hundred different trading books across the world each with around $1 million of capital at risk.

The drawbacks of this calculation are that all of the diverse and complicated risks in a trading book are combined into one number. Then that number is added up (taking into account diversification) across all the trading books globally and senior management sees this one number. That number has so many assumptions built in and so many caveats that on its own it is not that useful (Box 13.4).

Box 13.4 What VaR doesn't say

VaR of $1.8 million doesn't tell senior management:

- whether the bank is long or short global equities
- whether the bank is long or short global government bonds
- whether the bank is positioned to make or lose money if the economy worsens in Europe
- whether the bank is positioned to make or lose money if the US government is downgraded
- if there is one particular risk that the bank has, e.g. US house prices.

The concern about VaR is that during the 2008–2009 crisis even banks which did calculate VaR daily didn't necessarily have any less loss than those that didn't. The single act of calculating a number isn't risk management. Risk management is understanding what the number means, what the caveats are, what the assumptions are and ultimately what senior management's view on that amount of risk in that particular market environment is. Referring back to the post-credit-crisis analysis done on bank risk management, prudent, disciplined and experienced decisions need to be made about the risk over and above simply quantifying it.

| Senior Manager 1: | I don't like the economic numbers coming out at the moment globally. I feel like we're heading for another bust cycle. The treasury book can stay long but the other trading books need to flatten out. |
| Senior Manager 2: | I'm not sure I agree. The VaR numbers are pretty small at the moment. I think the books need to think about staying as neutral as possible. The biggest positions we have are in the US at the moment and I think that's where the biggest shocks will come from, so the other books are fine but the US books need to flatten out. |

Another approach to market risk management is **stress testing** and **scenario analysis**. Stress testing is when banks identify key assumptions which may be wrong or may change over time. Revaluing the bank's positions using these new assumptions will show how the bank's risk changes. Scenario analysis is when banks identify rational scenarios that are unlikely but could happen and they revalue the bank's positions using those scenarios. These have both become more popular since 2008–2009.

For example, one assumption that is generally made is that European equity markets are highly correlated to US equity markets. This assumption has been made because the United States is a large consumer of European goods and services. But what if Europe shifts its focus and is able to distribute its goods and services to Asia and is no longer reliant on the United States? What happens to the relationship between US and European equity markets? What does that mean for the US consumer? Another example is about the amount of liquidity in the financial markets. What if the daily trade volume goes down for an extended period of time to 50% of what it is today? The general view is that it will continue to grow, but what if it doesn't? What does that mean for risk? What does that mean about the bid–offer spread? What does that mean about our profitability as a whole? These are the types of questions that are being asked and should be contributing to the risk analysis that is done.

The obvious questions to ask now are: "How do banks lose billions?" "Do they have billions of VaR?" The answer to the latter question is no. Banks do not have billions of daily VaR. They generally report that they have a few hundred million of daily VaR; some even report less than $100 million of daily VaR. If a bank is making prudent risk management decisions, and calculating its VaR sensibly, it should not be possible to lose billions if the daily VaR is around $100 million. Box 13.5 answers the first question.

Box 13.5   How do banks lose $50 billion?

- Global Bank: 100 trading books, $1 million VaR each = $100 million of VaR.
- A loss of $50 billion means that each book loses 500 times its VaR.
- Is it possible for each trading book to underestimate by this much the possible price move in its financial products? NO

What happens? Scenario 1

- One or two trading books are long billions of dollars of notional to which they have assigned a few million of VaR only.
- Within a matter of weeks, the markets for those financial products no longer exist. There are no buyers for those financial products at any price.

What happens? Scenario 2

- One or two trading books are long billions of dollars of notional to which they have assigned a few million of VaR only.
- The size of the positions are far larger than the daily volume in those financial products. When the bank wanted to hedge those positions, it moved the market against it.

The assumptions and the risk in those specific products were grossly underestimated.

The fact is that every time a bank announces a large loss in a trading book it always gives an extraordinary reason for the loss, where, in truth, large losses happen so often there is rarely anything out of the ordinary about the loss at all. They range from fraud and model correction to market price correction and liquidity issues. These are generally excuses for bad risk management. All of these events do happen and they should be anticipated, internally regulated and managed to avoid losses in the billions when the stated risk is in the tens or hundreds of millions.

The three examples from Chapter 4 all have market risk. Megabank's trading books provided liquidity to do these trades and thus has taken risk. Some example VaR numbers are given in Table 13.2 to show the market risk that Megabank could have on each of those three trades. Obviously a big determinant in VaR is the size of the position itself. Notice that the Supermart interest rate swap trade has a very large VaR. As has been stated, this is a very large trade to do for any interest rate swap trading book.

TABLE 13.2 Chapter 4 Trades Market Risk Analysis

Trade	Megabank Position	Market Risk	Value at risk
PACAM treasury trade	Short $1 billion 5-year treasuries	YES: that the market price goes up	$2 million
Supermart interest rate swap	Receiving fixed on $7.5 billion 5-year interest rate swaps	YES: that the fixed rate for interest rate swaps goes up	$16 million
Structured equity product	Selling £200 million FTSE 100 5-year option	YES: that the price for options goes up	$1 million

Credit Risk

One of the most overused expressions on the trading floor is "That'll never happen." Some of the things that people have said would never happen include Lehman going bust and the US government's credit rating being downgraded from triple A to double A. These were almost inconceivable events. These are credit-related risks, which shows that credit in particular is one risk that people struggle with. When a bank gives a loan to Microsoft, the immediate response is that Microsoft will never default. However, there was a time when everyone said the same about Ford and General Motors.

When we think about what a bank is, we often think about an entity which gives out credit in the form of loans, mortgages or credit cards. It should follow that the majority of risk within a bank is credit risk. Because not all major banks give out loans this is not always the case, but it is a good generalization. Banks' expertise historically is credit risk. They have been in the lending business for hundreds of years. The source of credit risk obviously comes from the loan portfolio, but it also comes from the trading floor. Many financial products which are traded have a credit element as well. A corporate bond, for example, has market risk on the price but credit risk due to the issuer. We also have counterparty credit risk from derivatives (introduced in Chapter 10), which is sometimes as significant as the credit risk from the loan portfolios. Box 13.6 lists sources of credit risk.

Box 13.6   Sources of credit risk in a bank

- Loan portfolio (including personal loans, company loans, credit cards and mortgages)
- Bonds, loans and credit derivatives in trading books
- Counterparty credit risk across all derivatives

Credit risk is the risk that an entity cannot pay what is due. Treasury bonds were historically considered riskless but, post the 2008–2009 credit crisis, they are now considered to have some credit risk in them. This is the risk that the US government can't (or won't) pay back the money borrowed. The reason for that may be that it can't borrow from the financial markets in order to pay back the maturing debt. Or it may be that the US government doesn't approve a higher debt ceiling. Regardless of the reason, the idea has now been planted in the financial market that the possibility exists, admittedly remote, but it is there. On that basis, we can consider that all government and corporate debt has credit risk. Perhaps one way to put this in context is to think about the credit risk of McDonald's as compared to the credit risk of the US government. Which one is likely to default first?

Equity markets are not considered to have explicit credit risk. Certainly, if an investor owns shares in a company which has a bankruptcy, then that equity investor loses his investment, but that is considered market risk. The reason is because equity is not borrowed money. It is ownership in a company. The company is not required to pay the equity investors back. The equity price moving up and down has some relationship with the credit quality of the company but it is generally a loose relationship. Box 13.7 lists financial products with credit risks.

Box 13.7   Financial products with credit risk

Credit products: Bonds and loans and all derivatives on bonds and loans such as credit derivatives.

Equities have market risk as opposed to credit risk.

Distinguishing between market risk and credit risk on a financial product in a trading book is important in order to be able to manage its risk properly. Trading books which include bonds, for example, need to break down the risk between market risk and credit risk. This distinction can be made by looking at why the price moved (Box 13.8).

Box 13.8   Market risk vs. credit risk in a Supermart bond

Supermart bond

- Issued with a fixed rate of 3.15% and a price of 100% (note: this is different from the scenario we've been discussing of Supermart borrowing via a floating rate bond as originally introduced in Chapter 4, but it is more useful for this purpose).
- The price of this bond will move with general market price moves:
  - If there is a lot of selling of fixed income products then this bond price will go down as well. This is simple supply and demand.
  - If interest rates go up or down, the price of this bond will go down or up.
  - This is market risk.
- The price of this bond will move with market sentiment about Supermart:
  - If Supermart is performing well as a business, investors may want to buy Supermart bonds and the price will go up.
  - If Supermart is performing poorly or even struggling, investors may start to sell Supermart bonds and the price will go down.
  - An extreme scenario in credit risk is that Supermart goes bust and the investors don't get all their money back.
  - This is credit risk.

With bonds and loans, the notional amount of credit risk is clear. It is the principal of the bond or loan. If Supermart had a bankruptcy, it couldn't pay back the principal of its bonds and loans. What is not clear, however, is the notional amount at risk to Supermart in the derivatives that were traded with Supermart. As a result, in counterparty credit risk management we talk about the **loan equivalent** risk. This means, for example, when we do a $100 million interest rate derivative for five years with Supermart, what size loan would that be equivalent to? While an interest rate swap notional amount might be for $100 million, the two counterparties only exchange the interest payments. Also, those payments net with each other. So, it is not the same as giving a loan of $100 million, because a counterparty will never owe the full notional amount on an interest rate swap. Table 13.3 looks at an interest rate swap payment.

TABLE 13.3 Sample Interest Rate Swap Payments with Archery

	Megabank pays	Megabank receives	Net payment
End year 1	(Libor = 0.92%)*	1.07%	Archery pays 0.15%
End year 2	(Libor = 0.98%)*	1.07%	Archery pays 0.09%
End year 3	(Libor = 1.10%)*	1.07%	Megabank pays 0.03%
End year 4	(Libor = 1.18%)*	1.07%	Megabank pays 0.11%
End year 5	(Libor = 1.26%)*	1.07%	Megabank pays 0.19%

Libor is a rate for one year or less at which banks borrow and lend money to each other. In interest rate swaps, Libor is the floating leg which re-sets over time because interest rate swaps are generally several years long while the Libor rate is for one year or less.
*Numbers in parenthesis are payments.

The cashflows in Table 13.3 make some assumptions about where Libor sets each year. Using those assumptions, the net payments show that the amounts that a counterparty owes a bank on an interest rate swap are generally small. They are certainly not a huge percentage of the notional amount.

On day one, we assume that the trade was done at a fair market value but we know that interest rates move over time—this is market risk—and thus the value of the interest rate swap will change over time too. What we want to know on the day we do the interest rate swap is what the value might be in the future. We know that interest rates are as likely to move up as down so we are just interested in what the worst-case scenario could be. This is similar to the value at risk calculation. For example, a $100 million 5-year interest rate swap might have an $8 million loan equivalent risk. This means that lending $8 million to Supermart is the same credit risk as doing a $100 million 5-year interest rate swap. This helps to put into perspective the several hundred trillion outstanding derivatives trades globally. The counterparty credit risk on the outstanding derivatives is a fraction of the outstanding notional.

The key questions about credit risk are "What is the probability of a default of the borrower or counterparty, and if they default, how much will we lose?" To assess this risk for a counterparty, most banks will use a rating or a scoring system. A **rating system** is most common for corporate borrowers and a **scoring system** is most common for retail borrowers. There are public versions of these systems which are commonly known. Rating agencies such as Fitch, Moody's and S&P assign ratings to most of the large corporate borrowers, while a company like Experian provides credit reports and credit scores to retail borrowers.

TABLE 13.4 Corporate vs. Retail Borrowers

Corporate borrowers	Retail borrowers
Rating system based on:	Scoring system based on:
<ul><li>position and market share</li><li>strategy</li><li>leverage</li><li>profitability</li></ul>	<ul><li>how an individual has paid bills in the past</li><li>how much debt they have</li><li>what their current earnings are</li></ul>

TABLE 13.5 Chapter 4 Trades' Credit Risk Identification

Trade	Megabank Position	Credit Risk
PACAM Treasury Trade	Short $1 billion 5-year treasuries	Very small before settlement. None after settlement
Supermart Interest Rate Swap	Receiving fixed on $7.5 billion 5-year interest rate swaps	YES: approximately equal to $600 million loan
Equity Structured Product	Selling £200 million FTSE 100 5-year option	Very small before settlement. None after settlement

These ratings or scores are about grouping together similar credit risks (Table 13.4). The analysis for corporate borrowers is based on such considerations as position and market share, strategy, leverage and profitability. For retail borrowers it is based on considerations such as how individuals have paid bills in the past, how much debt they have and what their current earnings are. These considerations, along with a lot of historical data, help banks ascertain the credit risk they are taking and whether they want to take a particular risk. The rating or score then helps to quantify the risk to the bank across all its credit products.

The three trades from Chapter 4 don't all give credit risk to Megabank (Table 13.5). The PACAM treasury trade has a small amount of counterparty credit risk. Given that treasuries settle on the next trading day (as discussed in Chapter 10), the risk is almost zero. The equity structured product has a similar settlement risk to the retail client but, again, it is almost zero. The Supermart interest rate swap, on the other hand, has a large amount of counterparty credit risk. Not only does the trade have cashflows for five years but it is $7.5 billion. The loan equivalent is approximately $600 million.

RISK THAT DOESN'T MATTER . . .

One thing regulators hate to hear when they assess the risk in a bank is: "Well, we have this risk here, but we haven't accounted for it because if this happens we've probably already defaulted." In fact, in AIG's case, it was the opposite: those risks caused AIG's issues. AIG's financial product company, AIGFP, sold billions of dollars of insurance on events few believed were likely to happen. Because the likelihood of these events occurring was so remote, the insurance premium that AIGFP received was very small and didn't cover the losses when they ultimately came to pass. The point is that risk must always be accounted for, no matter how remote or in what sequence events might happen.

Other Risk

Liquidity risk is another big risk within a bank which was highlighted as a major issue in the 2008–2009 credit crisis. Liquidity in this context is about how much trades each day in a particular product (the daily volume) and how volatile the prices in that market are (which can be estimated from how wide the bid–offer spread is). This drives the cost of closing out or unwinding positions in a trading book. The issue being, if the bank decided to cut all its risk positions to zero, what the cost to get out would be (Table 13.6).

In the 2008–2009 credit crisis, liquidity dried up in certain products for months at a time and it wasn't possible to even get a firm market quote. Some of these products had quotes that were as wide as 20% at 80% of the principal amount of the bonds. This was a function of the extreme uncertainty in the financial markets. Liquidity risk was vastly underestimated by banks. They had assumed that liquidity in certain financial products would never go away. They may have considered it as an extreme scenario, but prior

TABLE 13.6 Sample Liquidation Cost

Book	Treasuries	US Equities	Total
Closing price	100–17	Average $60/share	—
Position	+$100 million	+200,000 shares	—
Cost of liquidation	½ of 1/32 $15,625	$0.05/share $10,000	$25,625

to the 2008–2009 credit crisis it was a risk they were willing to take when they decided to hold big positions in their trading books.

Funding risk was another risk highlighted in the 2008–2009 credit crisis. Banks often borrow money for short maturities, such as 3-months, and lend money (or invest money) for longer maturities, such as 5-years. Every three months, they need to re-finance. This is an extreme scenario. Banks borrow across a range of maturities and lend money in a range of maturities but generally comparing the two sides shows a mismatch. This is primarily a risk that comes from the loan business within a bank, but trading floor activity needs funding too, so to some extent it applies here as well.

For some banks this risk was larger than others. The most commonly associated blow-ups as a result of this mismatch were Northern Rock and Lehman Brothers. These banks had short-term funding shortfalls which meant that they ran out of money. In a scenario where no one wants to lend any money to anyone, if a bank needs to re-finance and it doesn't have a cushion, it can default. Today, the regulators are more focused on this issue and have proposed that banks need to manage this more prudently.

Operational risk is another big risk which has caused major disruption in the financial markets. Often this involves fraudulent activities. One trader, Nick Leeson, was in charge of trading options as well as booking them, which is normally a middle office responsibility. Because of the dual role Nick Leeson had, he was apparently able to hide some of the trades and the losses from those trades, which ultimately caused the collapse of Barings Bank, one of the oldest UK banks. Another trader did the opposite and famously booked trades in his book that didn't exist. With proper procedures in place, neither of these examples would have been possible. While this does fall under operational risk, classic operational risk is when trades aren't booked properly by accident as opposed to deliberately. Someone puts a plus sign instead of a minus sign and suddenly the trading book is long instead of short. These are all examples of operational risk. This risk is hard to anticipate but can be managed with proper procedures.

Reputational risk is another risk for banks which is often cited. This was a risk on which historically banks were very focused. It certainly feels in the last few years that banks haven't been as concerned about this risk as they have in the past. The risk is that banks lose their clients. In the past, if a bank was reputed to be doing deals that were bad for its clients or if it dealt with clients with questionable business practices, or if there were any hint of insider dealings, it would have been concerned that it would lose the trust of its clients. The ramifications of the 2008–2009 credit crisis have given the

TABLE 13.7 Chapter 4 Trades' Liquidity, Funding, Operational and Reputational Risk

Trade	Megabank Position	Liquidity Risk	Funding Risk	Operational Risk	Reputational Risk
PACAM treasury trade	Short $1 billion 5-year treasuries	Yes: if the position remains open	No	Yes: if the position remains open	No
Supermart interest rate swap	Receiving fixed on $7.5 billion 5-year interest rate swaps	Yes: if unhedged	No	Yes: whether hedged or not	Yes
Equity structured product	Selling £200 million FTSE 100 5-year option	Yes: if unhedged	Yes	Yes: whether hedged or not	Yes

impression that banks were often blinded by the profits and so reputational risk took a back seat. At the same time, it's not yet clear that this has made a big impact on client business for some of these banks. Perhaps the clients don't trust the banks but need to do business anyway. Or perhaps this is a more general statement that banks used to carry a position of trust with the public in general and this is simply no longer the case. Nevertheless, banks still do address reputational risk, the question is whether the threshold for business they will do versus business they won't do has changed.

Table 13.7 lists the various risks in the trades introduced in Chapter 4, which are:

- Liquidity risk: All three trades have liquidity risk if left open or unhedged. This is the risk that Megabank needs to hedge or close out all its open positions in one day. There will be a cost to this for each trade if it is necessary to do it immediately.
- Funding risk: In the extreme case, if retail investors all want to sell their equity structured product back to Megabank when Megabank is having trouble borrowing money, this could cause a problem; so the equity structured product has funding risk.
- Operational risk: If the treasury trade is closed out, there is no further operational risk. The other two trades (5-year Supermart interest rate

swap trade and the 5-year equity options trade embedded in the equity structured product) have significant operational risk because of the length of time there are cashflows to manage, regardless of whether they are hedged or not.

- Reputational risk: The treasury trade has negligible reputational risk but the Supermart interest rate swap and the equity structured product have real reputational risk. Treasuries are such a ubiquitous financial product that it is hard to imagine a realistic scenario where a bank suffers reputational risk from selling treasuries to a large investor. On the other hand, derivatives trades always have some risk of hitting the reputation of the bank that traded them, particularly when the counterparties are a corporate and retail.

Conclusion

Risks within a bank are complex because of how large and global many banks are today. They operate across products, across asset classes and across regions in very large size. The key risks on trading floors are primarily market risk and credit risk. These are risks for which there is generally market standard methodology to assess and identify them. However, the assumptions that go into the models are not always that straightforward. While the assessment of the risk may be complex or controversial because of the assumptions, the more difficult task is the management of that risk: this means the decision-making around whether the risk is sensible risk to have in the context of the business the bank does and at which point it is time to hedge or reduce certain positions. There are no easy answers to these issues, because much of the reason that a bank makes money in the first place is by taking on this risk.

Other risks which need to be assessed are liquidity risk of the positions in the trading books, funding risk of the bank as a whole, operational risk and reputational risk. All of these are complex to assess and manage; however, this is where judgment comes in. Determining whether a particular decision will affect the reputation of a bank requires judgment. Identifying where there are holes in the operations of a trading book which can be exploited requires deep knowledge of the system as well as judgment. Determining how much reputational risk a trade has requires understanding the client and the trade and, most importantly, it requires judgment. There is not a model in the world that can make these judgments.

Discussion Questions

Is the US government more credit risky than McDonald's?
Is market risk more important than credit risk to a bank?
Do banks care about reputational risk today?
Is operational risk significant in banks?

Please see www.terriduhon.co for answers and discussion.

CHAPTER 14

How Do We Manage These Risks?

This chapter will explore risk management procedures and their effectiveness on the trading floor. This is not just about the risk management team: risk is inherent in a bank's business. The risk management team only forms part of the risk management process. In particular, the risk management team runs the new product approval procedures and works with the trading floor to identify and quantify risk to then set risk limits. After that, decision-making about the market and credit risk that a bank takes, such as whether certain trades should be done or certain risks hedged, generally occurs on the trading floor by the traders and in some cases by trading floor senior management. For example, at one particular bank, traders call themselves risk managers rather than traders because that is what they see their role as being. At the same time, there is more than just market and credit risk in a bank, and what we really want to understand is how it all gets managed.

Often the trading floor is keen to do business which the risk management department is not so keen on. This causes a natural tension in the business which should produce a more effective risk management environment. Unfortunately, that is not always the case and the term "BPU" reflects that. This is what some trading floors refer to their risk management department as. It stands for Business Prevention Unit.

Because of the large amount of risk that banks have, there are often large teams of people employed in risk management; however, the risk management team's role is often misunderstood in the financial markets. The name of that team implies that it members control and manage the risk within a bank. It implies that risk doesn't get taken in a bank without their approval. In the 2008–2009 credit crisis, the question was continually asked, "Where were the risk managers?" This question was asked as if they had somehow shirked their duty.

The fact is that the risk management team only forms part of the risk management process. Its job is not to stop trades from happening on a trade-by-trade basis. In particular, the risk management team runs the new product approval procedures and works with the trading floor to identify and quantify risk and then to set risk limits. After that, decision-making about the market and credit risk that a bank takes, such as whether certain trades should be done or certain risks hedged, generally occurs on the trading floor by the traders and in some cases by trading floor senior management. For example, at one particular bank, traders call themselves risk managers rather than traders because that is what they see their role as being.

Analyzing risk on the part of the risk management team is a continual process because there is new information about financial markets every day. As we saw in the previous two chapters, a lot of the analysis is based on historical information and incorporates judgments about what might happen in the future. Remember that the traders sit in front of their screens all day and process market information in order to form a view about future market price moves. As a result, the relationship between risk management and the traders is an important one. At the same time, this relationship is similar to the one between traders and sales people in terms of the natural tension that should exist. Traders want to do trades that make a profit for the bank and risk managers want to identify and prevent excessive risk taking. One might say that this sounds like the same thing, because taking excessive risk does not necessarily lead to profits, but that is not the case in reality.

However, as we saw in the previous chapter, there is more than just market and credit risk within a bank. Thus the overall risk management within a bank is a responsibility that should be shared by everyone. It is not a responsibility that can be hived off and handed to one group of people. It should be part of the work ethic across different roles and responsibilities. It should be considered every day by every individual as they carry out their day-to-day business. Sales people should question whether trades make sense for their clients; traders should question whether they can properly hedge the risk they are taking on; quants should question whether pricing models make sense; structurers should question whether a product they originated is too complex; middle office should question the profit-and-loss calculations they see every day.

Unfortunately, that is not always the case and it is definitely not how many banks pay people. Human nature is to perform in the way an individual is incentivized. A trader who is paid as a function of the profitability of his trading book knows that to make more profits generally means taking more risk. At the same time it is hard to incentivize the risk management team to prevent excessive risk taking. How does a bank pay someone who stops profitable trades from happening? Obviously, this is a function of the definition of profit.

So who is making those prudent risk decisions that the regulators are calling for today? Sometimes, senior risk management individuals, for example the chief risk officer, do have key decision-making roles within global financial markets and they are able to control and manage risk appropriately. Sometimes, the senior trading floor management makes prudent risk decisions on a more disciplined basis. And sometimes there is a hole.

There is a commonly used phrase on the trading floors when dealing with very complex models. The idea is that the model is only as good as the information that goes into it. So if an assumption is wrong, the model results are wrong. It's interesting that we never blame the assumptions; we always blame the model and end up sometimes throwing out the baby with the bathwater. The phrase is "Garbage in, garbage out." Another is "All models are wrong; some are useful."

New Product Approval Process

Every bank has a new product approval process, which is the process by which the bank ensures that a new product will not create undue risk. It is a very sensible process, but it can feel very administrative. The process is generally to get the sign-off of identified senior managers in different departments of the bank who all agree that the new product makes sense and the risk can be managed (Box 14.1).

Box 14.1   Key signatures for a new product approval

- Senior management product champion
- Middle office team
- Documentation team
- Back office team
- Legal team
- Accounting team
- Finance team
- Tax team
- Quant team
- Counterparty credit risk team
- Compliance team
- Risk management team

Risk limits are probably the most crucial bit of the equation for any new product. They are set by the risk management team and can be limits of any sort which are designed to control the risk. Below are all examples of the type of risk limits that might be put in place in a new trading book (Box 14.2). They are designed to constrain the amount of business and test the systems and the market. Over time, they may be changed depending on how the test period went. Eventually, the trading book moves out of the test phase and into operations as normal, and the frequency of interactions with the risk management team goes dramatically down. In normal operations, there is no need to get approval on a trade-by-trade basis as long as the trader is trading a product that has already been approved and the risk is within the limits he has.

Box 14.2   Some examples of trading limits

- The total notional of trades that can be done in this new trading book is $100 million.
- The total number of trades that can be done is 10.
- The maximum maturity of trades that can be done is two years.
- The counterparties must be institutional investors only with collateral agreements in place.
- The maximum value at risk (VaR) for this book is $0.5 million (95% 1 day).

The trading floor sponsor of the new product will generally be a trader or a structurer who has identified a new opportunity in the financial markets. They will have had approval from senior management on the trading floor to proceed with the idea and dedicate the resources of the different teams above to create a framework for trading these new products. However, the risk management team will ultimately need to give the final approval to allow these new trades to be done.

New trading books are relatively rare in that most of the key asset classes and financial products already exist. The area that sees new product more often is typically in the exotic or structured product business. Either banks or investors come up with some pretty interesting and esoteric risk that they would like to trade. Because these are generally based on existing products, they are really derivatives of existing derivatives. It is rare that a full new product approval process (NPA) needs to occur (Table 14.1). The treasury trade with PACAM won't need an NPA because there is a treasury trading desk in existence. The trade is within the normal trading activity of the desk and fits within the risk limits. The interest rate swap with Supermart won't need an NPA because there is an interest rate swap trading desk and the trade is within the normal trading activity of the desk. Due to the size of the trade, it may not fit within the existing risk limits, but that situation comes under a one-off approval to breach risk limits rather than as an NPA.

The structured equity product is the type of product that may need an NPA process, for example a bank that hasn't sold an equity structured product to retail before but is now considering it will go through an NPA process or a bank that has sold structured product to retail before but not with an equity option like this. Structured products by definition are tailored. So just having done one structured product does not mean the bank is equipped to do another.

TABLE 14.1 Chapter 4 Trade New Product Approval Process Summary

Trade	Need NPA
PACAM treasury trade	No
Supermart interest rate swap	No, but will need one-off approval to breach existing risk limits
Structured equity product	For the first product like this: Yes

First, the structurer would secure the approval of a senior trading floor manager to get the NPA started. Then, he would tick off the NPA list for a structured equity product being sold to retail in the following way:

- **Middle office:** Because the structured product breaks down into a zero coupon bond that the funding department issues and an equity index option, the bank needs to think about these as two separate products. If equity options are already traded, and the middle office team already has a process to put these trades into the bank's systems, then the middle office team will sign off. The question the team will ask is "Who is the counterparty on the trade?" Most of their counterparties are institutional investors, so they will not want to book a trade several hundred times to represent the several hundred different retail investors. They will likely book the trade as one counterparty, which will be the name of the structured equity product, e.g. Megabank MegaReturn Bond I. The funding department borrows money by issuing bonds all the time, but it is unlikely that it regularly issues zero coupon bonds. It will need to look at its systems and confirm that it can manage a borrowing with a zero coupon cashflow structure.
- **Documentation:** If the bank hasn't done structured products before, the documentation team will not have a standard set of documentation that it will be able to produce. It will need to get a template from the legal department and will need to understand how the documentation in a trade like this will work. The documentation for most structured products like this are made up of the standard documentation of an equity option combined with the standard documentation of the normal Megabank bond issue. The documentation team will be responsible for maintaining a database of these documents rather than actually producing these documents. This is because the documents are normally so tailored that there is more involvement of the legal, trading and structuring team in them than on a standardized transaction.
- **Back office:** This team processes the cashflows for a trade. This team also looks at this trade as two separate pieces. It will see equity option cashflows and Megabank bond cashflows. It has dealt with these before so should be able to sign off.
- **Legal:** This team will need to do some work on producing a set of documentation for this transaction, but there is nothing overly complicated in this particular trade to cause it concern.
- **Accounting:** This team confirms how the trade will be treated from an accounting perspective. It will look at the two separate pieces as well and

confirm that there is no difference in how they are treated from a normal equity option and a Megabank borrowing with the exception that Megabank is offering secondary trading, which means the notional of the borrowing might decrease over time. The accounting team will need to take this into consideration.

- **Finance:** This team will calculate the valuation of trades for the general accounts. It will look at the two separate pieces as well and confirm that there is no difference in how they are treated from a normal equity option and a Megabank borrowing, with the exception that Megabank is offering secondary trading which means the notional of the borrowing might decrease over time. The finance team will need to take this into consideration.
- **Tax:** This team will confirm how the trade will be treated for tax purposes. It will look at the two separate pieces as well and confirm that there is no difference in how they are treated from a normal equity option and a Megabank borrowing.
- **Quant:** This team will confirm that there is a model to value and manage the risk of the product. It will look at the two separate pieces as well and confirm that there is no difference in how they are treated from a normal equity option and a Megabank borrowing, with the exception that Megabank is offering secondary trading, which means the notional of the borrowing might decrease over time. The quant team will need to take this into consideration.
- **Compliance:** This team will spend a lot of time considering the regulatory framework of selling structured product to retail as well as considering the risk to Megabank's reputation. Given the plethora of similar transactions in the financial market, it is likely to decide that this is a product that Megabank can trade. While this is not always the best approach, it is often the view that is taken.
- **Risk management:** It is unlikely that risk management will conclude something different from the other signatories on this form, primarily because this trade is really a combination of two products that the bank already manages. It will likely speak in depth with the equity trader, the structurer and the funding team to understand the driver and the overall approach to putting it together and managing the risk, but it will likely sign off on the trade.

The NPA process raises a few questions about the 2008–2009 credit crisis. If all those highly complicated mortgage products had gone through a process such as that described above, would they have actually been allowed to happen? The answer is that when a product originally goes through a process such as the one above no one knows exactly how the market around that product will develop. The reason for the process in the first place is to make different individuals think about issues that might occur in the future, but no one really knows what that will be. At the same time, as mentioned earlier, the risk management process is a continuous process of assessment. Just because the NPA has been signed off doesn't mean that the risk management team has done its job and can move on. It needs to be continually re-assessing the product, the market and the assumptions it made in its original analysis in conjunction with the traders and their developing understanding and assessment of the market. This is where the problem occurred during the 2008–2009 credit crisis: there was very little re-assessment of the risks as the mortgage securitization market evolved and grew. The profits became the focus of the business rather than the risk management, and the natural tension that should have existed between the trading floor and the risk management team just wasn't there.

A German bank had set up a business unit to invest in a particular type of structured bond. The bank allocated capital, raised the funding and started investing. It eventually had over $1 billion of investment in these products. The risk management team presumably had some knowledge of this happening, but it wasn't clear what that was because the team called a training business and asked it to educate the risk management team on the product in which the bank had already invested $1 billion. Although, as a rule, it's never too late to learn something new, this certainly sounded an exception.

Market Risk Limits

As mentioned above, risk limits are set for every trading book in a bank. These are generally market risk limits and are often determined by a specific market risk team within risk management. Depending on the type of trading book and the comfort level the bank has with the risk assessment, the risk limits can be simple or complex. Simple risk limits are just VaR (value at risk) based.

For example, the treasury trading book has a VaR of $2 million. As long as the traders don't exceed that VaR they can do whatever client trades make sense to them on that trading book. This gives the traders the ultimate freedom to make trading decisions. This does not mean that a trader can use the maximum VaR on a consistent basis. If he did that, he would not be able to do new client trades because as soon as he executed them he would immediately be over his risk limit. This would force him to close out the position from the client's trade before the end of the day, which may not be the best way to extract value from the trade. However, the only reason the trader would have his trading book at maximum VaR is because he had a view about the financial markets and wanted to make a profit on that view. The problem with this is that when a trader has a view on the financial market it is not a guaranteed way to make a profit. And, if he loses the trade-to-mid profit from a client trade because he didn't have the VaR room to properly close out the client trade, he is taking a different risk from the risk he's supposed to be taking. Explaining that not only did he not make money on a client trade because of a proprietary trade he had on but that the proprietary trade also lost money is very different from simply explaining that he didn't make money on a client trade.

At the same time, VaR is another way of saying "capital." This means that if the bank has assigned $2 million VaR to a trading book, it is recognizing that the trading book could lose $2 million. A bank will need to reserve (retain earnings or hold capital) against the potential loss of $2 million and, as a result, needs to make a return on that capital. So, while the bank is aware that VaR is actually capital at *risk*, it is really focused on making a return on that capital. This means that if all a trader does is lock in the trade-to-mid profit on client trades and take no risk, then it is likely that the return on the VaR will be lower than the target **return on capital** for that trading book. The reason is because market making books are often used to take proprietary trading positions to improve the profit and loss of those books. Thus, if capital and return on capital are assessed based on the previous year's performance, it's likely to be hard for the traders to only lock in the trade-to-mid profit on the client business. So often there is some encouragement on the part of senior management for market makers to formulate a trade strategy and take risk in order to achieve an appropriate return on capital to justify that trading book (and the trader's bonus).

Senior management on the trading floor doesn't encourage individual traders to put on proprietary positions without discussing their ideas with senior management. Formulating and articulating a view, looking at some historical data and setting profit targets and loss limits is a crucial process in allowing a market maker to put on (execute) proprietary trades that are not an integral part of his market making activity. These profit targets and loss limits are a form of risk management which is monitored by the senior management but driven by an individual trader.

Often there are several traders working on the same trading desk. For example, the treasury trading desk generally has several traders who have market making responsibility for different treasury products, as well as junior traders and a head trader. The individual traders will each make markets for clients as has been described throughout this book. The head treasury trader may not have specific responsibility for any one treasury product; he may simply sit on the desk and advise on large client requests, speak to some of the bigger clients of the bank with whom he has built up a relationship over the years and most importantly manage the risk across all the treasury positions. He will look at the financial markets and consult with the other treasury traders and decide whether there is an opportunity to take risk. He won't do this without consulting with his senior management and going through the risk management process described in the previous paragraph.

Another key consideration in market risk limits is when those limits need to be breached. The Supermart interest rate trade from Chapter 4 highlights an interesting situation of breaching VaR limits. If the VaR limits on the interest rate swap trading desk are $2 million and the VaR of the $7.5 billion 5-year Supermart interest rate swap trade is around $16 million (as given in the VaR discussion in Chapter 13), there will need to be approval to do this trade. Normally, the head of market risk would need to get involved in this trade to determine whether this is the type of risk Megabank should be taking. Given the importance of the client, it is unlikely that the market risk person would not give approval. It is also likely that a senior corporate finance banker and a senior trader will need to get involved in the conversation with the head of market risk in order to get the approval. Also, it is likely that the head of market risk would require some detailed plan of how the US interest rate swap desk will hedge this notional amount as well as a timeframe for achieving the hedge. The head of the US interest rate swap desk will need to send daily updates to the head of market risk about this trade.

Some trading books are so complex and so tailored that they are run entirely off Excel spreadsheets. The spreadsheets are created by the quants who sit on the desk and help price each of the trades at inception. These are often the most exotic of books and are called "hybrid books." These are books that trade combinations of different asset classes. One hybrid book in interest rate and currency derivatives was so complex that each night the hybrid traders would stay on the trading floor until midnight valuing their trades and calculating their VaR for reporting purposes. They had to do this because their

> trades weren't tied to a central system which ran automatically overnight. Also, the trades were all so exotic that even running the model and double-checking the results needed both the middle office team and the traders to go through each model individually.

Credit Risk Limits

While market risk limits are trading book specific, **credit risk limits** are client specific. These are determined by the credit risk limit team within risk management. There are a number of approaches to credit limits, but, very generally, the approach is to set general guidelines bank wide for different ratings, different jurisdictions and different industries. These limits will apply to all credit risk that the bank has to a client. This includes any lending the bank does as well as any derivatives and any credit trades on that client as issuer (e.g. bonds issued by that client or credit default swaps on that client) (Box 14.3).

Box 14.3   Supermart credit risk limits at Megabank

- Supermart Credit Limit: $1 billion
- $600 million in use in the loan portfolio
- $200 million in use in derivatives as counterparty credit risk
- $200 million available
- Credit Officer: John Doe

The credit limits for all clients will be in a central system accessible globally. There will be a specific **credit officer** listed next to each client in the system who has determined the limits and who monitors the credit risk globally. He will take the general limits given by a central credit risk limit team and adjust them for individual situations. Anyone in the bank possibly doing a trade which would create credit risk to an entity will need to check that system first. In the Supermart interest rate swap trade introduced in Chapter 4, the interest rate swap trader will confirm that the bank has limits to the counterparty in one of the initial conversations with the debt capital markets team.

Interest rate swap trader:	Here's an indication of where I can do that size interest rate swap, but you need to check that we have lines to the counterparty. A 5-year interest rate swap will have a credit exposure of around 8% of the notional. So, if we do a $7.5 billion interest rate swap, we're talking about needing lines of around $600 million.

The interest rate swap trader doesn't yet know who the counterparty is because Supermart is working on a big acquisition which is a secret until the announcement is made to the public. But, he knows that a big interest rate swap trade like this will create a lot of counterparty credit risk. He is telling the debt capital markets person that doing an interest rate swap of this size is the same as giving out a loan of around $600 million. While any company able to issue $7.5 billion in debt is obviously a large corporate and likely a counterparty to whom Megabank would lend $600 million, it may be that Megabank already has a lot of other exposure to Supermart and there is no longer "room under the line."

> Once a sales person in London breached credit limits simply by picking up the phone. One morning at 6:30, she was the only sales person on the desk and the phone started ringing. It wasn't her line, but someone had to answer the phone especially in case it was a client, which it turned out to be. The client wanted to do a derivatives trade. The sales person spoke to the trader and executed the trade. Unfortunately, the sales person didn't check the credit lines. It would have taken the sales person five minutes to check, but she didn't. The size of the trade was relatively small at one billion yen so the sales person thought it wasn't a big deal. The client actually knew it was over its credit limit and was happy to get a different sales person who didn't check the lines. Unfortunately, once the trade is executed, it is done and the bank's problem to deal with.

There is a slight nuance between the role of the credit officer and the market risk manager. The market risk manager can often be overruled by senior management on the trading floor because senior management considers that it is the expert in market risk assessment. The credit officer is much harder to overrule because he is the expert on the counterparty. In this situation, the credit officer has allocated a line of $1 billion to Supermart and there is only $200 million of room. If the credit officer is not comfortable extending the line to allow this trade, the corporate finance team will have had to come up with some alternatives to Megabank taking this risk. One solution is a **collateral agreement** with Supermart. This is where Supermart puts up cash against possible market moves on the interest rate derivative so that if Supermart defaults Megabank doesn't lose as much money due to counterparty credit risk.

> There are a few very conservative banks that are well known for being incredibly difficult with respect to credit limits. One bank in particular was a real stickler for giving out credit. A sales person was trying to get approval to deal with a new client in Eastern Europe but the credit officer wasn't interested in giving out a line. After much prodding, the credit officer turned to the sales person and said, "We didn't give a credit line to the Vatican because we don't know where their money comes from. Do you really think we're going to give a credit line to your client?"

Learn from Experience

Trading floors are full of stories about when it all goes wrong. The media in particular can't wait for banks to get it wrong so that they can be abused further. Sometimes these stories are entertaining and sometimes they are scary, but there is inevitably something to learn from them all.

- *No change is a small change:* There was a large 5-year credit derivative that was executed between two banks. It was on a portfolio of over a hundred different borrowers. A few years after it was executed, the middle office of the bank who bought credit insurance called up the middle office of the bank who sold credit insurance and said that there was a typo in the documentation. The middle office of the bank that sold the credit insurance saw the typo and considered it a small change and agreed to it. The change was that one of the borrowers had been included with a misspelling of the name. The name was ABC Inc. rather than ABC Co. The documentation was immediately changed to reflect that it was credit insurance on ABC Co instead of ABC Inc. The following week, ABC Co, which was a subsidiary of ABC Inc., went bankrupt while ABC Inc. remained an ongoing entity.
- *Documentation backlog:* Trading standardized derivatives can be a very hectic job. A trader can typically trade 5–50 different trades every day,

depending on the bank. Prior to the system automation, getting the documentation for this volume of trades was a nightmare for everyone. Every few weeks, the middle office person in charge of documentation would show up on the trading desk and leave a pile of contracts representing the hundred or so different trades each trader executed. Each trader then had to review the terms and sign each document. Inevitably, this would happen at the end of the trading day when the traders were ready to go home. So, rather than review the terms of each contract, the signature pages were tagged so the traders could simply sign the appropriate pages. It does raise the question of what was the point of the signature in the first place.

- *Complex system:* In the Nineties, trading derivatives was a complicated business for everyone. The systems in particular simply couldn't handle the volume of trades that were starting to be traded. In those days, the majority of trades were relatively simple compared to the trades that are done today. One day, a derivatives trader was handed a printout of his positions which had been re-calculated overnight. It turns out that there was a $1 billion position that had previously been missing and was suddenly in his book. It wasn't strange for this particular book to see new positions every day which needed to be hedged. But they would normally show up at least six months in advance so that the trader could manage them. This position showed up with only two days' notice. Given that volumes have grown exponentially and derivatives have become more complex since then, imagine what surprises occur today.

- *Wrong way risk:* Wrong way risk is when the risk of the counterparty defaulting and the valuation of the derivative are correlated. For example, imagine doing a cross-currency interest rate swap with a government on its own currency versus dollars. The local government owes US dollars in the swap against the bank owing the local currency. If the credit risk of the government deteriorates, this is because the government's economy is not doing so well. Often, governments will print more money, which devalues their currency. The local government can no longer afford the US dollars to pay the bank in the swap at the same time as the value of the US dollars has gone up. This is wrong way risk. This concept was often mispriced by banks and causes the banks who were the most conservative often to lose the business as a result. Sadly, the lesson that many traders and sales people learn from this is that it doesn't always pay to correctly calculate and reserve for risk.

- *Dodgy clients:* A sales person was trying to get a new client, which was a smaller bank, on board and was struggling to get past the credit risk officer. The sales person enlisted the help of the trader. The trader went and spoke to the credit risk officer. The credit risk officer took the trader into a small conference room and closed the door and said, "That client is associated with recent extortion attempts against a particular high-profile individual. The money from that extortion attempt was supposed to be paid into an account at that bank. The two most senior members of the board of that bank were recently shot in the street and no one's sure of the story. This is not the type of client we want to encourage."

- *Doing jail time:* A repo trader at a large bank got into a taxi one morning to go to work. The taxi driver asked the trader where he was going. The trader gave the address. The taxi driver said, "Oh I know that bank. What do you do there?" The repo trader was sure the taxi driver wasn't actually going to know what he did and wasn't particularly interested in having a conversation so he replied, "I trade repo." The taxi driver said, "Oh I used to trade repo." This got the attention of the trader. What in the world was this guy doing driving a taxi now? "I got involved in that treasury trading scandal a few years ago and did a few years of jail time. I'm banned from finance for life."
- *Training the regulator:* A regulator arranged to do some training on hedge funds. A group of 15 new hires within the regulator spent two days getting some expert training on hedge funds and their trading strategies. A year later, one of the large hedge funds called up the training company and said they had their regulator visit recently and had some questions about some recent changes in the settlement system for derivatives. The regulator wanted to speak to someone about it. The training company agreed to speak to the regulator. When the email was circulated introducing the regulator and the training company, it turned out that the regulator had been on the course provided by the training company only a year previously. One of the largest hedge funds in this jurisdiction had a regulator that only a year previously had been on a training course about how hedge funds worked.
- *Complicated documentation:* There was a large structured transaction done by a bank and sold to its investors. The bank itself retained some of the risk under the assumption that the risk was minimal. It turns out that the documents that the bank arranged weren't exactly clear and the risk it retained was the worst of the whole structured transaction, much to the bank's surprise and it lost almost $1 billion. Sometimes these products are too complicated even for the banks.
- *Best execution:* A derivative was executed between a bank and a client. The client came back to the bank two weeks later and said that there was a

problem with the derivative. The notional amount was wrong. Unfortunately, as is always the case, the market price had already moved so the derivative had a cost to unwind, which the client didn't want to pay. The situation deteriorated and eventually ended up in court. It turns out that the execution by the client was done while the client was on vacation and in a canoe and the reason it wasn't spotted as a problem immediately was because the client didn't look at the contract until a week after he got back from vacation. At that point, the trade was already underwater (pun intended).

Conclusion

Depending on the bank, the risk management team may be an integral part of the bank's decision-making process and consider itself part of the business or it may take a more adversarial view and the members may consider themselves police officers. Neither one of these approaches is perfect. When the risk management team is too close to the business, it may not be able to take a step back and make a rational disciplined decision. On the other hand, when its members view their role as one of policing the system, the trading floor would rather go around them than work with them. That is not a particularly healthy relationship either. The ideal relationship is one where the risk management team has enough power within the bank to create a natural tension between itself and the traders. Keeping this relationship balanced is the key for a bank to balance its risk and return.

In either case, the risk management team plays a key role in helping to assess and manage the risk despite not having the decision-making power to actively make trading decisions. Market and credit risk in particular are supposed to be managed by the trader who makes the "to hedge or not to hedge" or "to close out or not to close out" decision when he does trades with clients. Also, because the traders and their managers are the experts on their particular products and markets, it is hard to see how a risk management person could exert much influence on the overall market and credit risk position of a trading book other than by recommending to change the VaR allocation, which if it did reduce it, would cause huge push back from the trading floor almost irrespective of the reason.

At the end of the day, banks have more than just market and credit risk (e.g. operational and reputational risk). Thus, the risk a bank takes should be "managed" by everyone in the bank given how fundamental it is to the business of a bank. Unfortunately, that is not always an obvious part of the business culture at every bank, nor is it how people on the trading floor are incentivized.

Discussion Questions

Do banks add value to the financial markets?
Should they be allowed to take risk?
Should there be more regulation?
How should traders be paid?

Please see www.terriduhon.co for answers and discussion.

Epilogue

From a trader's perspective, the trading floor is the center of the financial market universe. Trading floors make the financial markets go round and financial markets make the world go round. What value do trading floors add?

- Trading floors intermediate between issuer clients and investor clients in the primary debt and equity markets.
- Trading floors facilitate access to exchange traded products for their clients.
- Trading floors provide liquidity for their clients in secondary, currency, commodity and derivative markets and as a result take risk.
- Trading floors intermediate between tailored derivatives for their clients and standardized derivatives, which are used to hedge and as a result take risk.
- Trading floors provide liquidity in all over the counter markets to their clients and as a result take risk.
- Trading floors provide liquidity in highly illiquid financial products and hedge using liquid financial products and as a result take risk.
- Trading floors provide liquidity for large size trades for exchange traded products for their clients and as a result take risk.

Trading floors are a crucial part of the financial market system whether products trade on exchanges or not. However, to play this role, trading floors take risk. All of these risks are complicated to quantify and manage. At the end of the day, critical judgment needs to be a crucial part of the trading floor mentality, whether it is making a market on a liquid product or making a market on an exotic product. No amount of regulation or legislation can take away the risk that the business of a trading floor often relies on individual judgment. This is where the thorny subjects come up. How do we properly incentivize individuals to make the right decision and is there even such a thing as the right decision? Everything is clear with hindsight, but no one has a crystal ball. At the end of the day, a business environment which encourages prudent risk management across roles and responsibilities and discourages the "star trader" system is probably one which will prove more sound through the business cycle.

Glossary

1 in 20—Chapter 12: Many value at risk (VaR) calculations are done based on a 95% confidence level, which means that the amount calculated is the maximum amount that should be lost in 19 out of 20 days. One out of 20 is the 5% chance that losses will be higher.

2 and 20—Chapter 2: This is a reference to typical hedge fund fees, which are a 2% management fee and a 20% performance fee.

Active investor—Chapter 2: When an investor is known for investing in financial products with a short time horizon such as days or weeks, an investor is considered a more active investor. A day trader is the most extreme of active investors.

Advisory agreement—Chapter 3: This is a formal legal agreement between a bank (generally the corporate finance department) and its clients to advise on financial matters, such as capital raising or mergers and acquisitions.

Analyst—Chapter 4: This is a junior individual working for a bank.

Arbitrage—Chapter 7: Arbitrage is when a market participant is able to buy a product at one price and sell it at a higher price without taking any risk. These opportunities generally only exist in illiquid or inefficient markets and often only on a small scale. Most arbitrage involves taking some risk.

Ask—Chapter 2: This is another word for "bid."

Asset management—Chapter 2: This is the process of investing money in the financial markets. This is also called investment management, fund management or portfolio management.

Asset manager—Chapter 2: These are financial companies who invest their clients' money. They are also called investment managers, fund managers or portfolio managers. Hedge funds are a specific subset of asset managers.

Assets under management (AUM)—Chapter 2: This is a term used by asset management companies to refer to the notional amount of cash their clients have invested with them.

AUM:—*See* Assets under management.

Axe—Chapter 6: When a trader wants to buy or sell a particular financial product and as a result gives a better price to a client than other banks in order to do that trade, he is said to have an axe.

Bear market—Chapter 5: This is when market prices for a particular asset class have been on a downward trend for weeks, months or years. This is generally associated with a weak economy.

Best practice—Chapter 4: This is the term used to refer to the procedure that ideally should be followed in various financial market activities, for example best practice execution or best practice risk management. This process is not necessarily always followed, but it should be.

Bid—Chapter 2: This is the price where one entity is willing to buy a financial product from another entity. When a trader makes a market, he provides a bid and an offer (which is a higher price than his bid). This is not necessarily the best bid or offer in the market, but it is where he is prepared to buy (his bid) or sell (his offer).

Bid–offer spread—Chapter 6: This is the difference between the bid price and the offer price.

Bid to mid—Chapter 7: This is the difference between the bid price and the mid-market price for a product.

Big figure—Chapter 4: Another word for "handle."

Black swan—Chapter 12: This is another reference to VaR from the book by Talib of the same name.

Black Wednesday—Chapter 5: The day (16 September 1992) when Britain had to allow the pound to fall out of the European Exchange Rate Mechanism after the government was unable to keep the pound above its agreed lower limit. George Soros made over $1 billion betting against the pound staying in.

Bloomberg—Chapter 3: Bloomberg is a large financial media and data corporation. On the trading floor, most traders and sales people use Bloomberg technology to look up historical financial data or price financial products. Bloomberg also has a messaging system which traders and sales people use to communicate, just like e-mails but they are referred to as "bloombergs."

Bonds—Chapter 1: A form of borrowing money that is generally for large companies and governments. Bonds are arranged and distributed by banks to their investor clients. They are generally considered public financial products.

Booking—Chapter 3: Booking a trade is the process that the middle office team goes through to input a trade into the bank's systems. This could entail typing in the details of the trade, producing the legal documentation and sending it to the counterparty and confirming the details of the trade with the counterparty.

Borrower—Chapter 1: The entity that receives the cash in a loan or a bond. In the bond market, the borrower of a bond is also called the issuer.

BRICS—Chapter 1: BRIC stands for Brazil, Russia, India and China. If there is an S on the end, it stands for South Africa.

Broker—Chapter 2: When an entity acts as a matchmaker between buyers and sellers of a particular financial product rather than acting as a liquidity provider (which involves taking risk), the entity is acting like a broker.

Broker/dealer—Chapter 2: This is a bank that will do trades on the exchange as a broker for its clients.

Broker trade—Chapter 2: When a bank brokers a client trade, which means the bank has not taken any risk because the bank acted like a matchmaker between buyer and seller, we say the bank has done a broker trade.

Broking—Chapter 2: Broking a financial transaction is to act like a financial matchmaker and find the buyer and seller to get a trade done without taking risk oneself.

Bull market—Chapter 5: This is when market prices for a particular asset class have been on an upward trend for weeks, months or years. This is generally associated with a strong economy.

Buy and hold investor—Chapter 2: When an investor is known for investing in a financial product and keeping that position until the financial product matures, for example buying a 10-year treasury and owning it for 10 years or buying a stock (which doesn't have a maturity) and holding it for several years, we say the investor is a buy and hold investor.

Buy, sell or hold—Chapter 9: This is a reference to the type of recommendation a research analyst might give for a company's shares or bonds. They recommend one of three options: to buy them, sell them or hold them.

Capital—Chapter 1, 7: There are two main uses of this word in financial markets: (1) this is generally used by corporate finance teams to refer to cash which a client can raise by borrowing money (debt), or for companies only, by issuing equity and (2) this money can be thought of as retained earnings which the bank is required to hold against the risk it takes.

Capital markets—Chapter 1: The capital market is generally a term used by corporate finance teams to refer to the financial markets that issuers can go to to raise either equity capital or debt capital, i.e. the equity market and the bond market.

Category 1—Chapter 12: For the purposes of this book, we refer to category 1 financial products as those products which have visible market prices and very liquid markets.

Category 2—Chapter 12: For the purposes of this book, we refer to category 2 financial products as tailored or illiquid products which use category 1 products to determine their price.

Category 3—Chapter 12: For the purposes of this book, we refer to category 3 financial products as tailored or illiquid products which use category 1 products to determine their price but also make several assumptions about the relationship to category 1 products.

Central market platforms—Chapter 2: This is the term used by this book to describe exchanges, interbank brokers and electronic trading systems.

Chinese wall—Chapter 3: This term is used to designate whether individuals have private market-sensitive information about a client or not. Often, individuals within corporate finance are within the Chinese wall and individuals within global financial markets are outside the wall.

Choice—Chapter 7: This is a market where the bid and the offer are the same.

Clearing price—Chapter 4: The clearing price is the level where a new bond or equity issuance needs to be priced to sell the target notional that the issuer needs.

Close out—Chapter 2: When a trader buys (sells) a bond or a stock, he wants to get rid of his market risk by selling (buying) the bond or stock. This is called closing out the trade.

Closing the books—Chapter 6: At the end of every trading day, the bank calculates the profit or loss for the day for each trading book, at which point the books are closed. This does not mean that trades can no longer be done but traders prefer not to trade after this point in order to keep the profit and loss calculations simple.

Collateral agreement—Chapter 14: When a bank takes risk to a client via a derivative contract, a bank will often ask for collateral (or some form of security) against that risk. For example, when an individual takes out a mortgage, his house is the collateral.

Commodity market—Chapter 1: The financial market where physical commodities such as oil and gold are bought and sold. It also includes all derivatives on commodities.

Company specific news—Chapter 5: This is all the public information about a company which could have an impact on the share price or bond price.

Compliance—Chapter 3: This is the team of people which ensures that the business that the bank does complies with all legal and regulatory requirements.

Corporate finance—Chapter 3: The business unit within an investment bank which manages the client relationship, provides capital raising advice and advises on mergers and acquisitions.

Corporates—Chapter 2: These are non-financial companies which are clients of banks.

Cost centers—Chapter 9: This is a term often used to refer to middle and back office teams that are not directly responsible for generating profit for a bank.

Countercyclical—Chapter 5: A countercyclical stock consistently performs well whether the economy is weak or strong.

Counterparty—Chapter 10: Each party to a financial transaction is generally called a counterparty.

Counterparty credit risk—Chapter 10: The risk that the counterparty to a financial product defaults before making all the payments required under the financial product.

Coupon—Chapter 1: The regular interest payments that a borrower must pay in a bond or loan in order to borrow the principal amount. It is generally a percentage of the principal paid annually.

Credit analyst—Chapter 9: The research analyst found in banks who analyses a company's debt products and publishes research based on that analysis. This research is circulated to as many clients as possible by the bank's fixed income sales force.

Credit curve—Chapter 4: The credit spreads for different maturities for the same issuer graphed over time.

Credit derivatives—Chapter 12: This is a derivative which is similar to an insurance contract against the default of a company or a government. This is also called a credit default swap, or CDS.

Credit officer—Chapter 14: Also called credit risk officer. This is the individual who sets the limits for each entity with whom a bank takes risk.

Credit risk—Chapter 13: This is the risk of loss due to credit deterioration of the issuer for debt or the counterparty in a derivative transaction.

Credit risk limits—Chapter 14: These are the limits to the risk of a single entity that a bank will take.

Credit spread—Chapter 3: Most borrowers borrow money at a higher interest rate than the government for a particular currency. This extra amount that the borrower has to pay to borrow money is called the borrower's credit spread. The more risky the borrower, the higher the credit spread. Sometimes this is calculated as the difference between the government borrowing interest rate and sometimes this is calculated as the spread over Libor that a borrower pays as a coupon.

Credit trading—Chapter 3: Credit trading is about bonds, loans and credit derivatives. These are instruments which are primarily characterized by credit risk or the risk that the borrower doesn't pay back the money borrowed.

Credit worthiness—Chapter 4: The credit strength of an entity or, in other words, the probability of survival of an entity.

Cross-currency swap—Chapter 4: A cross-currency swap is a subset of the interest rate swap market. The majority of interest rate swaps are an exchange of a fixed and floating coupon in the same currency without any principal exchange, whereas a cross-currency swap is an exchange of coupons in different currencies with an accompanying exchange of principal in different currencies.

Currency—*passim*: This is the type of money used in a country. Trading currency is about exchanging one currency for another. Another term for this is foreign exchange, or FX.

Currency market—Chapter 1: The financial market for the exchange of one currency for another, for example US$1 is equal to £0.6. This market also includes the currency derivatives that are traded. It is also called the foreign exchange, or FX, market.

Daily volume—Chapter 6: The notional amount of a financial product that trades on one day.

Dark pools of liquidity—Chapter 2: This is where a bank acting as an exchange broker has so many client orders that the bank is able to match-make between all its clients without using the bids and offers which are being shown on the exchange. If a bank didn't have all these clients, it would need to pass these orders to the exchange where they would show up as bids and offers on the exchange's system.

Day traders—Chapter 2: These are often individual investors who trade financial products throughout the day but close out all positions at the end of each day.

DCM:—*See* Debt capital markets.

Debt—Chapter 1: Borrowed money in the form of bonds or loans.

Debt capital markets (DCM)—Chapter 3: This is the team of people which straddles the corporate finance business and the global financial markets business. They help the corporate finance team navigate the new issue debt markets for the bank's clients.

Defensive—Chapter 9: The position an asset manager takes when they are concerned about market prices falling. They re-allocate their investment into more cash rather than have it fully invested in equity or fixed income.

Derivatives—Chapter 1: Financial products that are derived from the price of other financial products. Futures/forwards, options and swaps are derivatives. For example, the price of an equity option on Wal-Mart is priced as a function of the price of Wal-Mart shares.

Desk analyst—Chapter 9: This is a research analyst who does not publish research for clients but instead sits on the bank's trading desk and produces trade ideas or trade strategies for the bank's traders.

Desk quant—Chapter 12: This is a quant who sits on a structuring or exotic trading desk who builds models all day in order to help the traders price exotic or highly structured trades.

Diluted—Chapter 1: This generally refers to the smaller percentage of equity ownership a shareholder has when new shares are issued by a company. The original shareholder has a smaller percentage of the company now. His original shareholding has been diluted by the issue of new shares by the company.

Dividend—Chapter 1: The payment of some portion of the profits of a company to the shareholders.

Domain expertise—Chapter 2: This is the knowledge that individuals need to have to do their job properly.

Done—Chapter 4: This is a crucial word in the execution of financial products. Once all the terms have been agreed, when the client says "Done" to the bank, the trade has officially been agreed.

Dot.com bubble—Chapter 5: In the 1990s, many technology companies were able to issue initial public offerings with incredibly high price to earnings ratios due to the demand by investors to invest in technology shares.

Drinking the koolaid—Chapter 13: We use this term when people within an institution believe their own propaganda.

Due diligence—Chapter 3: This is the process an investor goes through to confirm that the investment is what he is expecting it to be. For example, in equities this is the process of confirming that the business the company says it does is the business it does do. It also includes a detailed review of the documentation associated with the investment.

Earnings announcement—Chapter 5: This is the official announcement of a company on a quarterly basis of the financial statements of a company for the previous quarter or the previous year.

Earnings per share (EPS)—Chapter 5: When a company produces its financial results for the quarter or the year, most investors are often interested in what the earnings per share break down into.

ECM:—*See* Equity capital markets.

Economist—Chapter 9: These are the research analysts who focus on macroeconomic market issues such as inflation or unemployment within a country or region. They publish research giving investment recommendations based on the research.

Electronic trading system—Chapter 2: In the context of this book, this is a system which is primarily used by liquidity providers (market makers) to hedge or close out their positions with each other. However, electronic trading systems will be familiar to many people as stockbrokers often have electronic trading systems available to their retail clients.

Emerging markets—Chapter 1: The financial markets that exist within countries that are considered less developed, such as countries in Eastern Europe, South America and Asia.

End of day (EOD)—Chapter 6: The point at the end of the trading day when the trading books are closed and the market prices are set for the profit and loss calculation for that day.

EOD:—*See* End of day.

EPS:—*See* Earnings per share.

Equity—Chapter 1: Ownership of some portion of a company.

Equity analyst—Chapter 9: The research analyst found in banks who analyses a company's equity and publishes research based on that analysis. This research is circulated to as many clients as possible by the bank's equity sales force.

Equity capital—Chapter 1: Equity capital is the cash that a company can raise by selling ownership in that company by issuing equity.

Equity capital markets (ECM)—Chapter 3: This is the team of people which straddles the corporate finance business and the global financial markets business. They help the corporate finance team navigate the new issue equity markets for the bank's clients.

ETP:—*See* Exchange traded product.

Exchange—Chapter 2: A company which provides a visible market consisting of bids and offers for the specific products which trade on it.

Exchange broker—Chapter 2: A bank or other financial company that can execute trades on an exchange either for itself or on behalf of a client.

Exchange traded product (ETP)—Chapter 2: A financial product that upon a trade is required to be reported to an exchange. These trades don't all happen within the exchange acting as a broker; they often happen within a bank's trading floor with the bank providing liquidity to a client or the bank acting as a broker between its own clients. Most stocks trade on exchanges. The companies that issue these stocks are said to be public companies.

Execution only—Chapter 3: This term is sometimes used to characterize the activity of the trading floor, which is that the trading floor executes trades that clients want to do rather than officially advising clients on their use of financial market products. The truth is that trading floors don't have official advisory arrangements with their clients but they do discuss markets and products with their clients.

Exotic derivatives—Chapter 3: These are derivatives that are less likely to be standardized and are often priced by reference to other derivatives and in many cases require some assumptions to price, such as the correlation between interest rates and currency rates. These are often tailored derivatives.

Facilitating—Chapter 1, 2: When a bank operates in a way to help a process occur. This is most often used in the context of a bank providing access to financial markets for its clients or a bank arranging and distributing an equity or bond issuance for a client.

Fair price—Chapter 5: The current market price for a financial product is said to be the fair price. For illiquid or tailored products for which there is not a visible market price, this is a price derived using current market prices for more liquid financial products.

Fair value—Chapter 10: The current valuation of a financial product based on a fair market price.

Financial companies—Chapter 2: These are clients of banks, which include insurance companies, pension funds, asset managers and other banks.

Financial market calendar—Chapter 5: This is the calendar with all the key dates for official releases of macroeconomic statistics in different countries.

Financial market participants—Chapter 5: Every financial product has different entities that transact in that financial product which together make up the financial market participants for that product. At the same time a wider group might be called financial market constituents, which means the different entities that have business in a financial product (which could include industry groups and regulators).

Financial markets—Chapter 1: A marketplace where buyers and sellers agree to exchange a specific financial product for a specific price. See Chapter 5 for a more comprehensive description.

Financial media—Chapter 6: The financial media are made up of large well-known companies such as CNBC, Reuters, Bloomberg as well as more specialist financial media groups such as Incisive Media and Euromoney.

Financial products—Chapter 1: A product such as a bond, a share or a financial derivative that is traded in the financial markets.

Firm—Chapter 4: Market bids and offers are firm when the trader has specified a size that he is willing to trade and has confirmed that he will trade on the bid or the offer.

Fixed coupon—Chapter 1: A coupon with a fixed percentage, for example 4%, which is paid each year on the principal of the debt.

Fixed income—Chapter 1: An asset class within financial markets that includes bonds, loans and all derivatives. In some banks it also includes currencies.

Fixings—Chapter 3: These are the fixed rates that are agreed for any index which is a reference for other derivatives. For example, Libor has daily fixings.

Flat—Chapter 4: Flat is another word for neutral and refers to a trading book position which should not make or lose money when markets move.

Floating coupon—Chapter 1: A coupon which resets on a fixed frequency but could have a different percentage due each period by the borrower. The most common is a Libor based coupon.

Foreign exchange (FX):—*See* Currency.

Founder—Chapter 1: The individual with the original idea for a company. Founders are often entrepreneurs as well, although entrepreneurs and founders aren't always the same individual. A founder has ideas similar to an inventor and an entrepreneur invests and builds a business around someone else's idea.

Four eyes rule—Chapter 4: The term used to refer to the fact that when a tailored derivative is being traded and priced more than one person should check the pricing being given to the client before the trade is executed.

Front office—Chapter 3, 5: These are often the sales people, traders, structurers, quants and research analysts on the trading floor.

Front running—Chapter 3: When an individual has private market-sensitive information and trades as a result of having that information. For example, if someone who knows about a big profit warning that is about to be announced for a company sells shares in that company, that is front running.

Funding department—Chapter 3: The department within a bank which focuses on borrowing money to fund the lending business in particular but also funds the trading floor activity.

Funding risk—Chapter 13: This is the risk of having to re-finance short-term borrowings against longer-term assets.

Future/forward—Chapter 1: A derivative product in which the buyer agrees to take delivery of a financial product at a specific point in the future at a specific price. Futures are traded on exchanges and forwards are traded over the counter.

FX:—*See* Currency.

GFM:—*See* Global financial markets.

Gilts—Chapter 6: This is the debt that the UK government issues. They are called gilts because the old certificates had a gold border.

Global financial markets (GFM)—Chapter 3: The business unit within a bank where the trading floor sits. The focus of this business unit is the trading floor activity. While there might be 1,000 people working on the trading floor, there are possibly 10,000 people within GFM who primarily work within operations which manage trade and cashflow processing.

Guarantees—Chapter 4: A guarantee is a promise. When used in finance it is often a promise to pay the principal due in a bond or a loan. Many structured bonds are guaranteed by the bank that structured the bond because the bank is also the issuer of the bond. The issuer of the bond promises to pay the principal back when due. Guaranteed structured bonds are also called principal protected bonds. It is a product where a bank guarantees that the investor will receive the principal back upon the maturity. This is similar to investing in a bond issued by the bank that is providing the guarantee.

Handle—Chapter 4: This term refers to the big figure in the price that generally doesn't move. For example, in bond pricing the numbers that are often quoted for the price are after the decimal (e.g. a bond with a bid offer of 101.46% at 101.48%, the bid offer might be quoted as 46 at 48).

Heavy on the offer—Chapter 7: This means that there are more offers to sell a financial product than bids to buy a financial product. This could move the market prices down but not necessarily, as we never have full information about how many bids and offers are in the market at any one point.

Hedge—Chapter 2: When a trader does a derivative trade with a client and wants to get rid of his market risk, we say he hedges his position by doing another derivative trade with another counterparty.

Hedge funds—Chapter 2: This is a subset of the asset management company client category. Hedge funds are considered more risky by asset managers and are not open to most individuals. Hedge fund managers are often referred to as speculators in the media.

High yield—Chapter 5, 9: We separate debt products into investment grade and high yield (also called sub-investment grade). Investment grade is triple A through triple B rated and high yield is double B and lower.

Hit the bid—Chapter 4: A market taker will have to sell at the bid where the bank is willing to buy. The term used is to hit the bid. This is selling at the lower price offered by the bank.

Hoot 'n' holler—Chapter 8: This is the broadcast system that traders and debt capital market and equity capital market syndicates use to make important market announcements to the trading floor.

Illiquid—Chapter 2: A product that is less liquid than other financial products is said to be illiquid; or when the entire financial markets were in distress just after the Lehman Brothers default in September 2008, we said every financial product was illiquid.

In comp:—*See* In competition.

In competition (in comp)—Chapter 4: This term is used when a client is getting prices from more than one bank for the same trade. The banks are being put in comp by the client so that the client can bet the best price.

Indicative—Chapter 4: Market bids and offers are indicative when the trader hasn't specified a size that he is willing to trade and has not confirmed that he will trade on the bid or the offer.

Indices—Chapter 1: A market index is generally a group of similar financial products which is used as an indicator of market sentiment. The price of the index is determined by the price of the underlying financial products in the index, for example the S&P500 is the price of 500 different US stocks.

Individuals—Chapter 2: A single person who is a client of a bank. This group of clients is also called retail.

Initial public offering (IPO)—Chapter 1: The first issue of shares to the public for a company which previously only had private shares.

Insider information—Chapter 3: Private market-sensitive information. Individuals who work within banks that have insider information are said to be inside the Chinese wall with respect to that company and can't trade the debt or equity of that company.

Institutional investor base—Chapter 2: These are financial companies (asset managers, insurance companies, pension funds and banks) which make up the bulk of the investor client base for the financial markets. They are also called real money investors. Often, hedge funds that are a subset of asset managers are excluded from this group because they are not considered real money. Hedge funds often borrow from banks in order to invest.

In sympathy—Chapter 6: When market prices of one product move in a similar direction as another financial product but aren't directly affected by the news that caused the move, we say they moved in sympathy.

Interbank broker—Chapter 2: A matchmaker for over the counter products such as derivatives between liquidity providers (market makers).

Interest—Chapter 1: The percentage of the principal that is due each year from the borrower to the lender in a bond or loan. The interest is the cost of borrowing money.

Interest rate swaps—Chapter 1: A financial derivative which is an exchange of fixed interest rates for floating interest rates.

Intermediating—Chapter 1, 2: When a bank sits between its issuer client and its investor client, it is intermediating. This term is used in the context of a bank providing access to financial markets for its clients or a bank arranging and distributing an equity or bond issuance for a client. This is also used in the context of a bank executing a tailored derivative with a client and hedging using a standardized derivative with another counterparty. We refer to the bank as the intermediator.

Intermediator—Chapter 1, 2: The bank that intermediates. *See* Intermediating.

Interpolate—Chapter 10: This is a process of figuring out a point between two known points. For example, if we have the price of the 5-year treasury and the 7-year treasury, we can figure out the price of a 6-year treasury by looking at the mid-point between the 5-year and the 7-year.

In the money (ITM)—Chapter 10: When a financial instrument has a positive mark to market or when there is a profit on the financial product compared to where it was originally traded.

Intraday—Chapter 5: This is a reference to the movement of a market price or a trading book position throughout the day.

Investing—Chapter 2: This is buying or selling financial products in order to make a profit.

Investment banking—Chapter 3: A bank whose primary client base comprises large entities such as corporates, financial companies and government entities. This could be the only business line the bank has or it could be a separate business unit within a larger financial institution.

Investment grade—Chapter 5, 9: We separate debt products into investment grade and high yield (also called sub-investment grade). Investment grade is triple A through triple B rated and high yield is double B and lower.

Investors—Chapter 1: Investors are the individuals, companies or government entities that take risk in the financial markets in an effort to make a return on their money. The simplest example of this is an individual who exchanges his cash for shares in a company in the hope that the price of the shares goes up. The risk is that the share price can go down.

IPO:—*See* Initial public offering.

Issuance—Chapter 1: "Issuer," "issue" and "issuance" are all related terms. The issuer of the bonds or shares is raising capital. The issue is the actual new bonds or new shares and the issuance is the same.

Issue—Chapter 1: To issue means to borrow money in the bond markets or to sell ownership in the equity markets.

Issuer—Chapter 1: In the bond markets, the issuers are the borrowers of the money, and in the equity markets the issuers are the companies in which a shareholder of a specific equity owns a portion.

ITM:—*See* In the money.

Kick the tires—Chapter 9: This is a reference to the due diligence which should be done before investing in any financial product.

Know your client (KYC)—Chapter 2: This is often associated with a compliance procedure required to identify money laundering. It can also mean getting to know your client so that you can provide the right service for them.

KYC:—*See* Know your client.

Large lot—Chapter 3: This is a larger than normal trade size.

Launch—Chapter 1: When a new financial product such as an initial public offering or a new bond is priced and sold to investors, we say it is launched.

Legal team—Chapter 3: Banks often have an internal legal team that focuses on the legal documentation necessary to do trades in financial markets. Derivatives in particular require a lot of documentation.

Lender—Chapter 1: The entity that gives money to a borrower. A bank is the lender of a loan. An investor is effectively the lender in a bond.

Libor—Chapter 3: Libor is the London Interbank Borrowing Rate. It is the rate where banks borrow and lend with each other in different currencies. Every day at 11 a.m. in London, Libor is set as a reference rate based on where Libor is trading on that day and the setting is then used by other products such as bonds and loans and interest rate swaps.

Lift the offer—Chapter 4: A market taker will have to buy at the offer where the bank is willing to sell. The term used is to lift the offer. This is buying at the higher price offered by the bank.

Liquid—Chapter 2: The size of a financial product that can trade at one time without moving the price is a measurement of how liquid a financial product is.

Liquidity—Chapter 2: A financial product can be described as liquid or illiquid, depending on the volume of trades that can be done each day.

Liquidity provider—Chapter 2: This is the term often used for banks that are willing to make markets in specific financial products for their clients. We say that they provide liquidity for their clients.

Liquidity risk—Chapter 13: This is the risk of having to hedge or close out all the positions in a trading book on one day.

Live—Chapter 3, 4: When prices are live, they are tradable for the stated notional. So a live bid is a firm price where the trader who put the bid is prepared to trade. Often, live prices have a time limit on them for clients to make a decision to trade or not. This is in contrast to indicative prices, which are not tradable prices.

Loan business—Chapter 3: The business unit within a bank which lends money to its clients. This is sometimes called the loan portfolio or the balance sheet of the bank.

Loan equivalent—Chapter 13: This is a term sometimes used in derivative counterparty credit risk quantification. The size of the credit risk in a derivative is often only a fraction of the notional of the derivative. This is called the loan equivalent.

Loans—Chapter 1: A form of borrowing money which is for all clients of a bank. A bank gives out the money in a loan and may distribute the loan to other banks but often retains the loan itself. These are generally considered private financial products.

Locked in—Chapter 1: An investor can lock in his gains by hedging or closing out his position.

Long—Chapter 4: When a financial market participant buys financial product, he is said to be long. His risk is that market prices for that product go down.

Long and wrong—Chapter 7: When a market participant owns (is long) a lot of a particular product and the price has or is expected to fall, we say he is long and wrong.

Loss leading—Chapter 8: A loss leading trade is a trade which either loses money or does not make enough money to justify the risk or the operational cost but is done to secure other business with a client.

M&A:—*See* Mergers and acquisitions.

Macroeconomics—Chapter 5: This is the focus on the economic health of a country using statistics such as unemployment.

Major bank—Chapter 2: An international bank that has an office in London, New York, Tokyo and Hong Kong and is a top 20 market maker in hundreds of different financial instruments. This term is used interchangeably with major dealer.

Major dealer—Chapter 2: An international bank that has an office in London, New York, Tokyo and Hong Kong and is a top 20 market maker in hundreds of different financial instruments. This term is used interchangeably with major bank.

Make a market—Chapter 4: This is the term used when a trader puts a bid and an offer on a financial product, thus making a market. The bid and the offer comprise the trader's market for a particular financial product.

Management fee—Chapter 2: Asset management companies charge management fees on the money they manage for their clients, which generally range from 0.10% to 2%.

Margin—Chapter 2: Margin is used in a number of ways which are all very similar. Sometimes it is the difference between the bid and the offer. Sometimes it is the difference between the trade price and the mid-market price. It is primarily meant to reflect the cost to the market taker, which is the opposite of the possible profit to the market maker for doing a trade.

Mark to market (MTM)—Chapter 7: This is a process of re-valuing financial products by comparing their original price to their current market price.

Mark to model (MTMdl)—Chapter 12: Similar concept to mark to market but the process for these instruments (category 2 and 3) are not observable and a model (which uses market prices) is used.

Market—Chapter 1: (1) A place where buyers and sellers agree to exchange a specific financial product for a specific price. (2) The price where a specific financial product for a specific size can be bought or sold. (3) The market participants in a particular financial product. See Chapter 5 for a more comprehensive description.

Market capitalization (market cap)—Chapter 1: The current market value of a company which is derived by multiplying the number of shares by the current market share price.

Market color—Chapter 3: This is the information about market prices, market liquidity, market flows and any key market news that is being currently discussed.

Market maker—Chapter 4: A bank's traders (excluding the proprietary traders) are market makers. They make markets. They determine the bid and the offer for a product where they will buy and sell. The clients are the market takers. They hit the bid or lift the offer.

Market risk—Chapter 13: This is the risk of loss due to market price moves.

Market standard—Chapter 3: This term is applied to financial products, documentation and quoting conventions. There are market standards of which financial market participants should generally be aware in order to know when a product or documentation in particular is non-market standard.

Market taker—Chapter 4: The clients are the market takers. They hit the bid or lift the offer when the bank's traders make a market.

Maturity—Chapter 1: The date when the principal amount of a bond or loan has been fully repaid or the date on which there are no further cashflows due in a derivative.

Mergers and acquisitions (M&A)—Chapter 3: This is the team of people within the corporate finance team which advises on mergers and acquisitions for their corporate clients.

Middle and back office—Chapter 3: These are the teams of people who focus on the operations of the financial markets trading activities.

Mid-market—Chapter 6: This is the midpoint between the bid price and the offer price for a product.

Morning market commentary—Chapter 6: Summary market information about market price moves the previous day and market price moves expected that day for a specific financial product. It is usually written or delivered verbally by the trader of that financial product.

Morning meeting—Chapter 6: The meeting for sales people and/or traders in each financial product to discuss any big market news or events anticipated for that day.

MTM:—*See* Mark to market.

MTMdl:—Mark to model.

Neutral—Chapter 4: When an investor or trader is not exposed to market prices going up or down, the investor or trader is said to be market neutral.

New product approval (NPA)—Chapter 11: This is the process a bank goes through to ensure that a new product does not create undue risk to the bank if it is traded.

Non-linear—Chapter 10: A product which cannot be perfectly hedged in the market and needs to be re-hedged every day based on current market prices is said to be non-linear. Options are classic examples of this.

NPA:—*See* New product approval.

Offer—Chapter 2: This is the price where one entity is willing to sell a financial product to another entity. When a trader makes a market, he provides a bid and an offer (which is a higher price than his bid). This is not necessarily the best bid or offer in the market, but it is where he is prepared to buy (his bid) or sell (his offer).

Off-exchange—Chapter 2: This is where a bank is able to match-make between two clients on exchange traded products or where a bank provides liquidity to a client on an exchange traded product.

Off-market—Chapter 6: When a price for a financial product is so far from the fair market price, it is considered off-market. Old derivative trades that haven't yet matured are often considered off-market because the market price which is documented in the contract is no longer the fair market price.

Off-market price—Chapter 4: A price for a financial product that is not at current market levels.

Offer to mid—Chapter 7: This is the difference between the offer price and the mid-market price for a financial product.

On-the-run—Chapter 4: This is the current benchmark product, for example the 5-year on-the-run treasury is the most recently issued 5-year treasury.

Open a line—Chapter 4: Often, sales people and traders refer to their internal speakerphone system as a line. Calling the trader quickly to do a trade often involves pushing a button on an open microphone on the trader's desk to ask for a price and agree a trade for a client. This is sometimes referred to as opening a line.

Open outcry—Chapter 2: This term is used to describe a rapidly disappearing form of trading on exchanges. The image is of men standing around screaming at each other. The movie *Trading Places* has a very good popular image of an open outcry exchange.

Operational risk—Chapter 13: This is the risk of input or calculation or systems error to a bank.

Option—Chapter 1: An option is a derivative in which the buyer has the right but not the obligation to buy or sell another financial product at a specified strike at a specified time in the future.

Option premium—Chapter 1: The price of an option.

Order—Chapter 2: When a client wants to trade a specific financial product at a specific price for a specific notional, he gives an order to a bank acting as a broker as opposed to the bank providing liquidity to the client. Not all orders get filled because the market price might move or might not be for enough size, whereas the client could have agreed to trade at a different price with the bank acting as liquidity provider.

OTC:—*See* Over the counter.

Other side of the trade—Chapter 6: If a bank buys bonds from one client, it needs to sell them on to someone else. The trade that it does with someone else is called the other side of the trade. This is the close out or hedge trade of a client trade.

OTM:—*See* Out of the money.

Out of the money (OTM)—Chapter 10: When a financial instrument has a negative mark to market or when there is a loss on the financial product compared to where it was originally traded.

Over the counter (OTC)—Chapter 2: A financial product that is not required to be reported to an exchange is said to trade over the counter. Most bonds and derivatives trade over the counter.

Oversubscribed—Chapter 4: When a new bond or equity issuance has more notional interest from investors than the size that the issuer originally wanted to issue.

P&L:—*See* Profit and loss.

Paper gain—Chapter 1: When an investor owns an investment which has increased in value but the investor hasn't sold the investment to realize the gain. This is called a paper gain.

Par—Chapter 1: This is when the price of a bond is 100%.

PE ratio:—*See* Price to earnings ratio.

Performance fee—Chapter 2: Some asset management companies charge a fee to their clients if they have a positive return on their assets under management. This fee is often a percentage of the positive return itself.

Pitch—Chapter 1: The marketing ideas for an investment are often called the pitch and they are presented in a presentation called the pitch book.

Position—Chapter 2: When a trader or investor has risk to market price moves in a financial product, he has a position in that financial product.

Post mortem—Chapter 6: A debriefing or informal investigation. When a transaction hasn't occurred after a client has asked the bank for a price, there is often a post mortem to discuss what happened and how the bank could improve in the future.

Premium—Chapter 4: This term is used in two ways in the financial markets: (1) when a financial market participant wants to do a trade for larger than the normal market size, there is a premium on the price or (2) the price of an option is referred to as the premium.

Price fundamentals—Chapter 5: These are the issues which affect the price of financial market products. They include macroeconomics and company specific news.

Price to earnings ratio (PE ratio)—Chapter 5: The share price divided by the earnings per share generally tends toward a certain number depending on the industry and the country.

Pricing models—Chapter 12: These models are used to price, hedge and value trades done. They are more commonly used for less liquid or tailored products.

Primary market—Chapter 1: The first time a bond or share is sold to an investor.

Principal—Chapter 1: This term is used in two main ways in financial markets: (1) the notional amount that a borrower originally receives in a bond or loan or (2) when a bank takes risk on a trade the bank is said to have done a principal trade.

Principal trade—Chapter 2: When a bank provides liquidity and takes risk for a client trade, we say the bank has done a principal trade.

Private banking—Chapter 3: A bank whose primary client base comprises high net worth individuals (also called private clients). This could be the only business line the bank has or it could be a separate business unit within a larger financial institution.

Private equity—Chapter 1: When the ownership of a company is not traded on an exchange but is held by a handful of individuals that often include the founder, the founder's friends and family and a private equity investment business.

Private equity company—Chapter 1: A company that specializes in investing in private equity.

Profit and loss (P&L)—Chapter 6: Every trading day, a bank calculates the profit or loss that each individual trading book has made based on the end of day market prices for the financial products in the trading book.

Proprietary trading (prop trading)—Chapter 7: Is done by traders at banks who are not market makers for the bank's clients. These traders are similar to hedge fund portfolio managers. They take risk by using the bank's capital.

Public equity—Chapter 1: When a company is large enough and well known enough, it can sell shares to the public and have its shares trade on an exchange. The investors in the equity of this type of company number in the hundreds of thousands.

Pulling the tapes—Chapter 3: This is a reference to the fact that most trades are transacted on a recorded line within the bank. When there is a trade dispute with a client or another bank, the bank can listen to the recording of the conversation in which the trade details were agreed. This is known as pulling the tapes.

Quant:—*See* Quantitative analyst.

Quantitative analyst (quant)—Chapter 3: This is an individual who builds financial models to price or risk manage financial products and risk. See Chapter 12 for more detail.

Quote—Chapter 4: A quote is another term for a bid or an offer from a market maker.

Rallying—Chapter 3: This is when market prices go up. A market that rallies for a long time is a bull market.

Range bound—Chapter 6: When a market price has moved between a tight upper and lower boundary for a long time.

Rating—Chapter 5: A rating is an alphanumeric indication of the credit worthiness of an entity.

Rating agencies—Chapter 5: These agencies assign public ratings to entities that provide a relative scale for credit worthiness. Moody's, S&P and Fitch are the most well-known rating agencies.

Rating system—Chapter 13: This is a system of analyzing the relative credit risk of companies and governments by assigning a relative alphanumeric rating to them.

Recognized—Chapter 7: We differentiate between a profit (or loss) that is realized and one that is recognized. A realized profit (or loss) is one that is calculated based on a hedged or closed out client trade, while a recognized profit (or loss) is one that has been stated on the accounts but is a function of mark to market rather than a hedged or closed out client trade. A recognized profit (or loss) could change over time, while a realized profit (or loss) is fixed because it is hedged or closed out.

Regional banks—Chapter 2: A bank that is not considered a major bank which operates in one particular financial product and/or one particular state, region or country.

Relationship banker—Chapter 3: These are the individuals within the corporate finance team who are responsible for the global senior relationships with the bank's clients.

Reputational risk—Chapter 13: This is the risk to a bank's reputation that may cause clients to transact with other banks.

Research—Chapter 3: These are reports written by research analysts that generally give trade ideas or trade strategies based on macro- or microeconomic analysis.

Retail—Chapter 2: In banking, retail clients are individual clients (e.g. retail loans are loans given to individual borrowers).

Retail banking—Chapter 3: A bank whose primary client base is made up of individuals. This could be the only business line the bank has or it could be a separate business unit within a larger financial institution.

Return on capital—Chapter 14: Every bank sets aside capital when it takes risk. Banks also have a target return on the capital it sets aside.

Revenue generators—Chapter 9: This is a term often used to refer to sales people and traders who are directly responsible for generating profit for a bank.

Reverse enquiry—Chapter 11: When a client asks for a tailored or structured product, we say the client has made a reverse enquiry.

Risk free—Chapter 5: This is the term used for the credit risk of many Western governments and any triple A rated entity. We no longer say anything is actually risk free, although the term is still used.

Risk limits—Chapter 14: These are the limits that all trading books are set on an annual basis.

Risk management—Chapter 2: This is a process of identifying financial risks, quantifying financial risks and mitigating the risks to the extent that they are larger than is deemed appropriate for a particular company or business. All entities employ risk management of some sort.

Risk management models—Chapter 12: These models are used to calculate different risk parameters for a financial product.

Risk management team—Chapter 3: This is the team within a bank which quantifies risk and sets risk limits. They also generally manage the new product approval process.

Road show—Chapter 1: The meetings with potential investors in a new financial product such as an initial public offering or a new bond issuance prior to the product being issued. This is also called the dog and pony show.

Runs—Chapter 8: These are the current market prices that market makers distribute to their sales force to let them know where the market is in the morning. For the more liquid financial product, this information is readily available on electronic screens, but for less liquid or structured products for which there aren't screens, a trader will distribute this information in other ways.

Sales people—Chapter 3: These individuals sit on the trading floor and cover a specific type of client (e.g. financial institutions) for a specific type of financial product (e.g. equity derivatives). The relationship is financial transaction oriented. The goal of sales people is to do as many profitable trades as possible with their clients. The sales person is the interface between the client and the trader.

Sales points—Chapter 8: These are the client trade profits which are allocated to the sales people on which their bonuses are based at the end of the year. They are generally a function of the trade price to the mid-market price for a product.

Sales-trader—Chapter 3: This is an individual who works in the sales team but focuses only on trade transactions with a client rather than relationship management. This is often a role only found on the equity trading floors, where the official sales person focuses on setting up road shows for initial public offerings and introducing the client to the research team, while the sales trader focuses on trade strategy and execution with the client.

Scenario analysis—Chapter 13: This is a form of risk management where rational market scenarios are constructed and applied to trading books to see the impact.

Scoring system—Chapter 13: This is a system of analyzing the relative credit risk of retail borrowers by assigning a relative rating to them.

Secondary market—Chapter 1: The second and following trades on bonds and shares.

Secondary market offering—Chapter 1: when a company that has already had an initial public offering has another share offering to investors so that the original private investors can sell their shares.

Settlement—Chapter 10: The settlement of a financial instrument is when the cash is exchanged for the product or when the price of the product has been received.

Share—Chapter 1: The financial product which represents ownership of some portion of a company. "Equity" and "shares" are often used interchangeably, although they mean slightly different things.

Shareholder—Chapter 1: The owner of one or more shares in a company.

Short—Chapter 4: When a financial market participant agrees to deliver a financial product in exchange for a price but doesn't yet own the financial product he has agreed to deliver, he is said to be short. His risk is that market prices go up.

Short-dated—Chapter 10: A financial product with a maturity of less than a year is considered short-dated.

Size—Chapter 4: Generally, this term is used to refer to a larger notional trade than normally trades in that financial product.

Speculators—Chapter 2: A speculator is someone who makes a bet on the direction of the market price of a financial product. This is the same as investing.

Standardized—Chapter 2: This is a financial product which has some agreed features that make it a more liquid product. Exchange traded products are considered standardized and many bonds and derivatives are considered standardized.

Start-up—Chapter 1: A brand-new company is often referred to as a start-up.

Stock—Chapter 1: Another word for shares. "Stockholder" and "shareholder" are used interchangeably.

Strategist—Chapter 9: These are the research analysts who focus on a particular asset class or product such as equity options or credit derivatives. They publish research giving investment recommendations based on the research.

Stress testing—Chapter 13: This is a form of risk management where modeling assumptions are tested to determine their sensitivity.

Strike—Chapter 1: A strike is a term used in option transactions. It is the price at which a financial product can be bought or sold by the option owner in the future.

Structured—Chapter 2: A structured product is generally used to mean a bond plus a tailored derivative such as the structured equity product described in Chapter 4. "Structured" is often used interchangeably with the word "tailored."

Structured product—Chapter 11: This is a term generally associated with a bond which has a tailored derivative embedded in it that is created by a bank specifically for an investment profile that a client desires.

Structurer—Chapter 3: An individual who liaises with traders and sales people on more complex and structured products. This individual will also coordinate with whatever other necessary areas (e.g. legal, tax, accounting, rating agencies) to make a structured trade happen.

Subscription period—Chapter 4: This is the period during which retail clients are offered structured investment products and decide whether to invest in them.

Suitability—Chapter 3: In financial markets, the concept of suitability is often applied to whether a trade is suitable for a particular client. For example, a complex derivative is not generally a suitable investment for a retail client because derivatives are generally considered investment and hedging products for institutional investors and not individuals.

Supply and demand—Chapter 5: The relative size of supply compared to demand will ultimately drive the market price of a financial product. This is the interest of investors in a new issue as well as general buyers and sellers in the secondary, commodity, currency and derivative markets.

Syndication—Chapter 3: To distribute, or the team which runs the distribution of, a particular product. We often say initial public offerings or new debt issues are syndicated to clients by the syndicate (or syndication) team.

T+0—Chapter 10: This is a reference to the settlement time for a financial product. "T" is today and "+0" means it doesn't take any time to settle.

Tail risk—Chapter 12: This is a reference to value at risk (VaR) and the 1 out of 20 chance that losses are higher than the 95% VaR.

Tailored—Chapter 2: If a client wants to trade a financial product that is different in any way from the market standard product, then that trade is tailored. For example, a 4.5-year interest rate swap is tailored because the market standard benchmark maturity is a 4-year or a 5-year interest rate swap.

Term structure of credit—Chapter 4: Another term for credit curve. This is the graph of credit spreads against maturity for one borrower.

Term structure of rates—Chapter 4: Another term for yield curve.

Theoretical price—Chapter 5: The theoretical price of a financial product may not be the actual price in the market because supply and demand drives the actual price.

Ticker—Chapter 9: This is the symbol which exchanges use for financial products that trade on the exchange. A ticker is mostly associated with the shares of a particular company. For example, the ticker for Facebook is FB.

Tight—Chapter 6: A market is said to be tight if the bid–offer spread is very small.

Trade—Chapter 4: To trade means to agree a price, a notional and a financial product that one party will buy from another. Often, the terms "buy" and "sell" don't have a lot of meaning for derivatives, so the terminology might be different, for example in interest rate swaps it is the fixed rate that one party agrees to pay to the other in exchange for Libor.

Traders—Chapter 3: These individuals sit on the trading floor and make markets in specific financial products (e.g. European equity derivatives).

Trading book—Chapter 3: Trading floors often split up the accounting of the trading activities into similar financial products. Equity indices in the United States will have one profit and loss, and equity indices in Europe will have another profit and loss. These can be thought of as individual bank accounts in which trades are transacted for specific financial products. The US treasury trading book might be split into different trading books based on the treasury maturity, while the US interest rate swap book might not be.

Trading floor—Chapter 2: The physical location where most financial trades are agreed.

Trading lines—Chapter 10: This is a reference to the credit limits that a bank has set with a counterparty.

Treasury—Chapter 4: This is the debt that the US government issues. US treasuries break down into T-bills, which are less than 1 year in maturity; treasury notes, which are 2-year, 3-year, 5-year and 7-year; and treasury bonds, which are 30-year.

Two-way market—Chapter 4: This is a bid and an offer.

Underlying—Chapter 1: Often, this term is used to refer to the financial product which drives the price of a derivative. For example, Wal-Mart shares are the underlying financial product when talking about an equity option on Wal-Mart shares.

Unwind—Chapter 1: When the two parties to a derivative decide to tear up the contract, it is called an unwind. It is usually the case that a payment is made from one party to the other in order to tear up the contract based on the market price move of the derivative.

Upward sloping—Chapter 3: This is the normal shape of a yield curve or credit curve. The longer the maturity, the higher the interest rate or credit spread.

Valuation—Chapter 10: This is the value of a financial product calculated by comparing the current market price to the traded market price.

Value at risk (VaR)—Chapter 12: This is an amount of money that might be lost for a particular portfolio based on some assumptions about future market price moves.

VaR:—*See* Value at risk.

Voice trading—Chapter 2: This is verbally agreeing a trade between two parties (as opposed to electronic trading, which happens via an electronic trading system without the two parties speaking to each other).

Volcker rule—Chapter 7: A reference to part of the Dodd-Frank Act enacted in the summer of 2010 in the United States which prohibits proprietary trading by US banks.

Yard—Chapter 3: A billion of any currency is a yard. Yen is often quoted in yards, given the exchange rates.

Yield—Chapter 5: The yield of a bond takes into account the coupon and the price of the bond. For example, a bond that is trading above 100% will have a yield that is lower than the fixed coupon on the bond.

Yield curve—Chapter 3: All entities borrow at different interest rates for different maturities. Generally, the longer the borrowing, the higher the interest rate. A graph of this picture of interest rates over maturity is a yield curve. It is also called the term structure of interest rates.

Zero coupon—Chapter 4: A bond that is issued at less than 100% of the principal (e.g. 70%), pays no coupons and then matures at 100%. The borrower only receives 70% of the principal on day one but pays back 100% at maturity in exchange for not paying coupons.

Index

Note: Page references in *italics* refer to Figures; those in **bold** refer to Tables and Boxes